Like the Morning Sun

A Personal and Family Spiritual Portrait

RON UNRUH

DEDICATION

'In memory of Murray,'
unthinkable words to write.
Often, I told Murray, "Mom always loved you best."
What was not to love about Murray? Blue eyes like mom's,
naturally curly hair, a beautiful boy. And then a beautiful man.
People responded with affection and attention,
to the man with a winsome smile and spontaneous humour.
Five years younger than me and solid friends in our teens.
Murray was friendly. God gave him friends.
He trustingly let God lead him in marriage and career.
Diane and Murray were a spiritual team. It was more than good.
People found Christ because of Murray and Diane.
Not everything in life came easily.
Challenges and disappointments visited.
God managed the contests and always restored hope.
Murray faced his end of life, eternity occupied his mind,
until the moment hope converted to reality,
"like the morning sun, shining
ever brighter till the full light of day."

Murray Dennis Unruh Sept 7, 1947 – Nov 14, 2023

LIKE THE MORNING SUN

"The path of the righteous is like the morning sun, shining ever brighter till the full light of day." Proverbs 4:18

ACKNOWLEDGMENTS

Thanks to Christine, to whom I became engaged to be married on New Year's Eve 1966, and with whom I exchanged wedding vows on August 12, 1967, and in whose company, I have lived and served God with joy. Thanks to our parents, Edward and Tina Unruh and James and May Langlois, who provided us with the necessities of life, the comforts of loving homes and encouragements during the diverse seasons of all our lives. Thanks to our two children, Carinne May (Cari) and Ronald Jeffrey (Jeff) for their love for us, for their devotion to Jesus Christ, and for the cherished people they have brought into our family. I am grateful for the informational input of Les Willems, Ruth Willems Low, and Esther Willems McIlveen.

1 LIKE THE MORNING SUN

THE BOOK TITLE, 'LIKE THE MORNING SUN,' derives from scripture. It was inspired by a birthday greeting from Diane, my sister-in-law on my 75th birthday six years ago. She assured me that "the future is very bright indeed!" She quoted Solomon, who wrote "*The path of the righteous is like the morning sun, shining ever brighter till the full light of day.*" Proverbs 4:18

Reflecting on this emphasis prompted me to view this project as broader than the story of my own life. It must contain my very large family, both extant and earlier. The spiritual heritage of both paternal and maternal sides of my family, accounts in large measure for all that is good and worthwhile in my life. Therefore, this is a family wide story rather than an autobiography. I purposely draw attention to the maiden names of my mom and my two grandmothers and in the case of my maternal grandmother, both of her married names. I have done that because all five families, Unruhs, Loewens, Fasts, Doerksens, and Willems are rooted in the same socio-religious heritage.

As far back as I can trace my lineage, my forebears carrying the Unruh name have been followers of Jesus Christ. They were heirs of theology that emerged out of the Protestant Reformation, and they have lived the convictions of a stream of Anabaptist believers known as Mennonites. From 1500-1900 AD, Mennonite beliefs occasionally collided with the State church or other faith traditions or with political leaders. Intermittently their lives were threatened and sometimes extinguished. Wherever they settled after fleeing from their homelands, most Mennonites continued to practice faithfulness to the God of scripture. They cleared land, tilled ground, raised crops and animals and became known for capability and competence. As time went on, many Unruhs were invested in community leadership, churches, international mission ventures, education, and scholarly pursuits.

For centuries this extended line of people have been illuminating a path so vibrantly that my brothers and I joined them. That is, we embraced fundamental aspects of biblical Christian faith. This is how I explain the improbability that three brothers (Murray, Neale, and myself), would become pastors and missionaries. We were the sons of a factory assembly-line labourer named Edward and his multi-competent wife Tina. In their own ways our parents encouraged our faith. Fortuitously for Murray, Neale and me, the best possible soul mates entered our lives, Christine for me, Diane for Murray, and Kathy for Neale. Like most families, ours is a family with warts and pain. In mercy God applies the ointment of grace on us frequently.

***

The Willems family name occurs within our Unruh story by relationship but not by bloodline. There is no biological lineage connection between Unruhs and Willems. Nevertheless, it's a vital relationship that will become clear as I include significant references to the Willems family tree. I have dedicated some chapters to their story.

***

The project is almost too late in starting. An eye blink ago I was 50, 60, 70. I consulted relatives and Mennonite historians for 25 years. I began to write on my 75th birthday. Between writing and painting, I planned to finish by September 13, 2022, my 80th birthday. In 2019 an autoimmune illness interfered for three years. 2023 became the new target. Finally, I can say, the book is complete. I am 81. It's a rich history resource for the generations who follow my brothers and me.

The relatives who know the stories first-hand are almost all gone. Of the Willems clan, Aunt Ruth Willems Low is now the surviving member. Her sister, Esther Willems McIlveen died on October 17, 2022. I have done my best to gather relevant data.

I have woven my own story in some of the family history and in two closing chapters. My own path in life has been guided by the God who sustained generations.

I am the eldest surviving Unruh of our lineage. The history that I document can endure beyond my time. It will remain available to the generations that follow me, and it will offer lessons of devotion and tenacity and faithfulness. My earnest prayer is that everyone in the vast family will shine ever brighter, moving steadily with us toward the full light of day.

2 THE WOMAN UNDER THE COVERS

HER FORM WAS SO SMALL, curled into a foetal position and concealed under the sheets and bedspread. The figure might have belonged to a small child. It didn't. She was lying in a bed in the long-term care unit of Tabor Manor in St. Catharines. She was nearing the end of her earthly days.

I visited infrequently. I lived far away but now I was there with my wife Christine and with my two children Cari and Jeff, ages twelve and eleven. I stood beside her bed. She was asleep. She slept most of each day. Touching the blanket that covered her, I was hoping to stir her to wakefulness. She was unresponsive. Naively I was thinking she would communicate as cheerfully as she always did. Not until that moment did I realize she had little time left. My mind was suddenly overcome with a flood of memories that involved her and the many ways she had factored into my life. She had been a woman of great strength and many aptitudes. It was offensive to me to see her defined by this tiny shape in the bed. She was my maternal Grandma Willems. Her story is captivating.

***

The Unruh family tree has deep and distant roots. While I could hastily take you back to the 1600's to speak about Unruhs, I am starting more recently at the end of the 1800's to speak about this

4

lady who never was an Unruh. She was my mother's mother. She was Maria Fast, sometimes known as Marie. I will use her given names interchangeably depending on the documents cited or the people quoted. Maria was born on April 27, 1894, in Marion, South Dakota. She was born to Peter P. Fast (277123) and Katarina Duerksen (#103949). Her Mennonite parents raised her to understand the Christian faith and she personally committed her life in faith to Jesus Christ. She was baptized by immersion in water at the age of eighteen on June 1, 1912.

The bracketed numbers correspond to references within the database known as GRanDMA OnLine7, which is a Prussian/Russian Mennonite Genealogy resource. Exceedingly helpful. Anyone can subscribe for $20.00 per year.

Maria was fifth among Peter's and Katarina's fifteen children.

1 Fast, Abraham P. (#20023), born 12 October 1889, Marion, South Dakota. Died 2 July 1966, Mountain Lake, Minnesota.

2 Fast, Anna (#277286), born and died 12 October 1890.

3 Fast, Peter P. (#277287), born 1 October 1891, Mountain Lake, Minnesota. Died 8 February 1968, Lebanon, Oregon.

4 Fast, Katarina P. (#70571), born18 February 1893, Mountain Lake, Minnesota. Died 15 May 1978.

5 Fast, Maria P. (#277288), born 27 April 1894, Marion, South Dakota. Died 22 September 1983, St. Catharines, Ontario.

6 Fast, Elisabeth (#277289), born 27 June 1895, Marion, South Dakota. Died 21 October 1993, Mountain Lake, Minnesota.

7 Fast, Johann (#277290), born and died 1897.

8 Fast, Johann (#277291), born and died 1898.

9 Fast, Jacob Peter (#115510), born 3 March 1899, Marion, South Dakota. Died 5 January 1978, Dallas, Oregon.

10 Fast, Heinrich P. (#244329), born 25 August 1900, Mountain Lake, Minnesota. Died 20 April 1991, Abbotsford, British Columbia.

11 Fast, David (#277293), born and died 18 September 1902.

12 Fast, Anna (#277294), born and died 8 December 1903.

13 Fast, Anna Erna (#277295) born 24 May 1904, Mountain Lake, Minnesota. Died 11 July 1987, Mountain Lake, Minnesota.

14 Fast, Franz P. (#277296), born 18 May 1905, Mountain Lake, Minnesota. Died 8 September 1985, Mountain Lake, Minnesota.

15 Fast, George Paul (#277297), born 24 April 1909, Mountain Lake, Minnesota. Died 20 March 1977, Minneapolis, Minnesota.

***

Three years earlier on another continent, a baby boy was born, whom Maria Fast would one day meet, love and marry.

Jacob and Maria (Richert) Doerksen were expecting their seventh child. They already had four sons and two daughters. Their eldest two children Marie and Jacob were twins. Did you notice that the children's names are identical to their parents? At first glance it seems like flagrant parental narcissism or a failure of imagination. Instead, this was common practice. The patronym and matronym was a centuries old practice and was a symbol of family fealty in many cultures. These twins, Marie and Jacob were twelve years old when Isaac R. Doerksen was born on August 9, 1891, in Waldheim. Waldheim was a town in the German Mennonite Colony of Molotschna in southern Russia. He was child number seven. His parents were church members of the Waldheim Mennonite Congregation.

There is a grand story waiting for you in this book about why these German speaking (Plautdietsch) people lived in South Russia. Ukraine and Crimea were under Russian rule.

***

Isaac R. Doerksen was the seventh of eight children born to Jacob Doerksen (#353284) and Maria Richert (#34158). Here are Isaac's siblings.

1 Doerksen, Marie (#353289), 22 September 1879, Russia. Died 7 September 1956, Abbotsford, British Columbia.

2 Doerksen, Jacob R. (#700261), 22 September 1879, Waldheim, Molotschna, South Russia. Died 4 January 1940, Saskatchewan. He was the pastor of Langham Evangelical Bible Church from 1908 to his death in 1940.

6

3 Doerksen, Heinrich (#353286), About 1882; no further information.

4 Doerksen, Margarethe (#353290); no further information.

5 Doerksen, Johannes (#353287), About 1886. No further information.

6 Doerksen, David R. (#329532), 17 September 1886, Waldheim, Molotschna, South Russia. Died 16 October 1970, Salem, Oregon.

7 Doerksen, Isaac R. (#353288), 9 August 1891, Russia. Died 13 June 1920, Dalmeny, Saskatchewan.

8 Doerksen, Abraham R. (#1147518), 1 March, 1894, United States of America.

Isaac's birth happened at a time in South Russia when the Russian government introduced changes that threatened the Mennonites' religious freedoms and their special status that included exemption from military service. Isaac was one year old when his parents made the difficult decision to leave their Russian farm home and community to join many others in the first Mennonite migration to North and South America. The Doerksen family emigrated to the United States of America in 1892 and settled in Minnesota. They relocated to Dalmeny, Saskatchewan, Canada in 1901.

***

Maria's family came to America settling first in South Dakota and then moved to Minnesota. As seen here, young Maria was looking forward to so much that life could offer. She could not know that she would soon become a homesteading wife and mother. Within a few years incredible challenges settled upon her. The strength of this lady is astounding to contemplate.

In time Maria met and married Isaac Doerksen. Maria and Isaac and Isaac's younger brother Abraham R. Doerksen, left their family enclave in 1917 to homestead on readily available acreage far away in Montana. They held title to a quarter section of land, 160 acres on which they grew grain. The brothers built a substantial log house, a cottage we might call it, with two sizeable spaces. One was their living quarters, and the other was the barn. In this meagre shelter the smell of farm was ever present. Two cows, chickens, a pig, and horses lived in the adjoining room.

Homesteading life was grim, demanding and yet hopeful. Maria worked hard on their Montana farm, preparing meals, and doing household tasks for her husband Isaac and brother Abraham. She also gardened and cared for the animals. During those first years of their marriage and farming, Maria gave birth to two children. First, a son whom Marie named Peter in honour of her father Peter P. Fast, and then a daughter whom she named Tena (my mom) in honour of her sister Katarina. 'Tena' is on her birth certificate.

Then the unthinkable occurred. Isaac became ill and his condition rapidly deteriorated. A specific illness or cause is not mentioned within any records. Maria's parents had found farming difficult in Minnesota because of poor soil conditions. Canada was open to immigration and land was available in Alberta and Saskatchewan, so her parents had moved to Saskatchewan. When they heard that Isaac was critically ill, they invited Maria to bring Isaac and the children to live with them in Saskatchewan. Maria needed to make a decision. It was a choice that would dramatically change her life; her children's lives and would ultimately affect my brothers' and mine. Maria and her two children, Peter and Tena, and her ailing husband Isaac came to Canada.

***

Maria's brother-in-law Abraham Doerksen remained in Montana to work the land that she and Isaac had jointly shared with him. He married and had a family and later deeded the land to the Fast family, Maria's clan. Abraham died in Salem, Oregon. Maintained now as a family heritage building, the log home/barn stands after all those bitter Montana winters and burning summers on a vast farm acreage retained by members of the Fast family.

Christine and I have seen and walked inside this heritage site homestead. The extended Fast family, most of them citizens of the United States, has held a reunion every five years for three decades. In 2007 Christine and I made a long summer drive from British Columbia to Montana to join my mother and father (Tina and Ed Unruh) and my Uncle Les Willems. The three of them had driven from Ontario. Mom was there because Maria was her mother. Uncle Les was there for the same reason. Maria was also Les Willems' mother. Same mother but different fathers. That will become clear as this story continues.

Eighteen years earlier on September 8-9, 1989, in Mountain Lake, Minnesota, Les attended the first 'Fast Cousins Reunion.' Les wrote a letter to all the Fast cousins, dated November 30, 1989.

"I attended an event which was called the 'Fast Cousins Reunion.' It may have been a reunion for some, but it was an introduction for me. What an experience. I am still mesmerized. What happened? It was mystical; it was spiritual, it was uplifting and at the same time it was exhausting. What had I expected to find? As I told the group at our Saturday gathering on Sept. 9, I hoped to find 'kin folk,' which meant people who loved me. But why should I expect this from strangers? Because they were my mother's people. Perhaps this was the simplest trust that I have ever known. It was born from the love of a mother for her son. My mother who taught me about love, not by words but by being love personified. And my trust in that love was rewarded as I had expected it would be. But far more than my expectations of finding people who loved me, I found people whom I loved. More importantly I found forgiveness in my heart for resentments I thought I had buried as a boy. Suddenly some people that I had determined would only exist on the fringe of my consciousness, became very dear to me, and yet we hardly had time to speak

9

together. I had a wonderful time and I hope that you did too."

Here is the rest of Maria's noteworthy story. It reveals how Tina and Les could have the same mother but different fathers.

***

In Dalmeny, Saskatchewan, Maria's husband Isaac Doerksen succumbed to his illness and was dead at the age of 29. It was Sunday, June 13, 1920. Maria was now sole caregiver for two small children, Peter, age four and Tina, almost two years old.

Maria was brave, resourceful, and determined. As a young woman Maria was proficient at tailoring, a trained seamstress. With the death of her spouse and with two small children to feed and to clothe, she began to make her livelihood. She stayed with a farming family for as long as it took to complete an entire wardrobe for the family, as well as curtains and bedspreads. By word of mouth and for room and board, she did this work and moved from farm to farm, from family to family.

When her parents made the decision to return to the USA, they told Maria that she should come with them to live in Minnesota. She agreed but she had one work assignment that she wished to honourably complete.

If her choice to come to Canada altered her own life and future, her next personal decision affected and influenced several generations. In Saskatchewan she met a man named Abraham A. Willems. When she decided to marry him, he became my mom's stepdad, so while not related to me by bloodline, he is the man whom I remember as my maternal grandfather.

Abraham A. Willems was born in Cottonwood County, Minnesota, U.S.A. on February 27, 1883. He and his brothers and sisters helped in the operations of the family farm. As they became young adults, they wanted their own farming properties. Farmland ownership opportunities were no longer available in Minnesota.

The children began to move to other states, like the Dakotas and Nebraska. Some members of the family took advantage of Canada's offer of prairie farmland. They moved to Saskatchewan.

When Maria Fast met Abe (Abraham A.) Willems, he owned a small farm and he needed someone like Maria. He too was grieving the loss of a spouse. His wife, Anna Wiens died on December 30, 1921, at the age of forty. They had been married at the Ebenfield Mennonite Brethren Church on February 6, 1908. Anna was buried at the Hepburn M.B. Church cemetery. The death of his dearly loved Annie, as he called her, left Abraham as the sole caregiver to their seven children. This was catastrophic. The children ranging in age from toddler to teens had adored their mother. From the eldest to the youngest, they were Menno, Lilly, Rose, Annie, Edwin, Abe, and Grace.

As Abe and Maria got to know one another, Maria's parents' invitation for her and her two children to join them in Minnesota was still on her mind. She needed to explain to them why she would consider marrying a man who was eleven years older than she was. A man who owned only a small farm but had seven dependent children, the youngest of whom was twenty-one months old. Her parents were not impressed and were understandably concerned. She would become stepmother to all these children, and she was herself the biological mom of Peter and Tina.

She agreed to marry Abraham. It was in large measure a marriage of mutual convenience. Each one needed what the other could contribute. One needed a companion and helper and caregiver to children. The other needed a home and a provider. Was there love? Who can know now? Initially there was attraction and eventually came respect and love for one another. Grandchildren like me who came along much later, viewed them as two interesting old people who were comfortable with one another. We knew no history.

Maria (Fast/Doerksen) Willems was now stepmother to seven children. This was a demanding full-time responsibility complicated by initial reluctance of the original seven Willems children to accept a new mother figure. Relational frictions existed for Maria's biological children, Peter, and Tina, trying to fit into this crowd of stepsiblings. There were tensions. It took time for these forced relationships to enjoy the affection of family. It was not entirely successful. The depth of the struggle between family members was never shared with succeeding generations. It was not a subject spoken about to any of us. The marriage itself between Abraham and Maria was often strained with so many mouths to feed. Maria tried to be all things to all people, but that was too much to expect. Not only did nine children have to co-exist but they also had to make room in their hearts and home for more children. Yes, more children. This union between Abraham and Maria eventuated in the births of five more children. That's right, Maria gave birth to Leslie, Gladys, Ruth, Esther, and Ruby. These are my uncles and aunts. Les, Ruth, and Esther have shared many of these details with me. My own mother never did. Candidly, I never thought to ask her. I sensed her lack of ease, even discomfort. I will never understand what held me back.

The reality is that Maria had three families of children, the first two biological offspring, the seven adoptees, and the latter five biological children. She loved and she cared for all her children, her own and her adopted children. No wonder she was exhausted. She gardened and cooked and sewed for them. She nursed them when they were unwell. During all these years, heartache ripped through this blended family. Lilly and Annie died as children. When Maria became pregnant with Ruby, she found herself incapable of coping with yet another child. In the home of her parents in law, Abraham S. and Katharina, she found temporary refuge, a day or so at a time, enough time for the in-laws to care for her and to pray with her and to pledge their support throughout her pregnancy. Maria carried on. Ruby was born.

Maria's firstborn child, Peter Elmer Doerksen was twelve years old when he was baptized on September 12, 1929. By his seventeenth year, he had experienced enough of life with the Willems brothers on that small farm. Harmony was not consistently in evidence in this blended family. Peter did not want to be a member of the Willems' clan. He refused to be called by the Willems surname. He retained his birth surname 'Doerksen.' How painful it must have been for Maria, Tina (my mom), and Peter, as he left the farm and boarded a train in Hepburn. His destination was the farm home of relatives in Minnesota. Something different happened. In Mountain Lake, MN., he stayed with a lovely couple, who owned Balzer Manufacturing and he was employed there.

Peter attended the Mennonite Brethren Church with the Balzer family, and that is where he met Evelyn Ysker. They were married on October 3, 1941, in Mountain Lake, Minnesota. They had two children, Jane, and Rodney (my dear cousins). Jane relates that before her mother Evelyn passed away, she told Jane that her father Pete had made such a good impression on her that she could hardly believe he had looked at her, and that mutual gaze became love at first sight for both. Very sadly for Evelyn, Jane, and Rod, on February 9, 1957, Peter died at the age of forty. I can still recall the shock and sorrow in our home as my mother read a telegram informing her of her brother's death.

***

As years passed the older Willems' sons left home for work elsewhere in other provinces. Life was changing. My Uncle Les Willems, before he passed away, wrote so ably his personal journal that describes those years. I have included his account in a later chapter.

Tuberculosis was a highly contagious, rampant disease and it struck members of the Willems clan. Gladys, Ruth, and Esther were isolated in the Sanatorium in Saskatoon many miles from home. Grandma Willems went to be with them as often as she could. The sickness consumed months and years of the girls' lives. Esther remained there for three years. Grace had been admitted earlier. She never left the hospital. After several years of isolation, Grace died at the age of twenty-six. Grace and my mother Tina were stepsisters, and they were the same age. My mother had already been working outside the family home for several years when Grace died. My mom (Tina) was married and had given birth to her first child, a son, me.

We don't know when or why Maria's given name was changed

to Marie. It was not a momentous modification, but it is noteworthy because most people remember her as Marie. My Aunt Esther (Willems) McIlveen remembers her mother with love and admiration. In her story included below, Esther refers to her mother as Marie.

Esther told me that one might have said that Marie sewed her way through life. Her sewing machine was her livelihood and with it she developed a reputation. She was known for her ability to sew coats, wedding dresses, drapes, and costumes, and she supplemented family income this way when she could get the work. Imagine her loss when during the Great Depression, her sewing machine was repossessed because of lapsed payments. Esther remembers being a little girl, holding the fabric of older dresses or pants as she sat across from her mother, who used a razor blade to cut the threads of the seams. She then washed the material, sewed, and recreated and ironed a newer garment. Marie would create her own patterns and if a child pointed at a style in a picture, Grandma Willems could create it. Esther and Ruth and her siblings appear in photographs that seldom convey how poor they were because they looked fashionable for their time. When I spoke with Esther, she still possessed her mother's metal thimble with a tiny hole pierced by the constant poking of needles over the years.

Marie lived among proven craftswomen who gathered to stitch their stories and their losses into beautiful quilts. Quilting bees were like community therapy sessions where news of unplanned pregnancies and of deaths in the families and of failed crops and the consequent hardships were shared. It was a sisterhood of quilters who could laugh and cry together. For many years Esther treasured a peach and white coloured quilt with impeccable stitching done by her mother. Esther could wrap the quilt around herself when she longed for her mother's arms. It was natural to have those longings for a mother whose gentle hand once rested on Esther's shoulder as she knelt at her mom's knees, and they prayed together.

Esther passed away peacefully on October 17, 2022, surrounded by her children, Kathryn, Kirsten, and Anthony. At their request, I officiated her memorial service. Married to Howard, a Presbyterian minister, Esther, in my later years, was my kindred-spirited, literary, poetic confident. As I began retirement, after 45 years of work as a clergyman, I struggled. I could become an interim or supply preacher, or I could restart my interrupted desire to be a fine artist. She held my hands, and blue-eyed, charismatic prophetess that she was, she told me to pick up my paint brushes and paint. She assured me that God was satisfied. Esther had learned so much of the Spirit from the woman who stitched her quilt.

***

When WWII ended in 1945, the Prairie economy was shattered and the small farm on which Abraham A. Willems had raised his family could sustain them no longer. There was no future there for his youngest son Les or for his youngest daughters, Gladys, Ruth, Esther and Ruby, the children of Marie's third family one might say. Of her second family consisting of the seven Willems stepchildren, some had moved away, and some had died. Menno, the eldest, as well as Rose and Abe, remained in the West.

Menno married Sarah Fadenrecht on October 21, 1932. They raised seven children on their family farm, Irvin, Maurine, Lorne, Leonard, Harvey, Maurine, and Bob.

Rose married Jacob (Jake) Nickel, a school teacher, on August 16, 1936. They lived in Saskatchewan, Minnesota, and moved eventually to British Columbia. Rose and Jake had three children, Sheldon, Shirley, and Larry. Jake passed away in 1988. Rose died on October 11, 2008. She lived in Abbotsford and since Christine and I moved to B.C., we visited her frequently. She became blind in her last few years, yet she specialized in joy. She asked me to officiate her funeral. She said, "when I am gone, tell them all that I can see."

Abe moved to Ontario, joined the army in 1942. At the conclusion of the war, he married Patricia Purdy from St. Catharines. They had three children, John, Debbie, and Betsy. In later years, Abe moved to Burnaby, B.C. where he died in 1990.

Edwin was already married to Alma Baerg and had moved to St. Catharines, Ontario in 1941. Two children were born, Gerald Kenneth and Marilyn Joyce.

Of the original Willems offspring, Lilly, Annie, and Grace were deceased.

Many Westerners had moved to Ontario where job opportunities reportedly abounded. Some of Willems' friends had relocated in St. Catharines, located amid the productive Niagara fruit belt where there were Mennonite churches. The appeal was real. So, Abraham and Marie made the decision to move to Ontario. They were both in their seventies when they moved with their grown children.

My take on the fifteen years that Grandpa Willems lived in Ontario before his death on March 21, 1965, is that these were years of contentment for him. He held occasional part-time jobs as did Grandma. Grandma's first family consisted of Peter and Tina. Peter was gone, residing, and working in Minnesota. He was married to Evelyn. Tina, married to Edward Unruh was still in Hepburn at the time of the Willems move east in 1942 but Tina and Ed soon moved to St. Catharines as well in 1945. And I came with them.

It was during Grandma's St. Catharines years that I, and many of my cousins, knew Grandma Willems. I turned five when we arrived in St. Catharines. From then on, Grandma W. was always in my life. She was industrious. She cleaned other people's homes. She sewed garments for others. She drove a car. She spent time with me. I went berry picking with her on Peter Bergman's farm. When I dislocated a bone, not just once, Grandma drove me to her unlicensed Mennonite chiropractor for instant relief. She listened well. She loved me. I can write that. It's my auto-bio moment. The truth is, she loved each one of her grandchildren and each of us knew it.

Grandma Willems was unresponsive to me in that Tabor Manor bed from which her soul would go to heaven. There was finality in my visit with her. I sensed that inevitability as I stood there and that is why I broke into spontaneous uncontrollable sobbing. With tears on my face, I thanked the Lord for this woman in this tiny form under the covers. Unaccustomed to seeing me with tears, my children saw me weeping. They could not understand. I explained later that I had been overwhelmed by love and gratitude for Grandma that I could no longer personally express to her.

Sisters: Elizabeth, Katherine, and Maria Fast

3 HE SAID, "GOOD NIGHT SWEETHEEART."

IT WAS ANOTHER EVENING SPENT WITH THE WOMAN HE LOVED. Tina stood on the steps of the front porch wearing a knee length wool coat over a mid-calf length patterned dress. Ed didn't want to say good night. He didn't want to leave her. Her dark hair was highlighted by the full moon overhead. She was twenty-one years old, and she was lovely. It was 1940 and in just one month the two of them would be married. Ed wore gabardine slacks and a cotton long sleeve shirt over which was a brown leather jacket. Ed removed his fedora, leaned forward, enfolded Tina in his arms and kissed her, a long kiss. Still holding her, he looked into her eyes and said, "good night sweetheart. I'll see you tomorrow." Putting his hat back on his head, he turned and without looking back, strode down the road, whistling as he walked.

***

Marie Doerksen was in labour. She was about to give birth to her second child. It was a sunny Montana day, on the 4th of June. The year was 1919. Her two-year-old son Peter was playing on the floor in the main room. Marie began to have serious contractions shortly after her husband Isaac left for town. He would be gone for some time. There was no way to summon a midwife or a neighbour woman. No time left. The baby was coming now. Her shouts were heard by their hired man, who opened the front door and said, "Allens in de Reeg?" (Is everything okay?"). "Büst up Stee?" ("are you okay").

She shouted, " Kümm in! (Come in).

Once inside that humble birthing bedroom, the hired man saw her condition. The baby came. He was quickly told to take the scissors and to cut the umbilical cord. My mother Tena Martha Doerksen was born on the fourth of June 1919 in Wolf Point, Montana and the birth was registered in Oswego, Montana. Much later in life, Tena learned about the 'hired man maternity' anecdote from her own mother Marie. Tena was my mother.

***

In most ways I will tell Tena's story as a journalist would write it, objectively, yet I cannot resist occasions when her life's tale touches me personally. 'Tina' as she later spelled her name, lived to celebrate eighty-eight birthdays. She has been away from all of us and with the Lord Jesus since November 2007. Time passes and memories blur. Photographic images help our recall.

As I sit to write, I see her in my desk photo in a glass frame. She is a young woman, and slender and beautiful. As I look at her face in the photo, I myself am an old man, looking back at the beginning of her life, and I know how her story turned out. It's good for me to think about her. Perhaps hearing me talk about her will help you to revive your memories as well. Or maybe it will introduce you to a lady who lived an ordinary life in an extraordinary manner.

Tina Doerksen was two years old when her father, Isaac Doerksen died. She was fatherless for a couple of years and then just like that, she was in this other large family in a small Saskatchewan farmhouse with other children that belonged to this new man. Her mommy told Tina that Abraham A. Willems was her new father. As a little girl she slept with three other girls who were not her sisters, but who suddenly were her 'steefsesta' (stepsisters), she was told in low German. Rose was twelve years old, and Anna was six years old. Grace was four months older than Tina, and both were four years of age. One year later Anna died at the age of seven. One can only imagine the grief in the Willems household where children had lost their mother two years earlier. Another Willems daughter named Lily had died in 1916 at the age of six. Tina had new stepbrothers too. Menno was twelve years old; Edwin was eight, and Abram was two years of age.

Tina grew up in the farming communities of Waldheim and Hepburn. Most of Tina's years, as a child and teenager in the Willems' family, are an untold story. She did not speak about those years to me or anyone it seems. Her youngest sisters confirmed to me that Tina was largely silent about the past. In many respects those were severe years, and they were not a topic she wished to review.

Her birth mother Marie began bearing more children. Half-siblings came along. When Tina was five, Gladys was born in 1924. Leslie was next in 1927. Then Ruth in 1930, Esther in 1933 and Ruby in 1937.

The 1930's were economically depressed years on the prairies. She wanted to study but was prevented from proceeding past grade nine. Necessity forced her to go to work. She needed to look after herself. She was industrious. She knew how to sew, how to bake and how to cook, the skills learned by most girls in small prairie towns. The only work available to Tina other than farm work, was domestic help in other homes and clerking in a store. She landed a job as a switchboard operator for the Hepburn town telephone service.

Tina was a Christian in a Mennonite community, and her faith was sincere. She was a church going woman as were most residents in town. She had a pleasant singing voice, a kind of unfinished contralto. She sang with others, duets and trios and choir.

Tina was not far away from a brand-new life filled with love. At 21 yrs of age she met 26-year-old Edward Richard Unruh. They were acquainted for a long time, but they got to know one another when they were both employed in the Hepburn Red and White Store.

***

I will also tell Edward's story with editorial impartiality until those moments when I cannot resist the personal touch that Dad makes upon me.

Edward was the youngest child of Cornelius Kornelius Unruh (best known as C.K.) and his wife Katharina Loewen, best known as Katrina to some friends and affectionately as Tina to C.K. When Edward came into the world on March 8, 1915, C.K and Katharina already had three older children. Edward was the baby, thirteen years younger than his sister Annie who was the eldest child. The first son born to them was named Cornelius like his father, but he soon preferred to be called Neale. He was eleven years older than Edward. Then came Harry who was five years older than Edward. It has fascinated my two brothers, Murray, Neale, and I that we have the same time interval between the three of us, as did Uncles Neale, Harry, and Edward. I am five years older than Murray and eleven years older than my brother Neale.

Edward was a likeable young man around the town of Hepburn. As a youth he played hockey on the outdoor rink, hung around with friends, and listened to the radio. He completed grade eleven before working at occasional jobs wherever he could find work. His hair left his head in his late teens. By age eighteen he was bald on top. What hair remained on the sides was dark and then he grew a thin, trimmed black mustache. There was more to the man named Edward whom Tina came to know and to love. He had a pleasant voice and a constant whistle. The tunes he whistled in downtown Hepburn (Main

Street), were often popular tunes, dance band music. He knew them all, tunes and words. He whistled them when he walked. He was five foot six and he walked with confidence. He wore flat caps and fedoras slightly set to the right side and he was attractive. Tina saw him that way. He was romantic in her eyes.

As perfect as he seemed, Edward had a weakness. In the eyes of the Mennonite Community, his deficiency was spiritual. Edward Richard Unruh had no recognized spiritual commitment, had made no public profession of faith in Christ, and had not been baptized by immersion in water. As a child and youth, he had attended church with his parents. He no longer attended.

Tina was a believer. She had been baptized. If Tina chose to marry Edward, she would be marrying someone outside the faith. She would be unequally yoked (linked) to an unbeliever. That was a theological conviction within the Mennonite community. That Edward came from a respected family was not at issue. He was a very fine man. His seeming faith-less life was the concern.

Edward was a private man. He expressed opinions and viewpoints to Tina that no one else heard. Did he not believe in God? Did he not believe in Jesus Christ? Did he not believe that God had sent his son Jesus to be the Saviour of sinners? Tina knew he was not without faith. Ed knew Christian fundamentals but had not yet subscribed. What hesitations did he have? Why was he reluctant to commit in a public manner? She knew.

Mom loved Dad. In the Mennonite town of Hepburn, Saskatchewan in 1941, her decision carried public shame. What must it have meant to Mom to choose Dad over the advice of family, church, and community? She would not be allowed to be married in her Mennonite Church. Out of principle and conscience her pastor would not officiate. What impact did this church stance have upon Dad? Did Mom view her choice as defiance of belief and custom and tradition? Probably not, and none of the questions matter now.

Their wedding on June 12, 1941, took place outside the church, not because they wanted that. A Saskatoon justice of the peace solemnized the ceremony. Mom did not wear white. It was not 'appropriate.' She wore a soft pastel pink suit with a matching pink broad brimmed hat. Why she felt it necessary to comply with this hurtful distinction we cannot know. That's how their marriage began. Yet following the wedding, they found that people accepted them. They both were well liked. Life went on. And that's only a small part of their story.

World War II had broken out, and Canada became involved because it was a member nation of the British Commonwealth. The immediate cause of the outbreak of WWII in Europe in 1939 was the German invasion of Poland. England and France had guaranteed that they would protect Poland's borders. When Germany invaded, France and England kept their promise and declared war. It was not automatic that Canada would engage in the war, but Canada's government and people were united in support of Britain and France.

On the 10th of September 1939, Canada entered the war. During the first two years of Tina's and Ed's married life, this military conflict interrupted them. What kind of conversation must the two of them have had? Ed's inclination to enlist was counter cultural. Hepburn's dominant Mennonite community were pacifists. Ed was not prepared to make a faith-related claim as a conscientious objector that most Mennonite peers were making. But what could you expect from a man who was not a professing Christian? That may have been the thought of some church folk. It never crossed Dad's mind to ask for an exemption.

Dad's father C.K had purposely emigrated to Canada. Canada was now the family home. The uncertainties and threats in Russia had been left behind. In Canada freedoms existed, freedoms that needed to be secured. Dad was born in Canada. Contrary to the pacifism of the Mennonite culture, Dad felt that he must make a citizen's contribution. Mom let Dad do what his heart and conscience informed him to do, enlist, and serve his country. He enlisted. I was born on September 13, 1942, and Dad was a member of the Royal Canadian Air Force. Imagine our mom in 1943, with a newborn baby boy, and having to kiss Ed and let him go? And here I am at 81 years of age, grateful for Dad's courage to take such a stand.

Following brief preparatory postings to Gananoque and Vancouver, Dad was commissioned to the Yukon Air Services. He spent much of his tour at RCAF Station Whitehorse which had originally been the Whitehorse Airport owned by the Canadian Department of Transport. In 1942 it was transferred to the Royal Canadian Air Force as part of the system called the Northwest Staging Route. This route consisted of a series of airstrips and radio stations from Alberta, British Columbia, Yukon, and Alaska. This provided a secure air route to send assistance to Russia through Northern Canada, across Alaska and the Bering Sea to Siberia and eventually to the Eastern Front of battle. Dad was among the team that operated and maintained the airport facilities, processing 450 planes per month.

The RCAF provided regular leaves from his duties during the four years of his military service. Dad would arrive at home each leave time, handsomely dressed in his uniform and cap. Mom would excitedly greet him. I was two and three years of age yet I remember this pleasant familiar person bringing me small gifts. Then finally in 1945 the war was over. He came home to stay, and he was my father, and I don't recall any impression of this being strange to me.

The post war years began with Mom and Dad opening and operating a Coffee Shop in Hepburn. It was popular, particularly because Mom baked the tastiest pies on the planet. It was an ordinary achievement in a small town where no one had much money. When I was four years old and with mom pregnant again, it was apparent that Hepburn could not provide long-term opportunity for the family. Non-farming prairie families were moving either west to the coast or to Ontario. As Mom and Dad discussed their future, they were convinced that employment and a viable future existed either in British Columbia or in Ontario. They had a choice to make.

Dad's brother Neale, married to Agnes (Aganetha Hiebert), had already made the move to B.C. They had one child, a daughter named Verna Catherine. Why Dad did not opt to move West to B.C., I have never learned but he did move from his hometown and from the Prairie past. Dad and mom decided to go east. Mom's parents, her birth mom Marie (Doerksen) Willems and her stepdad, Abraham A. Willems had already made the move to St. Catharines, and that is where our new home and future would be. Dad left behind his mother and father, C.K. Unruh, and Katharina (Tina) Loewen as well as his sister Annie and her husband George Friesen, and his brother Harry and his wife Ann Peters.

Our little family, my dad, my pregnant Mom, and I moved to St. Catharines, Ontario in 1947. Shortly after our arrival, my brother Murray was born on September 7, 1947. Six days later I celebrated my fifth birthday. Neale, the youngest son came much later, when I was eleven and Murray was six.

***

Mom and Dad rented accommodation for many years, first a condemned two-room shack on Geneva Street for a few months. Next was a downtown St. Paul St. third floor apartment, followed by a detached bungalow house in Rosedale Gardens that was a subdivision outside of St. Catharines. Within two years we moved to a large brick house at 10 Clark St. Five years later we made the move to an even larger two-floor house on James St. Finally, Mom and Dad, aged 37 and 41 respectively, purchased their first home. It was a 3-bedroom bungalow with a basement. It was located on Bunting Rd., #531, with a private back yard, well outside the city of St. Catharines. It was wonderful to each one of us. Murray, Neale, and I loved it. I was twelve years old.

During all those years while her children grew, Mom did housework for other women, some occasional sewing of garments. She was hired to sew costumes for the local skating club. She worked in her church, Calvary Church, always in the kitchen. It was what she knew best to do, and the skill for which she became known. In fact, over time, she operated her own Catering Business and prepared grand dinners for large gatherings. Wealthy people hired Tina Unruh. Her happiest employment was as Day-time Food Services provider for Ontario Paper head office. She even prepared a cookbook of her many recipes and those of others. She asked my brother Neale and I to design a cover and chapter art work. She self-published 1000 copies and sold them all. What a lady.

Perhaps Mom's greatest personal fulfillment was found as she

worked with her local church women's group and took on a
leadership role. She became recognized as a woman of integrity, of
spirituality and she was elected eventually to the presidency of the
Women's Ministry for the entire southern Ontario region of
Associated Gospel Churches. She led meetings, gave talks and
presentations, and while she was humbled and sometimes terrified,
she amazed herself that she could do this and that her leadership
was valued. By the time of this latter achievement and service, her
three sons, Ron, Murray, and Neale, were each of us in some form
of Christian ministry ourselves. She would say over and over that
we were a constant source of joy for her.

She was a much-loved mother and grandmother and great
grandmother.

***

Job opportunity for an unskilled worker like dad and the urgent
need for an income to support his family, meant taking a factory
job as soon as he and mom moved from Saskatchewan to Ontario.
First, he worked on the assembly line at Ontario Paper Mills, then
Thompson Products pumping out General Motors parts, and then
for over 40 years at Anthes Imperial that manufactured furnaces.
He had a few different tasks at Anthes but most of his working
years in that plant until he was 65 were spent on an assembly line,
standing up and kneeling all day long, screwing in metal parts. I
remember the years we lived on Clark Street when he would walk
to and from work covering several miles each way. We marked
distance in miles rather than kilometres in those days. Dad was a
hard worker and as his sons we respected him. When we were
older, in our thirties and forties, we asked him why he had stuck
with that job all that time instead of looking for some other
employment, and his response humbles me still. "I did it for my
boys."

I was ten years old when my father walked to church one
Sunday night. I can't remember that dad had ever before attended a
church meeting by himself. It could be viewed as a divine
appointment. On that occasion my dad did what he hesitated to do
or could not do as a younger man. Dad made a decisive choice to
believe that Jesus Christ is the Son of God and to accept Jesus as

his Saviour and LORD. Years later I asked him why he had hesitated for so long to make this decision. He told me that it was because every morning of his childhood and youth, his mother left the kitchen and made her way to the barn. Many times he watched her and listened to her as she knelt in the straw of a stall to pray to 'Unse Vader in'n himmel!' our Father in heaven. Her disciplined example overwhelmed him. He concluded that if that was required to be a Christian, he could never measure up. I assume my Grandma Unruh's barn prayers were realized on that Sunday evening when Dad walked to the front of the church and gave his life to the LORD. Dad was not a theologian, but he tried to understand scripture and he sought to live by its principles. Mom's and Dad's dependability, authenticity and love most certainly affected the three of us sons. All of us cherish the legacy of those who have gone before us.

Their marriage vows were genuinely lived. My mom and dad loved each other for all their 66 years together. There were occasional differences of opinion between them, but I cannot remember a time that my father raised his voice in anger to my mom. She was blessed by a gentle man.

The enduring memory my father has left me, is of his love for our mother. She was always his sweetheart. He encouraged her, supported her, protected her, helped her, and loved her unmistakably. Acting this out became difficult for him only when her dementia was so acute. She was a patient in Tabor extended care facility, and he was still healthy and able to live in his own apartment. He didn't know how to spend time with her. Dad found it incredibly grim to see his loved one so helpless and distant. At last, he asked Murray to accompany him when he visited. That was the support he required.

Our dear mom, Tina Unruh, died on November 6, 2007. As the extended family stood at mom's coffin, dad spoke to her, saying, "Good night, Sweetheart. I'll see you soon." Six months later, on May 1, 2008, Dad, true to his word, followed her in a typical quiet way. He was 93 years of age when he turned to walk to his couch and had a weak spell and lay down on his carpet and fell asleep.

Among Dad's and Mom's favourite songs was a spiritual sung by Stuart Hamblen. The lyrics became familiar around our childhood home. "When I close my eyes in sleep, say amen but don't you weep. I've got so many million years I just can't count them."

What material stuff did my parents leave behind? There were dishes and silverware, coins, and jewellery. All modest pieces shared among children and grandchildren. Yet get this. After purchasing their first home for $10,000 in 1954 when dad was 39 and mom was 35, and after living in it for 40 years, they sold it in 1985 for $65,000 when dad was 70. They then lived off that money, a modest company pension and government pensions for another 23 years. They enjoyed winters in Florida and a few trips to the West Coast where I have lived since autumn 1991. Still, when the estate was settled, dad left $39,000 to his three sons. I consider that remarkable.

I have five grandchildren. They were born when my mom and Dad were elderly and no longer able to travel. They saw only baby Kailyn when Tim and Cari and Christine and I made a trip to Ontario. They never did see Ryan or Jayden or Kale or Kadence. Nonetheless, whenever I visited dad, he asked me about each of his great grandchildren and he used each of their names.

Tina on her wedding day
June 12, 1941

4 WHY WAS MY DAD BORN IN HEPBURN?

AS I WRITE THIS PERSONAL STORY ABOUT MY
FAMILY, I am always conscious that my two brothers, Murray,
and Neale, share so much about which I write. It is to be their
cherished memory as well as mine. Why was our Dad born in
Hepburn, Saskatchewan?

Our father, Edward Richard Unruh was born on the 8th day of
March in 1915 on the family farm outside of Hepburn where each
of his older siblings Annie, Neale, and Harry were born. Edward
was the youngest son of Cornelius K. Unruh and Katharina
Loewen.

***

Eddie's Boyhood

When Eddie was born in 1915, WW1 had begun in Europe. The
British declaration of war on Germany automatically brought
Canada into the war, because of Canada's legal status as a British
Dominion. On August 4, 1914, the Governor General Robert
Borden declared war between Canada and Germany. When the war
began Eddie's two brothers, Harry, was four years old, and Neale
was ten. The First World War lasted from 1914–1918.

Life for Eddie was spent out of doors as long as the weather
cooperated. A most exciting day for him would be a day when his
father was helping a neighbour raise a barn. There were scores of

men who showed up, and they could frame a barn and cover it in one day. The men came with their children, usually the boys, but sometimes entire families showed up. Women busied themselves with cooking food for their men. Girls huddled on the farmhouse porch playing with rag dolls, and corn husk dolls they had made. Boys hung out within sight of the construction. They swapped stories, or played marbles, and spun wooden tops they had carved with pocketknives.

Summer days were long, always enjoyable, and sometimes surprising. Eddie never knew what new experience would occur. "Eddie, come with me," his dad said. Eddie's dad was going to clear a part of an acre of land and Eddie came along. He watched as his dad, who always seemed a large, powerful man, cut down willows, pine trees, cottonwoods, and poplars. Eddie didn't feel like he was much help. His dad never made him feel like he was a nuisance. He was a companion. He brought his dad water from a large thermos. His mom had prepared sandwiches for them, and Eddie opened them up at noon, when his father, perspiring and exhausted, sat beside the truck with his back against a tire.

During the long cold winter months, Eddie read. Occasionally his father would buy him a book, such as 'Just William' by Richmal Crompton, or 'Emil and the Detectives,' by Eric Kastner. Gramophones were a luxury, and a radio was hardly affordable but C.K. said it was necessary. The home radio was a lifeline to the world. Their tall floor vacuum tube model cost $150. Eddie could lie on the floor and listen to favourite programs. Low-power stations were within range and produced music, comedy, drama, education, preaching, news, poetry or narrated stories. As years passed, imported shows such as Amos 'n' Andy, Fibber McGee and Molly, and The Great Gildersleeve were added.

Most of the family acreage was in grain. Crops were crucial to family income and sustenance. Hail was always a threat. In some years, the waving wheat so large and colourful, could be the best of a decade. Within hours hailstorms would steal 2,000 dollars. Eddie's dad became the local hail adjuster for an insurance company. He was respected because he equitably assessed damages that farmers suffered. As Eddie grew into his teens, he wielded the 3-foot axe to cut trees to extend the grain farm, or he manned the thresher. Whatever the task, he knew what it was to work. And on a day that wasn't pressing with responsibility, he took the family shotgun and walked, far into the land, out of sight. Beautiful country, wild grasses up to his knees and then walking slowly, quietly to one of the sloughs full of ducks. With a couple of quick shots, he brought supper home, a delicious surprise for his mom and dad. No one cooked poultry as well as his mom did. At church potluck suppers, he walked past all the meat dishes on the serving tables, to find his mother's contribution.

Eddie grew up and wondered what he could do with his life. He was reliable and hard worker and he didn't mind putting in a good day's work for anyone who hired him. But in this town, opportunities were scarce, that was, apart from toiling on farms. Eddie often wondered why was he there?

Why was Edward Richard born in Hepburn? The constructive response is one that explains where Dad's parents, Cornelius K. Unruh, and Katharina Loewen, came from and why they chose to come to this small Canadian town. That's an enormous transcontinental story and it reaches into an unfamiliar and distant time.

***

Katharina Loewen (My paternal grandmom)

The S.S. Silesia was a late 19th-century Hamburg America Line passenger and cargo ship. The Silessia had a capacity of 600 passengers. It transported European immigrants, primarily Russian, Prussian, Hungarian, German, Austrian, Italian, and Danish individuals, and families. The ship ran between the European ports of Hamburg, Germany and Le Havre, France, to Castle Garden and later Ellis Island, New York.

The Silesia was built by Caird & Company of Greenock, Scotland, and she was 340 feet (100 m) in length and 40 feet (12 m) from side to side. Silesia had both a steam engine and a set of traditional masts. She had a steel hull, two masts, and one steam funnel. Her two engines drove a single 10 ft. (3.0 m) screw with 2,200 horsepower making 54 revolutions per minute.

Aboard the S.S. Silesia on this ocean crossing were Jacob and Helena Loewen and their four children, Jacob Jr. (7 yrs), Maria (4 yrs.), Helena (2 yrs.) and Katharina. Yes, that's her, Katharina, my grandma. Murray's and Neale's paternal grandma. Katharina was only five months old when her parents brought her to the United States.

The Loewens and other passengers aboard S.S. Silesia daily saw the dark smoke rising from her stacks and blackening her twelve sails. They may not have been aware that twelve men shoveling coal continuously from her four coal bunkers kept her engines running around the clock, consuming 75 tons per day of her 1,100-ton capacity of coal. All the steam generated in her boilers was recovered and reused during the several days of her journey from Hamburg, Germany to Ellis Island, New York. The Loewen family arrived and disembarked from the S.S. Silesia at Ellis Island, New York, NY, on the 8th of July 1874.

Ellis Island was sometimes called the Isle of Hope. For some people it was the Isle of Tears. It was the 'Golden Door' to a new life for half a century. Immigrants of every ethnic background arrived there after treacherous trips across land and harrowing passages across oceans. They disembarked to start life in a new land. The immigration experience was challenging but Mennonites were accustomed to trials.

Immigrants with farming background were directed to American states where there was available land for homesteading. The Jacob Loewen family settled in Turner County, Dakota Territory. My grandmother Katharina Loewen lived in Turner County throughout her childhood and teen years. Hers was a God-fearing, church-attending family and she made a public expression of her own faith at the age of fifteen when she was baptized by immersion in water on July 21, 1889.

Only when she was older did Katharina learn the details of her birth in a distant country that had been home to the extended Loewen family for several generations. Katharina was born on February 26, 1874, in Bruderfeld village, within the Molotschna Colony in Crimea, South Russia (Ukraine) to Jacob and Helena Loewen. She was only five months old when she was brought abord the S.S. Silesia.

Katharina's father Jacob Loewen was born in the village of Hierschau, Molotschna Colony, South Russia on August 23, 1842. Her mother, Helena Unruh, that's right, did you catch that Unruh surname? Helena Unruh was born on March 5, 1849, in Waldheim,

Molotschna, South Russia. She married Jacob Loewen, and her own maiden name was Unruh. Yes, my grandma Katharina Loewen's mother's maiden surname was Unruh? It could be a coincidence. I have news for you. I have a notable revelation for you. It's a feature of our family history that I have uncovered and that was never shared and may not have been known beyond Helena's own generation.

Helena Unruh was the daughter of Kornelius Unruh, a man born on Nov. 11, 1820, in Sofievvka, Volhynia (Prussia). She was the second of five siblings, the eldest of whom was her brother Kornelius K. Unruh. According to common practice, he was bestowed his father's given name as his middle name, and then he was also saddled with Kornelius as his own first name. He was Kornelius Kornelius Unruh. Kornelius K. was six years older than his sister Helena. He was born on March 17, 1843, in Waldheim, Molotschna Colony, South Russia.

Kornelius K. was 24 years of age when he married Aganetha Kroeker on the 5th of December 1867 at Schwesterthal, Crimea, South Russia. Kornelius K. and Aganetha had eight children. They named their second born child, Cornelius K. Unruh (my grandfather). A little mercy there, his first name was spelled with a 'C'. So, Helena, Kornelius K.'s sister, was my grandpa C.K. Unruh's aunt. He was her nephew. Aunt Helena's daughter, Katharina Loewen, was Kornelius K.'s niece. Katharina was our Grandma. And yes, you are catching on.

Breaking news: At the age of twenty, Helena's daughter Katharina married Helena's brother Kornelius' son, Cornelius K. Unruh. And there you have it, Grandpa and Grandma Unruh, my dad's parents, were first cousins. Their wedding took place in Hillsboro, Kansas on December 2, 1894.

Something else that may be news to you. In tracing Grandma (Loewen) Unruh's ancestral information, I learned that she bore two more children than the four children with whom we have always been familiar. We knew of Aunt Annie (Anna), Uncle Neale (Cornelius), Uncle Harry and Edward (my dad). However, two daughters preceded them, Hannie born June 16, 1895, and Susanna, born April 3, 1897. Hannie died at or near her birth. Susanna died on 8 February 1898 in her first year of life.

***

C. K. Unruh (My paternal grandfather)

For several weeks in 1893, Kornelius Kornelius Unruh. and his wife Aganetha and their eight children spoke about leaving the family home and farm in Temir Bulat, Crimea, and crossing land and ocean to go to America. We can imagine the emotion involved in taking with them nothing but essentials. And then, how many tears were shed as it became apparent that the family had only meagre financial resources and could only afford to send two of the children, the two eldest. They would report back to the rest of the family. It was hoped that the others could follow later. Not all could.

Their eldest child was Aganetha, born September 11, 1870. You read her name correctly. Yes, her mom and dad did that to her, gave her the same name as her mom. No wonder, she opted for Agnes when she was of school age. My grandfather, Agnes' brother Cornelius Kornelius Unruh, the second born child of his family, was born in the town of Temir Bulat in South Russia (Crimea, Ukraine) on the 20th day of April 1873. Today the town of Temir Bulat is known as Rozdol'ne.

At the time that this immigration discussion was underway, Cornelius was twenty years old, and he was single. His sister Agnes was 23 years old, already married and she had two small children.

Agnes' husband was Heinrich Kroeker, whom she married on the 19th of November 1889. Heinrich's birth date was September 28, 1867, in South Russia. At the time of their trans-ocean trip, their two sons, Cornelius and Heinrich, were three years old and one year old respectively. In 1893 these three adults, Cornelius (C.K.), Aganetha and Heinrich, and their two small children embarked by ship to emigrate to the United States of America to start life that offered hope.

Upon arrival, like so many others, they docked in New York and then proceeded to their destination by train and settled in South Dakota. They stayed there for three years before moving to Harvey, North Dakota where they lived for seven years.

***

Why were the parents of Cornelius K and Katharina born in Ukraine (South Russia)? Their lineage pointed to Prussian origin with ancestral homes near the Baltic Sea. Why did their parents and grandparents move from there to South Russia? Was it a matter of choice, necessity, or desperation? Was it their preference to live in these vast collective colonies containing scores of small villages? Was it their desire to spend their lives turning the vast steppes of South Russia into productive agricultural farmland? What was happening in Europe culturally, politically, and spiritually that can answer these questions? The answers reveal why my dad was born in Hepburn?

Their surnames, Loewen and Unruh suggest some of the answers. In some cultures, a surname or family name indicates the person's tribe or community. That's true here. The ancestral names mentioned in this book are associated with a vast ethnic group called Anabaptists and Mennonites. They settled in northern Poland from the early 1500s to the late 1600s. From where did they come? The names, Willems, Fast, Doerksen, and Loewen are patronymic surnames of Dutch origin. Unruh appears more identifiably of German origin. Whether all these families came from the Netherlands, or Switzerland, or Belgium or Germany, they all found Poland to be a place with a measure of religious freedom. In 1772 a large part of Poland was partitioned and assigned to Prussia. A second partition called West Prussia was where most Mennonites lived.

Cornelius K. Unruh (C.K) and Katharina Loewen Unruh came to Saskatchewan when farmland was made available to them by the federal government of Canada. They located near Hepburn. The area was almost exclusively populated by Mennonite families who had emigrated from South Russia, spoke Plautdietsch (low German), and attended worship in Mennonite churches, many of them Mennonite Brethren. Hepburn had a Mennonite Brethren church.

So, dad, Edward Richard Unruh was born in Hepburn.

Oh, and so was I.

Cornelius K. Unruh (C.K) and Katharina Loewen Unruh

Back: Peter Friesen, Annie, Neale, Agnes, Harry
Front: C.K., Edward (Dad), and Katharina
Bottom right Note from Neale & Agnes

5 IN BED TOGETHER, 1-500 AD

I KNEW THAT TITLE WOULD GET YOUR ATTENTION. A titillating chapter title. Spoiler alert: The title refers to the unexpected relationship between the ancient Roman Empire and Christianity. It was not an immediate union, yet it did eventually happen, but first ...

***

Our family history cannot be told without referencing Christian faith. A life of faith was fundamental to our featured families as far back as I can trace them. Distant ancestors preserved their unique faith expression by living in settlements comprised exclusively of like-minded people. They became known as Mennonites, a name derived from one of the movement's founders, Menno Simons. Mennonites had distinctive beliefs. Faith should be voluntary rather than compelled. Living lives of love, reconciliation and peacemaking was their calling. Injustice was to be overcome with good. Life was to be lived simply. Happiness was more than material well-being. Nature was God's gift and was to be cherished with stewardship and gratitude. The highest expression of faithfulness to Christ, was loving, sacrificial service. Today, our North American generations have embraced faith more privately, attending both Mennonite and non-Mennonite churches, pursuing diverse careers, and valuing the ancient principles passed down to us.

***

Growing up in Hepburn during the 1920s and 1930s, Eddie Unruh did not prioritize Christianity. He wasn't resistant, just apathetic. A decade later at Calvary Church in St. Catharines, he agreed with God and trusted exclusively in Jesus Christ. His understanding and commitment grew as he listened to sermons at church and on radio, and as he read the Bible. Years later, he expressed both wonder and satisfaction that his three sons were bible college graduates. The attributes of his character and temperament modelled the Christian life for his sons. Surprisingly, he had little knowledge of his Mennonite heritage, but in the 1980s, I was able to share some of that with him.

In 1991, Christine and I were settled in British Columbia. Dad knew I was studying our family history. During our annual visits my 76-year-old Dad had many questions for me. He wanted to know about his faith, salvation, hope, and his family story. I told him that many relatives were missionaries, church pastors, and bible college teachers. I reminded him that our daughter Cari, was studying music and piano performance at Mennonite Brethren Bible College (MBBC) in Winnipeg. Then I surprised him, informing him that the first president of that college was his own second cousin, Abraham Heinrich Unruh. A.H. Unruh had also previously founded Winkler Bible School and served as its president for nineteen years. We spoke about the origins of faith and the church and the Mennonite story. At some points he wiped tears. He realized he was part of something much larger than he understood. He listened eagerly. Then predictably after a discussion, he said, "I'm going to lie down now for a little while".

***

An Inconceivable Relationship
Here is a tale I never got to share with my Dad. This is a whirlwind trip of history, travelling back to 800 B.C., and moving forward to meet 15th-century Mennonites. This helps us to understand our family's world and how they embraced Christianity, leading to Eddie's birth in Hepburn.

In 753 B.C. the city of Rome was founded on the Tiber River. From 753 B.C. to 1 A.D. Rome rose was a kingdom, a republic and an empire with unmatched military might, conquering tribes and kingdoms. Religion played a crucial role in Roman life, depending on a pantheon of gods and goddesses for prosperity, success, and victory. This dependence furthered imperial ambitions. By 300 B.C. the Empire absorbed the entire Italian peninsula. By 1 AD it controlled Spain, modern-day France, the North African coast, Greece, Britain, and much of the Middle East. The Roman Empire was a superpower. While Rome governed Palestine, Jesus the Messiah was born. Rome would be a channel by which Jesus' life and teaching would have its profound impact on world history.

***

The Words "Follow Me."

Jesus selected individuals to whom he said, "Follow me." So compelling was his presence that these self-employed and independent men followed him. In daily conversations, Jesus spoke knowledgeably about the Kingdom of God. These followers became disciples. He taught standards they should live. His coaching, his compassion for people, and his power to heal were evident. Crowds of people were attracted to him. In time large crowds celebrated him as King of the Jews.

As his popularity increased, so did the opposition. Spiritual leaders within the Jewish community viewed Jesus with suspicion and disapproval. They perceived him as challenging their traditions and upsetting their scruples about the Law. They disliked him. Most of all, many Jews hated Jesus with homicidal fury because he claimed to be the Christ, the Son of God. He asserted equality with God.

His life ended abruptly on a Roman cross. He was impervious to death. This is where our vital trust matters. His resurrection was medically inexplicable, but plausibly undeniable. Hundreds saw him, touched him, and spoke with him following his resurrection. Jesus commanded and they obeyed. *"Go into all the world and preach the gospel to every creature,"* Mark 16:15.

***

The Church in Rome Asserted Primacy

Predictably, as the gospel spread, it arrived in Rome. Roman citizens became Christians. Paul the apostle wrote a letter to the Romans. *"Paul, a servant of Christ Jesus ... to all those in Rome who are loved by God and called to be saints"* (Romans 1:1,7). Since their faith was exclusively in Jesus Christ, Christians naturally renounced all other faiths. That viewpoint was contrary to syncretic Roman culture. Localized opposition and persecution followed. Both apostles Paul and Peter were executed by the Roman regime. Persecution became a defining feature of Christian self-understanding for the first three hundred years. Yet during those first three centuries, the numerous house churches in Rome became known collectively as the Church of Rome. Predictably, since Rome was the capital city of the vast Roman empire, it was presumed that the Church of Rome was the foremost congregation of all other Christian churches. Eventually The Church claimed to be the supreme Christian authority on earth. It was uncontested.

One reason for the claim was the traditional belief that Peter was founder and first bishop of the church of Rome. My problem? No first century historical accounts mention Peter being Bishop of Rome. The Church did not allude to it until the late second century. There is no explicit scriptural text to support it. Roman Catholics insist that Christ's words attest to it in Matthew 16:18. *"You are Peter, and on this rock I will build my church."* I prefer the following linguistic interpretation. The scripture passage submits that Jesus would build his church, not on Peter himself but rather on the truth of Peter's confession, that Jesus is the Christ, the Son of the living God.

Jesus asked the disciples, *"Who do people say that I am?"*

They answered, *"Some say John the Baptist, others say Elijah, and others say Jeremiah or one of the other prophets."*

Then Jesus asked, *"But who do you say that I am?"*

Simon Peter answered, *"You are the Christ, the Son of the living God."*

Then Jesus blessed Peter for his wise answer, and told him that, yes indeed, he would build his church based upon that exact truth, that Christ is the Son of the Living God. (Matthew 16:13-20).

Another feature of the Roman Church surfaced in the second

century when Ignatius of Antioch, a church father and bishop, alluded to four characteristics for the Roman Church. This was formalized in 381 AD as doctrine. The Nicene Creed states, "We believe in one, holy, catholic, and apostolic Church."

According to the Roman Catholic Church, the concept of a Papacy with a succession of popes also traces its origin to the apostle Peter. Yet no reference is found in scripture for papal successors, so the Papacy has a dubious origin. Then how did this develop? It is probable that Roman imperialism influenced the Roman mind so much that it shaped the Roman Catholic institution.

***

Power Sharing Between Big Church and Big State

Diocletian. In 286 AD Emperor Diocletian, believing that the Empire was too vast to manage from Rome, divided the Roman Empire into two sections with two co-emperors. Rome governed the Western Roman Empire. Byzantium, ruled the Eastern Roman Empire, known as the Byzantine Empire. Christianity was tolerated.

Constantine. Constantine became Emperor in 306 AD. His mother Helena had already adopted Roman Catholic Christianity. He himself professed to become a Christian in 312 AD. Constantine legalized Christianity. He did not ban polytheism, but Christianity was the dominant religion of the empire. This launched the era of the State Church of the Roman Empire. Constantine reigned from 306–337 AD.

Theodosius (347-395 AD). He was baptized as a Christian in 379 AD and went a giant step further than Constantine by declaring Christianity as the official state religion in 380 AD. This established the Church-State union. The Church and State were inseparable. The ruler's faith became the faith of the people. Identifying as a Catholic Christian was mandatory. Non-adherents were considered heretics. Pagan worship was forbidden. Catholicism remained the sole official religion of its allied Empire until 1555.

***

By now you should have a contemplative smile. Neither Christianity nor the Roman Empire anticipated the intimate connection that would develop between them. Rome had crucified Christ. Now the Roman Empire embraced Christianity. It's unthinkable, isn't it? An unexpected relationship between the ancient Roman Empire and Christianity. It wasn't a romance, and it wasn't a marriage. It was an ugly, messy affair, far more grim than my quick synopsis reveals. Their relationship was often a tug-of-war union and it existed for the next two millennia.

Why and how could this happen? Nothing is out of God's control. I must accept that the all-knowing God intended for the gospel of Jesus Christ to impact the world. Rome would be a vehicle.

***

I'll save the suspense. This apportioned Empire, Western and Eastern, (Roman and Byzantine), did not endure. Only the Eastern (Byzantine) empire survived. In 476 AD., the barbarian Germanic leader Odoacer staged an assault and deposed the Roman Emperor, Romulus Augustulus. Romulus was the last Western Roman emperor. No Roman emperor ever again ruled from a post in Italy. The Eastern Byzantine empire continued to flourish, and the Roman Catholic Church was still alive and extending its reach.

6 EMPIRE AND CHURCH IN THE EARLY MIDDLE AGES, 500-1000 AD

"WHY WAS I BORN IN HEPBURN?" MY DAD ASKED. Trust me, in my pursuit of the answer to Dad's question, I was forced to explore political and religious world history.

The early Middle Ages, or Medieval times or Dark Ages, are all descriptors that historians use for the same historical period from 500 AD to 1000 AD. 'Dark Ages' is appropriate because after the fall of the Roman Empire, the Empire's land was up for grabs. Kings and Lords fought for domain. Warfare and bloodshed were everywhere for hundreds of years. And with the central government gone, written records were no longer kept.

And yet, the Roman Catholic Church carried on. It relied upon the Eastern Roman Byzantine Empire that continued to function in its eastern provinces. And in time it relied on Western European monarchs who identified with Christianity.

Justinian. In 527 AD Justinian I, became Emperor of the Eastern Empire with its capital in Constantinople. Much of Justinian's desire to reunite and rebuild the empire came from his views concerning Church and State. Whereas Constantine had legalized Christianity, and Theodosius had made it the official religion, Justinian articulated the Church-State relationship. He wrote, "There are two great gifts which God, in His love for man, has granted from on high: the priesthood and the imperial dignity. The first serves divine things, while the latter directs and administers human affairs; both, however, proceed from the same origin and adorn the life of mankind." Justinian thought that if these God-ordained purposes were being carried out appropriately, then the world would have general harmony, a united empire!

Justinian strengthened the empire. As a sociopolitical team, Justinian and his wife Theodora introduced reforms. Theodora inspired legislation that prohibited sex trafficking and infanticide. She also instituted the death penalty for rapists. All their progressive policies together with all existing Roman laws in hundreds of documents were rewritten as the new Justinian legal code called Corpus Luris Civilis (Body of Civil Law). The expressed ideals within the code were strongly Christian and anti-unbeliever and were assimilated throughout Europe. In fact, Justinian made apostasy punishable by death. He closed famous schools in Athens because of their pagan teaching. He enforced laws in support of Christian morals and teaching. He established churches, the most famous being the Hagia Sophia in Istanbul, a supreme architectural achievement and still today a tourist attraction. He did much to solidify the concept of the Church and State ruling together in society. From the perspective of developing the Church-State relationship, Justinian's reign as Emperor from (427-565 AD) was one of the most effective in history.

***

The Franks, Charlemagne, and the Holy Roman Empire

The Franks

'Franks' was a name associated with several Germanic tribes. They migrated from northern Europe into Gaul. Gaul encompassed present-day France, Belgium, Luxembourg, most of Switzerland, parts of Northern Italy, and Germany west of the Rhine.

The Middle Ages were defined by the Franks. The Franks developed feudalism. Feudalism was a construct of society that was based on relationships of loyalty. Land was granted in exchange for labour and service. Lords and barons pledged loyalty to a king who conferred land to them. In turn, they provide soldiers (knights) to defend the king's interests. Each lord possessed enormous acreage on which there was a castle or manor. Around each manor a village grew as the lord gave portions of land to peasants to grow crops. Peasant loyalty was pledged to the Lord. Ninety percent of the people were peasants. The lord lived in the manor and people gathered there for protection or celebration. Peasants owned nothing, yet they were more than slaves. Peasants were considered free people, and could operate businesses as blacksmiths, bakers, and carpenters as well as farmers. The lord owned it all, manor, village, peasants, and crops. Peasants' lives were hard and brief, and they often died in their thirties.

The Catholic Church was powerful in most parts of Medieval Europe. A Bishop was the top church leader in the kingdom and managed an area called a diocese, consisting of many village churches. The church received a tithe of 10 percent from all the people, so the church became wealthy.

Two dynasties ruled the Franks during the Middle Ages, the Merovingian Dynasty, and the Carolingian Dynasty.

In 509 AD King Clovis founded the Merovingian Dynasty which ruled the Franks for the next 200 years. King Clovis converted to Christianity and was the first king of the Franks to be recognized as king by the Pope. This connection between Church and Government was considered vital and routine.

Imagine being stuck with this name, King Pepin the Short. When he took power, he inaugurated the Carolingian Dynasty that ruled the Franks from 751 to 843. Carolingian, the dynasty's name, derives from the many family members named Charles. Most notable was Charlemagne.

Charlemagne

Charlemagne was the most celebrated Carolingian ruler, with a reign lasting from 742 to 814 AD. He was already regarded as the leader among European monarchs, when on December 25, 800 AD, Pope Leo III crowned Charlemagne as the first 'Holy' Roman Emperor. A shocking tactical action by the Pope. It was the start of the 'Holy' Roman Empire. The Church and the Empire in powerful alliance again. The old Roman Empire was long gone. The Byzantine Empire still functioned in the East. But Pope Leo envisioned Europe as a new domain for Christendom. With Frankish and then German kings, this Holy Roman Empire ruled over western and central Europe for ten centuries from the 9th century to the 19th century (800–1806).

The Empire consisted of dozens of countries governed by kings, dukes, counts, bishops, abbots, and other rulers, collectively known as princes. The lesser potentates elected the Emperor and were ruled by him and were required to be loyal to the Emperor. Throughout the Middle Ages the Holy Roman Empire coexisted uneasily with these princes of the local territories who often tried to take power from the Empire. To avoid being deposed Charlemagne and succeeding emperors were forced to grant increasing autonomy to local kings, dukes, princes, nobles, and bishops.

Emperor Charlemagne was known as Charles the Great or King Charles I. He stimulated a Renaissance in Europe, a cultural and intellectual revival. He brought many reforms such as a strong government, written laws, education, a monetary standard, and support for the arts. He eventually founded the French and the German monarchies and successfully united what today is France, Germany, and northern Italy.

The last Emperor to be crowned by a Pope was Charles V in 1530.

So, What About our Ancestors, our Predecessors

The earliest dates of birth I have found for members of the five families, Willems, Loewens, Fasts, Doerksens, and Unruhs, are the following. The families predate the following birthdates, but their stories are lost to us. Record keeping was inadequate or vanished in the ravages of time and the changeover of governing powers.

Cornelius Willms born September 30, 1730, in Lakendorf, Gross Werder, Prussia. (Yes, this surname Willms belonged to an original progenitor). Heinrich Loewen's estimated birth year is 1750 in Neustaedterwald, West Prussia. Jacob Fast was born about 1752 in Waldheim, Molotschna, South Russia. Johann Doerksen's estimated birth was in 1820 in Waldheim, Molotschna, South Russia. Heinrich Unrau was born about 1640, and son Hinrich Unrau about 1665. The next generation was Martin Unruh, born in 1760 in Brenkenhofswalde, Brandenburg, Prussia. Notice the spelling change in the surname, from Unrau to Unruh. No explanation is found. Martin's son was Benjamin Martin Unruh, born in 1783.

But what about faith for earlier ancestors than these? I believe that there was little option about faith for members of the Unruh, Loewen, Fast, Doerksen and Willems families who predated my earliest recorded ancestral lifetimes. By the 9th century over fifty percent of Europe was under the control of the Roman Catholic Church and by the 12th century the authority of the Church was universal. I assume that our earliest ancestors complied with the dominant faith in their locations. That is unless they already associated with some early reform-minded people.

History informs us that reformers were at work for centuries, protesting what they perceived as Roman Catholicism's errors in belief and practice. Those protesters were routinely shut down or eliminated. Over time, the protestations of some individual reformers became movements and through both debate and violent conflict, concessions were granted by local governments. Only gradually, there were lands and nations where Protestants were given autonomy of faith. Our ancestors who shared the convictions of reformers were willing to leave their own homelands, to relocate to places where they enjoyed such freedom.

7 EARLY REFORMERS & PERSECUTION
1000-1500 AD

CATHOLIC HISTORIANS ACKNOWLEDGE THAT PURITY IN THE CATHOLIC CHURCH WEAKENED during the centuries of the Middle Ages. Parish priests should have been well-educated, yet many were illiterate, hardly capable of performing religious services. Successive popes were either in conflict or collusion with monarchs. Corruption was rampant. The Church desperately needed reformation. It was a long time coming. Protestations came from within the Church but were unwelcome. Catholic priests, Martin Luther, and Ulrich Zwingli are credited with fathering the Protestant Reformation. However, long before Luther and Zwingli and John Calvin, there were others, most of whom the Catholic Church condemned as heretics.

Pre-Reformation Movements and Heroes

Many reform-minded Christians, movements, factions, and sects tried to return their Church to what they perceived as the purity of the apostolic church. They protested perceived errors and excesses of the Roman Catholic Church. The seeds of reformation began with them. Although met with fierce resistance, their opinions foreshadowed Protestant ideas that were later enunciated by the Reformation.

In this simple list of 12 early reformers, there are three men whose names I have highlighted and about whom I will elaborate,

Pierre Valdo, John Wycliffe, and Jan Huss. There is so much more to the lives of the others but I have presented primary notes.

1. Gottschalk of Orbais, (b. 808 – d. October 30, 868 AD) was a Saxon theologian, monk, and poet. He advocated two-fold (double) predestination, meaning God grants grace to a select few while denying grace to those destined for Hell. For that he was condemned as a heretic. He was forced to burn his writings, was whipped, and beaten and imprisoned for 20 years in the monastery of Hautvilliers.

2. Ratramnus, (died 868AD) was a Frankish monk in France who similarly favoured double predestination, namely that God predestinated the fates of both the elect and the damned. He also advocated a spiritual view of the eucharist, rather than the actual body and blood of Christ.

3. The Pataria was a movement that began in Milan, Italy in 1075 AD and ended the same year. Aiming at reform of church and clergy, it opposed the papacy and moral corruptions. It was declared an heretical sect. Group members were assassinated and the group lost its energy.

4. Berengar of Tours, France, (died January 6, 1088) was a bishop who like Ratramnus, denied transubstantiation, that is, the real presence of Christ in the sacraments. He was excommunicated, threatened with death and he recanted.

5. Arnold of Brescia (b. 1090 – d. June 1155), an Italian church clergyman, taught the merit of following apostolic poverty. He was exiled, arrested, and hanged under order of the pope. His teaching gained recognition among Waldensians.

6. **Peter Waldo** or Valdo (b. 1140 – d. 1205); and Waldensians.

7. The Friends of God (German: Gottesfreunde; or gotesvriunde), was a mystical group of Catholic clergy and lay people founded in 1339. They were centered in Basel, Switzerland, and in Strasbourg and Cologne. They criticized the corruption of Catholicism and believed in an imminent judgement from God on the church. Many group leaders were executed for heresy.

8. **John Wycliffe** (b. 1328 – d. 31 December 1384), and the Lollards.

9. **Jan Huss** and Hussites, (b. 1370 – d. 6 July 1415).

10. Johann Ruchrat von Wesel, (died 1481), a German theologian, held that scripture is the sole rule of truth; he opposed

indulgences and the infallibility of the church. He died in prison under a life sentence.

11. Wessel Gansfort, (b. 1419 Groningen, Friesland, Netherlands – d. October 4, 1489), was a theologian who believed in grace-oriented salvation; and protested the paganizing of the papacy, indulgences, and the superstitious uses of sacraments.

12. Girolamo Savonarola, (b. September 12, 1452, in Ferrara, N. Italy.), was excommunicated on May 12, 1497, and together with two other friars was hung and their bodies burned on May 23, 1498

***

Foremost among those forerunners, were Pierre Valdo in France in the 12th century, John Wycliffe in England in the 14th century, and Jan Hus of Prague in Bohemia in the 15th century. Their doctrine influenced Luther and the reformers of the 16th century. Of paramount importance was their emphasis upon confidence in scripture.

Pierre Valdo (1140-1217) **and the Waldensians.**

Different sources ascribe different names, Pierre Valdo, Vaudès or Valdès, to identify this courageous forerunner of reform. Valdo was a wealthy merchant in Lyons, France. By reading the four Gospels, he was persuaded to live a simple life and to tell others about Christ and the Christian life. He sold all of his assets and adopted an austere life of poverty. He became a preacher. (Nudge, nudge. Sometimes in my life I have said that poverty and preacher are synonymous). Valdo arranged for the writing of a translation of the Bible in his vernacular language. In time his preaching drew many followers who were called Waldenses.

Following Valdo's example, unordained Waldenses, became travelling preachers. They were called Barbes, meaning 'uncles,' to distinguish them from Roman Catholic priests ('fathers'). Valdo did not request permission from the Roman Catholic Church to launch this lay movement. Why would he, since the Waldenses disagreed with the Roman Catholic Church about many aspects of theology. Waldo and his followers believed and taught many of the same Protestant doctrines, including sola scriptura, sola fides, and the priesthood of all believers. Hus and Luther would champion these too. Waldenses opposed the papacy, its wealth and power and its institutional nature. Waldenses rejected purgatory and indulgences, and what they called the cult of the saints. However, the Waldenses took part in mass and the sacraments of the Catholic Church.

At the Council of Verona in 1184 the Waldenses were excommunicated. Thereafter, their worship and preaching were done in private houses. Despite persecution, the Waldensian movement continued to expand in France, Italy, Germany and as far as Hungary and Poland. Many segments of the Waldenses survived until in 1532 when they formally aligned with the Reformation. Waldensian churches exist today in Italy and have spread to some parts of the world (including South America).

John Wycliffe (1320-1384) and the Lollards.

Wycliffe, a brilliant Oxford theology professor, became familiar with the teaching of the Waldensians. As the Waldensians lost energy in the fourteenth century and fled from persecution, many found refuge in England. Wycliffe became the impetus for the rise of another reform movement, the Lollards. 'Lollards' was the derisive name given to them by detractors using the Dutch word that means 'mumblers', or 'babblers.' What were they babbling? Here is what happened.

Wycliffe disdained the doctrines of transubstantiation, and of purgatory. He felt the Catholic Church was too institutionalized and had become corrupt. He believed and taught that God has a true church of chosen people quite apart from the visible Roman church. He promoted a personal kind of Christianity, consisting of piety, humility, and simplicity. Wycliffe revered the Bible as the exclusive criterion for faith and practice. He wrote boldly about the Bible's superiority to all church tradition. Intuitively, he promoted access to scripture for everyone. However, Latin, which most people could not read, was the language of the Bibles used in churches. The Bible should be in English vernacular. He made that happen. However, printing of Bibles was financially impractical, and purchasing a Bible was too expensive. Wycliffe trained people to understand and to memorize large sections of the English Bible and sent them out as evangelists. These were the Lollards.

Most were volunteers who were modestly educated. Only a few were university trained. They wrote and printed tracts. Tract content asserted that Catholic practices of baptism and confession were unnecessary for salvation. Praying to saints and honouring their images was considered a form of idolatry. Oaths, and fasting, and prayers for the dead had no scriptural basis. They denounced the trappings of the Catholic church, such as priestly vestments, holy bread, holy water, bells, organs, and church buildings. They circulated the tracts all over England and Wales.

In 1381, three years before his death, Wycliffe was expelled from Oxford because of his criticisms of the Catholic Church. Forty years after his death, the Church called him a heretic and under orders of the Pope, Wycliffe's body was exhumed, his bones burned, and the ashes scattered into the waters of the River Swift.

As a movement, Lollards survived and functioned under a cloud of antagonism from 1300 to 1500. During successive waves of persecution many Lollards lost their lives. Lollards endured long enough to merge into other non-conformist groups in England.

Jan Huss (1369–1415) **and the Hussites.**
Condemned as a heretic, John (Jan) Huss was burned to death in 1415 AD for preaching reformation themes long before Luther penned them in his theses. It was astounding that it should have happened. A century later, Martin Luther dusted off a book of Huss' sermons and found a new hero in Huss, his ideas, and his commitment. Martin Luther said, "I was overwhelmed with astonishment ... I could not understand for what cause they had burnt so great a man, who explained the Scriptures with so much gravity and skill."

Huss was born in 1369 while Wycliffe was still alive. Recognizing that his own theology was confused, Huss began to read Wycliffe's writing, and that of Pierre Waldo and the Waldensians. His appetite for scripture grew. He trusted the scriptures and wrote, "desiring to hold, believe, and assert whatever is contained in them as long as I have breath in me."

Prague was already a centre for reform in Bohemia (region in Czechoslovakia). Huss was influenced by some of his professors who held strong anti-papal views. He completed bachelor's, master's, and doctoral degrees and by 1398 he was teaching at the university of Prague. He was quickly promoted to dean of the philosophy department. In 1401, Bethlehem Chapel, the most popular church in Prague, hired Huss. He was an eloquent speaker. True to the progressive trend in the city, Huss preached in his native Czech language rather than in Latin. 3,000 eager worshippers clamoured to hear him.

The Pope's authority was in question as Huss proclaimed that the Bible was the final authority for the church. Huss's popularity increased as he raged against the corruption of the Pope, the clergy, and the State church. He taught that humanity obtains forgiveness of sins by true repentance, not money, and therefore Huss deplored the Pope's endorsement of indulgences (pardon of sin for money). The Bohemian King received a monetary share from indulgences, so Huss had also antagonized civil power. The King in response, arrested three men from the lower classes who openly called the indulgences a fraud, and had them beheaded. They were later considered the first martyrs of the Hussite Church. Huss' Czech followers amplified their calls for reform. The Papacy was not pleased.

The pope excommunicated Huss and placed a ban against any Prague citizen receiving Communion or being married or buried by Huss. In 1412, to spare the city, Huss withdrew to the countryside. There he devoted his time to writing treatises arguing that Christ alone is head of the church, and that to rebel against an erring pope is to obey Christ. Huss was summoned to the Council of Constance in November 1414 to explain his doctrine to the church bishops. The Holy Roman Emperor assured Huss safety, but upon arrival, he was arrested. Instead of a hearing, while standing in chains, he was asked to recant. He did not. His arrest and death sentence were shocking. Imprisoned for months Huss was finally condemned as a heretic by Pope John XXIII. On July 6, 1415, he was taken to the cathedral and was stripped of his priestly garments. He was taken to the public square, tied to a tall wooden stake, and given one last chance to recant. Huss refused, and said, "Lord Jesus, it is for thee that I patiently endure this cruel death. I pray thee to have mercy on my enemies." As flames engulfed him, he was heard reciting psalms. At the age of 46, he died in the flames.

Bohemians were furious with the execution and repudiated the council for the action. Over the next several years, a coalition of

Hussites, radical Taborites and others refused to submit to the authority of the Holy Roman emperor or the church and fended off three military assaults. They became the foundation for the Moravian Brethren who eventually played an influential role in the conversion of the Wesley brothers, John and Charles.

***

Persecution

The Canadian Charter of Rights and Freedoms insures freedom of expression, freedom of assembly, and freedom of religion. For those of us who are in relatively safe, twenty-first century North America, we read the following definition with incredulity. 'Religious persecution' is the systematic mistreatment of a person or a group of individuals as a response to their religious beliefs or affiliations or their lack thereof.

Of the 7.9 billion people in the world, 2.6 billion are Christians (mid 2023). There are 195 countries in the world, 75 of which are not tolerant of Christianity. In those 75 countries there are 245 million believers, who risk isolation, ridicule, imprisonment, loss of their homes, torture, rape and even death for their trust in Christ.

In the entire universe, only planet Earth is known to host life. Of all life forms on earth, humans have the most highly developed intelligence. That begs this question then. Why in our lengthy history of thousands of years have humans been killing fellow humans over the subject of religion? We're still doing it today. It points at something intrinsic to human nature that is very, very wrong, doesn't it? Could we acknowledge that it is sin?

The explanation for the extreme violence may simply be that by nature we humans are sinful creatures. Good ideals and purposes can be misunderstood, confused, distorted. Something as pure as the Christianity that stemmed from the life, teachings, death, and resurrection of Jesus can be mismanaged. I believe that it was.

When Christianity became acceptable as the official religion of the Roman Empire, the simplicity of the Christian gospel mutated. It was still recognizable but inflated by exaggeration in formalism, ceremony, iconography, clerical vestments, and pageantry. The emperors were often more in charge of church than the clerics during the Middle Ages.

Naturally one wonders how religion that purports to be right, good, and holy, could provoke such vitriol? One explanation may be the perceived role of the Church to convert a heretic and to protect society. The heretic who won't be converted must be punished. How far will the Church go to protect society, and how far will it go with punishment? Is violence justifiable? In the Middle Ages, the Church and the State approved of it in the name of God.

8 PROTESTANT REFORMATION THEOLOGIES
Lutheran, Reformed/Calvinist, Anglican, and Anabaptist
Theologies, 1500-1700 AD

I SPOKE WITH MY DAD ABOUT SOME OF THIS. We come into life, and take it as it comes, yet underneath there is a bedrock of spiritual heritage. The Protestant Reformation helped to shape my entire life. Our people chose to identify with reformers. Fifteen generations ago, my ancestors were impacted by the reformation movement and the reformers themselves. God used our ancestors' experience of the reformation, to put us in a position to know him. Generations of Loewens, Unruhs, Fasts, Doerksens and Willems have followed Christ. Faith born and sustained through suffering became an instructive heritage for us all. It helps to explain why Eddie Unruh was born in Hepburn. This legacy of faith influenced my parents' lives, my life, my brothers' lives, the lives of our wives and our children. I have made personal choices, and yet, who I am, what I have believed, and how I have lived, is linked to the histories of my ancestors and to the testimonies of the two generations that most immediately preceded my own.

***

Why the Reformation?
The center of town life was the local Catholic church. Parishioners felt that the Church was politically and economically driven. They paid a tithe in money or in kind (seeds, produce,

animals) for all weekly services. They paid fees for sacraments of marriage, child baptism, confirmation, and burial. Priests exhorted worshippers to buy 'Holy Relics' endorsed by the Vatican. Relics such as feathers from the dove that rested on Jesus, straw from Christ's manger, and wood from the cross. Fraud was overlooked as wealthy buyers purchased official church offices. The most profitable and objectionable practice was selling indulgences with the approval of the Pope. Papal pre-signed pardons of sins committed or yet to be committed.

The Church was institutionalized, having changed dramatically from the humble community of believers in which the Holy Spirit was invested in century one. By the 1500s, reform-minded Catholic people were protesting with increasing persistence and fearlessness.

With greater access to scripture, reformers supported the credo, 'sola scriptura,' meaning that 'scripture alone' should be the source for faith and practice. There were longstanding concerns that the Church had cultivated interpretations and practices that were not derived from scripture. Catholic historians now acknowledge that through the centuries lamentable deviations did occur with respect to the gospel message and practice. This necessitated reform.

Reformers were themselves Roman Catholics. They began to question several church dogmas. The veneration of Mary, the mother of Jesus, was a major cause of concern. Mary was deemed 'The Mother of God since she gave birth to second person of the Trinity. Mary's 'Immaculate Conception,' asserted that the Virgin Mary was free of original sin from the moment of her own conception. Perpetual Virginity was the proclamation that Mary was a virgin before, during and after giving birth to Jesus. Naturally, protesters cited that Mary had other children than Jesus. There was biblical proof. "Is this not the carpenter's son? Is not His mother called Mary? And His brothers James, Joses, Simon, and Judas? And His sisters, are they not all with us?" (Matthew 13:55–56). The Assumption of Mary stated that she did not die but rather, she was transported body and soul into heaven as Jesus had been. No biblical support exists. Church theologians simply drafted them as dogma.

Rosary beads, instituted as a Catholic ritual, derived from the testimony of a priest named St. Dominic in the 13th century. He said that Mary had appeared to him and instructed that instead of praying the psalms, Christians should pray the prayers called, Hail Mary, Our Father, and Glory Be. By 1139 AD, married priesthood was abolished. The promise of celibacy was required of all priests and candidates for priesthood.

***

Along Came Luther, Zwingli, Calvin, and Anabaptists

Although most accounts swiftly cite Martin Luther as the initiator of the Protestant Reformation, it is better to acknowledge that Martin Luther and Huldrych Zwingli are the co-originators of the Protestant Reformation. The reform movement was broader than one man and his theological preferences. Both men were Roman Catholic priests/pastors. They only intended that their interpretations of scripture could reform the Catholic Church. In essence they defied the Church. Martin Luther, Huldrych Zwingli and John Calvin considered their choices to be an emancipation from perceived church exploitation and corruption. They would not backpedal on their convictions. They survived the recoil from the Catholic gatekeepers and each of them began reforming movements. They are the respective patriarchs of Lutheranism and Reformed Theology. This was the formation of Protestantism as a Christian entity distinct from Catholicism. Today ecclesiologists classify Roman Catholicism as a branch of Christianity.

The result was that four major theology and church streams emerged and rapidly developed, Lutheran, Reformed/Calvinist, Church of England (Anglican), and Anabaptist. Please notice I said 'four' streams and I have mentioned Anabaptists, that are seldom regarded as reformation contributors in historical accounts. But they should be mentioned. They are decidedly significant.

***

Because I want readers to understand the story of Anabaptists from which Mennonites derive, I am mentioning them right off the top. In naming the key Reformation figures and their theologies, I will give them their due, but I am telling you now that all Protestants and Catholics while they were at odds with each other, had one resolution in common, and that was that Anabaptism had to be eliminated.

Of the five families profiled in this book, our earliest ancestors became devotees of this Anabaptist expression of Christian faith. The Anabaptist group with which they identified was called Mennists and Mennonites, because the movement's significant protagonist was Menno Simons. Some Anabaptist convictions challenged Catholics and Protestants. Consequently, Anabaptists and Mennonites were insulted, slandered, exiled, pursued, and slaughtered. Resisting such coercion at the risk of death became part of a family legacy at the beginning. For a brief period, Anabaptists became one of the most despised sects in world history.

My Dad had heard about this. His father had related to him a story or two concerning family members who suffered for their faith.

***

The Catholic Church, during both 1500s and 1600s, maintained its traditional sacramental theology and hierarchical structure. Catholic doctrine emphasized the authority of the Pope, the seven sacraments, including infant baptism. The Church maintained its rich liturgical traditions, including the use of Latin, elaborate ceremonies, and the veneration of saints. The Mass remained the central act of worship, with the belief in transubstantiation in the Eucharist, that the bread and wine when taken, became the actual body and blood of Jesus.

Four Protestant Reformation Streams:

The Lutheran stream began with Luther's protest against Johann Tetzel's scandalous sale of indulgences. In October 1517 AD, Luther's action of posting his 95 theses for public display in Wittenberg, Germany, was the catalyst for the birth of the Protestant Reformation. Lutheran theology was based on the teachings of Martin Luther. Lutherans emphasized the concepts of justification by faith alone and the authority of Scripture. They held to the sacraments of baptism and the Lord's Supper, acknowledging the real <u>presence</u> of Christ in the Eucharist, rather than transubstantiation. Lutheran churches retained elements of Catholic liturgy, including the use of liturgical vestments and rituals. Lutheranism emphasized congregational singing and the importance of preaching the Word. The vernacular language was used in worship services, and the sermon became a central component.

The influential figures in this movement were Martin Luther (1483-1546), Philipp Melanchthon (1497-1560), Martin Chemnitz (1522-1586), Lucas Cranach (1472-1553). Their theology is articulated in **the Augsburg Confession** (1530), and **the Book of Concord** (1580).

The Reformed stream originated with the priest named Huldrych Zwingli and was later influenced by John Calvin. These men emphasized the authority of Scripture and the importance of a disciplined Christian life. Reformed theology stressed the sovereignty of God and predestination, namely, that God elects some to eternal life and others to damnation. Reformed churches adopted simpler forms of worship, removing some Catholic practices they considered idolatrous. Emphasizing preaching and the study of Scripture, their worship services were characterized by simplicity, psalm singing, and the reading of sermons. When Zwingli preached systematically through the book of Matthew in Zurich in 1519, he effectively replaced the Catholic mass with the preaching of the Word as the central focus of church services and it marked the beginning of expository preaching. Reformed churches still practiced infant baptism and viewed the Lord's Supper as a memorial rather than a literal presence of Christ as did Lutherans.

The influencers of the movement were Zwingli (1483-1531), Martin Bucer (1491-1551), Henry Bullinger (1504-1575), John Calvin (1509-1564), and Theodore Beza (1519-1605).

Zwingli's role in shaping the theology of the Reformed tradition was eclipsed by a second-generation reformer named John Calvin. John Calvin was a young contemporary of Zwingli, who built on his elder's teachings. Calvin was born in France in 1509, and studied theology and law, but was forced to flee in about 1534 after becoming involved with a group of university students who were circulating Protestant ideas. He settled in Strasbourg, where he joined a group of reformers who helped him formulate and solidify his ideas. Later, he moved to Basel where, in 1536, he published the first edition of his masterpiece. Reformed Theology is enunciated in '**The Institutes of the Christian Religion**,' (final version 1559), and in the **Heidelberg Catechism** (1562).

The Church of England (Anglican) separated from Rome in the mid-1530s through the Act of Supremacy. People invested in this stream were Thomas Cranmer (1489-1556), William Tyndale (1494-1536), Hugh Latimer (1487-1555), Nicholas Ridley (1500-1555), Richard Hooker (1554-1600). Its theology is evident in the Book of Common Prayer (1549), and Thirty-Nine Articles (1563). I will not elaborate further on church development in England, Wales, Scotland, or Ireland since their stories are unrelated to Eddie Unruh's birth in Saskatchewan.

The Anabaptist movement arose when some of Zwingli's enthusiastic followers lost confidence in him. This group had been gathering to study with Huldrych Zwingli. With him they studied the Greek classics, the Latin Bible, the Hebrew Old Testament, and the Greek New Testament. They were committed to the church reforms that Zwingli proposed. Zwingli wanted to abolish the Catholic Church Mass and images. All changes had to be approved by Zurich's city council (the Reformed Church and State coalition). Council was not ready for such radical changes. Zwingli chose orderly change and did not break with council but carried on officiating the Mass and preaching the gospel in the vernacular.

Among the study group were Conrad Grebel, Felix Manz, and George Blaurock. By 1523 these came to believe that Zwingli was too conservative and that the reforms he advocated were too few. They broke with him. The breakaways were squarely against the Mass, against icons and images, and against priestly celibacy. They wished to re-create a kind of Christianity described in the New Testament. In applying the Sermon on the Mount, that meant disposing of things like swearing of oaths, usury, military service, participation in civil government, and infant baptism. They claimed that the City Council had no business legislating on matters of religion. They met covertly in homes for Bible reading and prayer. Two years later, Mass was abolished in Zurich in May

1525, but an impetus for greater reform was off and running.

On a wintery February evening in 1525, these Christian friends met in the home of Felix Manx. Only eight years earlier, Martin Luther had posted his 95 theses that caused its enormous commotion. After discussion and prayer, these folk baptized one another. That was unusual in their circles, unheard of. Re-baptism, or simply believer's baptism, was perceived as an act of defiance by Zwingli, by the Reformed Church and the Swiss State. Church and State had been amalgamated since the fourth century when Christianity was made the official religion of the Roman Empire. These re-baptized friends had been baptized as infants. Infant baptism is what the Catholic Church and the State required but these believers could find no justification for infant baptism in the Bible. This seeming defiance as I have stated before, led to the persecution of Anabaptists by both Catholic and Protestant authorities.

They were Anabaptists now. They rebaptized. Anabaptists emphasized the idea of a voluntary adult baptism, viewing it as a public declaration of faith and commitment. They rejected infant baptism practiced by the Catholic and Protestant churches, both Lutheran and Reformed. They emphasized the priesthood of all believers and sought to establish a more egalitarian church structure. They rejected the use of force in religious matters and believed in a voluntary church membership. Some emphasized pacifism and practiced communal living and advocated separation of the church from the state and the world. A few others integrated more with society and allowed infant baptism.

Zwingli supported a Council decision to outlaw private meetings and to require all children to be baptized. The men resisted. Grebel was exiled and died of the plague. By order of the Council, Manz was executed by drowning in the River Limmat, the first Anabaptist martyr. On the day of Manz' execution by drowning in the village of Zollikon near Zürich in 1525, another leader, George Blaurock, was beaten and expelled from the city. From there, he travelled to Bern and eventually left Switzerland, never to return. Bern became the center for Anabaptism in Switzerland. Blaurock was burned at the stake near Klausen in 1529.

The movement spread, both by evangelistic zeal and persecution, from Switzerland into Germany, Moravia, Poland, Russia, the Netherlands.

The principal protagonists were Balthasar Hubmaier (1485-1528), Thomas Müntzer, the warring one (1489-1525), Pilgrim Marpeck (1495-1556), and Menno Simons, the peace-minded man (1496-1561). Their theology was initially detailed in the Hutterite Chronicle (1525), and **the Schleitheim Confession** (1527).

Was the Death Penalty Warranted?

A comment by John Calvin typifies the treatment afforded to Anabaptists by Catholic, Lutheran, Reformed, and Anglican Churches. Anabaptist were among those whom Calvin categorized as Libertines about whom he wrote to the Protector Duke Somerset, that Anabaptists, "deserve to be repressed by the sword, which is committed to you, since they not only attack the King, but strive with God, who has placed him (the king) upon a royal throne and has committed to you the protection as well of his person as of his majesty." (Calvin on the Church of England – Part 1, Steven Wedgeworth; February 15, 2022; in Ad Fontes a quarterly online publication of The Davenant Institute.)

Historians invariably call these reformers 'radical.' I don't like the term associated categorically with all Anabaptists because it insinuates violence. Only a few were violent in defense of their beliefs. 'Radical' is an appropriate descriptive only for their intention to bring greater change than the other reformers supported. Call them radicals, because they were uncompromising enough that they were ready to die for their vision.

The Schleitheim Confession of Swiss Brethren (Anabaptists)

This is the first expression of the fundamental Anabaptist idea, that the true church is not a Christian society, but a company of believers separated from society. It's proper title in German was, 'Bruderliche vereinigung etzlicher Kinder Gottes siben Artickel betreffend.' It means, 'Brotherly Union of a Number of Children of God Concerning Seven Articles.'

The seven statements of belief distinguished Anabaptists from Catholicism and the first wave of Protestant reformers.

Barely two years after the start of the Anabaptist movement, this confessional agreement was written. Customarily, it takes much longer for religious movements to develop statements of faith. Luther's Augsburg Confession came 13 years after he nailed his 95 theses to the Wittenberg door. Haste was necessary because the best Anabaptist leadership were being killed, and furthermore, some followers were unprincipled, and some wanted to take up arms.

The chief author of the Seven Articles of Schleitheim was Michael Sattler of Stauffen, Germany. Sattler was originally a Roman Catholic priest. He had become a leader among the Swiss Brethren, who believed in adult baptism, separation of the elect from society and refusal to accept the authority of the state over born-again Christians. The State as well as the Church considered him a dangerous radical because of his rejection of civil government. Michael Sattler was tortured and burned alive on May 20, 1527. On his way to the execution site, he called on the crowds to repent, and prayed for the judges. Eight days after her husband's death, his wife Margaretha was drowned in the River Neckar. Death by drowning was mockingly called, "the third Baptism." Margaretha said she would have rather gone to the fire with her husband. Under Zwingli's influence, the city of Zurich became the first Reformation government to execute 'heretics'.

The Mennonite Church Confession of Faith

It can be said that the Mennonite Church had its beginnings during the sixteenth century in the Swiss-South German part of Europe, where the Schleitheim Articles were adopted in 1527. When the Anabaptist/Mennonite movement began, it relied upon the element of this confession. Since then, Mennonite groups have produced numerous statements of faith, to which the Schleitheim articles and historic creeds of the early church have been basic. In time, Mennonites accepted additional confessions: the Dordrecht Confession (Holland, 1632), the Christian Fundamentals (1921), and the Mennonite Confession of Faith (1963). In 2004, the 21 member conferences in 19 countries of the International Community of Mennonite Brethren (ICOMB) unanimously approved an International Confession of Faith.

9 MENNONITE ANCESTORS IN PRUSSIA

THE ANABAPTIST MOVEMENT IS ONE OF THE MOST TRAGIC IN THE HISTORY OF CHRISTIANITY. However, it was the first explicit appeal in modern history for a new type of Christian society. It was like an announcement to the modern world that church should be an absolutely free and independent society. It should be free from the State and free from a controlling mother church or command centre.

Our people, our family ancestors, were drawn to this understanding. And I am telling you this because ultimately this is why Ed Unruh was born in Hepburn. The appetite for freedom explains why all five named clans in our family lines came to Canada. They were involved with other believers on the run or on the move. Not constantly, but periodically because they desired and promoted freedom. A free church and freedom of religion that were independent from the state were unthinkable concepts to both clerical and government leaders in the 15th and 16th centuries. In fact, the ideas were equated with anarchy. A freedom of personhood, and of faith and place were intolerable to both the political and religious authorities of their eras. Magisterial (the dominant) reformers absolutely rejected religious liberty and the State was determined to suppress it.

Religious Freedom Championed by Anabaptism

Here is the incredible outcome of that sixteenth century freedom announcement by Anabaptists. Not all historians will agree, but I consider this a defensible view. The elevated principles of freedom of conscience, separation of church and state, and voluntarism in religion, have become basic to North American Protestantism and to our democracies. These ideals were derived from Anabaptists of the Reformation period. They were the first spokespersons to openly enunciate them and to challenge the Christian world to practice them. The Canadian Charter of Rights and Freedoms, and the U.S. Constitution speak to the separation of the church from the State and to the freedom of religion. The debt to original Anabaptism is unmistakeable. (This substance of this acknowledgement was ably presented in 'The Anabaptist Vision', given as a presidential address before the American Society of Church History in 1943, by Harold S. Bender.)

And here is how it has played out for me. My parents did not raise me in a Mennonite (Anabaptist) Church. Even though I have never been a card-carrying Mennonite, I have been a member and a pastor of four churches whose members are voluntary, baptized believers. These churches value the autonomy of the local church. Each church was a voluntary autonomous member church in an association of churches or a denomination. Their affiliation was entirely cooperative and designed to accomplish ministries together. Two of the four autonomous churches I pastored were linked with Associated Gospel churches of Canada and two with the Fellowship of Evangelical Baptist churches. I then finished my formal ministry career as president of the Evangelical Free Church of Canada (EFCC). The EFCA (America) and the EFCC (Canada) originated in Scandinavia where the term 'free' denoted freedom from the State. So, believe me, I am grateful for the astounding dedication of Anabaptists and Mennonites.

As I have mentioned already, during the years 1527-1560, Catholic, Lutheran, and Zwinglian authorities endeavoured to crush the Anabaptist movement with a frightful savagery in Switzerland, the Netherlands, South Germany, and in all the Austrian lands. I have been repeatedly sickened by images and accounts of torture and executions. In 1529 the imperial Diet (Council) of Spires approved the sentence of death on all

Anabaptists with the words, "every Anabaptist and rebaptized person of either sex should be put to death by fire, sword, or some other way." This was repeated at subsequent councils and in 1551 a decree ordered that all judges and jurors who had scruples against the death sentence on Anabaptists, should be removed from office and punished with fines and imprisonment.

***

Menno Simons and Mennonites

Slightly later than in Switzerland, Germany, Tyrol, and Moravia, Anabaptism appeared in the Netherlands by 1530. Melchior Hoffman was an outspoken German lay preacher who left Lutheranism to convert to Anabaptism and to add his own zealous eschatology. He preached extensively, coming to Emden where he baptized over 100 adults who converted to Anabaptism (some sources say 1000).

In 1531, a Dutch, Frisian, Roman Catholic priest by the name of Menno Simons (1496–1561) learned about the Anabaptist movement, which he said, "sounded very strange to me." It was less strange to him after he began reading the Bible, something that he had never done during his training for the priesthood. He didn't want the Bible to confuse his theology. His brother Pieter already was an Anabaptist and when Pieter was among a group of Anabaptists who were killed in 1535, Menno "prayed to God with sighs and tears." He converted to Anabaptism around 1536. He rejected the Catholic Church and the priesthood and cast his lot with the Anabaptists. He was re-baptized as an adult in 1537 and became part of the Dutch Anabaptist movement. He was a preacher among them and soon their leader.

Within the broad scope of Anabaptism in the Netherlands, there were some people who clearly ignored the Schleitheim Confession's emphasis on peace. Instead, they had the spirit of vigilantes rather than the spirit of Christ. Those fringe groups had apocalyptic, vengeful, and amoral ideas and intentions. They were militants.

But there were Anabaptists who distinguished themselves from such insurgents. They found in Menno Simons, a godly biblicist and an advocate of peace. Hence the characteristic of 'peace' for which true Mennonites have been known. By means of his writings, Menno Simons conserved the teachings of early Swiss founders. He wrote that "true evangelical faith . . . clothes the naked, feeds the hungry, consoles the afflicted, shelters the miserable, aids and consoles all the oppressed, returns good for evil, serves those that injure it, prays for those that persecute it."

Rather than saying that the Mennonite movement was founded by Menno Simons, the movement took his name. These were Anabaptists who preferred his biblical interpretations and emphases. Simons founded Mennonite congregations in his homeland of the Netherlands, yet he also was very active in organizing congregations in German states of Lower Saxony and Schleswig-Holstein. In the ensuing decades, members of our five families were exposed to the values and teaching of the Mennonite Church and they embraced them. They came out of State churches or unbelief to belong to an endangered religious group, because freedom to express personal faith in Jesus Christ by being baptized as a believer, and freedom to practice this faith among like-minded believers was so important.

Simons is the only well recognized reformer of Dutch descent, yet he is as familiar as Luther, Calvin, and Zwingli. Mennonites (or Mennisten or Doopsgezinden {baptism-minded}) are named for Menno Simons. It is wise to distinguish Mennonites of those early years from Anabaptists in the Netherlands because Simons fostered the vision for discipleship and congregational life with which our families are familiar.

Some Dutch Mennonites seeking religious asylum were already crossing borders into Poland. Menno Simons visited the city of Danzig, Poland and surrounding area in 1549. He perceived it to be a refuge for Mennonites.

Menno Simons was born in Witmarsum, province of Friesland. That's where he died in 1561 at age 65. He was buried at home, in his garden. Soon after Menno's death, his followers in the Netherlands fragmented into several local factions. There were Waterlandic, Frisian and Flemish denominations. Waterlanders, a branch of the Dutch Mennonites, derived their name from Waterland, a region in the province of North Holland. Flemish were a branch of Mennonites that originated in 1566 in opposition to the Frisians. Frisian and Flemish are important to our families since they associated with one or the other. In the second half of the 16th century many Frisian and Flemish Mennonites seeking to escape persecution in the Low Countries (Netherlands = low countries) especially Friesland and Flanders, moved to the Vistula Delta in the Kingdom of Poland. They established settlements that flourished until the 1770s. During this time Poland became Prussia and that is an important aspect in our family story.

Migration to Poland-Prussia, a Temporary Refuge

Early members of Unruh, Willems, Loewen, Fast, and Doerksen families, whose given names we do not know, were among those who fled from the Netherlands, Belgium, Switzerland and Germany. They were seeking to avoid Spanish Catholic persecution as well as harassment by Dutch and Swiss Reformed Churches in the Low Countries. (Given names of the earliest family members are unknown; perhaps lost during migrations or inadequate record keeping in their communities.)

Our ancestors were among the Mennonites who fled to the Vistula Delta region in the Kingdom of Poland. Four, maybe five of the families described in this book, have originated in the Netherlands. Only the Unrau/Unruh family appear to have come from Germany, but I find other authors named Unruh telling me that our people came from the Netherlands too. I am okay with that. I will seek to confirm that data before the book finishes. By the time all of them made the migration to Poland-Prussia, they had subscribed to the Mennonite vision and beliefs.

As early as the 1530s, Dutch Mennonites, refugees from the Netherlands and Belgium, moved and settled in the Vistula River delta between the present-day Polish cities of Gdansk, Malbork and Elbing. It was known that the Mennonites of Holland were industrious farmers and were experts at using dikes and canals to reclaim swampy, unfruitful lands. Prussia was desirous to have its marshy lowlands turned into productive land. Dutch farmers were welcomed.

Settling in the Vistula delta was strategic because of its access to the city of Danzig, Poland's principal seaport. Produce could have a vital connection to the Low Countries by traditional grain trade. All that was needed was for wetlands to be turned into productive farmland. Windmills, typically used in the Low Countries, drained the swamps. Cultivation began and crops were grown, and Mennonites promoted trade relations with the Netherlands.

Religious toleration was the negotiated policy between Poland authorities and Mennonite immigrant farmers and tradespeople. From 1550 and during the 1600's, northern Poland offered an environment in which thousands of Anabaptists/Mennonites could live their faith. Many more Mennonites arrived in succeeding decades. More than the availability of land, the compelling attraction that Mennonites enjoyed was the religious freedom and tolerance in Poland. This freedom was officially confirmed with the Warsaw Confederation of 1573. Soon about 1,000 Mennonites lived in the city of Danzig, and very many more in the Delta. In 1569 Dirk Philips founded the first Mennonite Church in Danzig (Gdańsk). Mennonites could build churches in their communities and were allowed to run their own schools but had to pay school fees for the public school as well. Initially, the emigrants led quiet, undisturbed, even isolated lives. Their numbers grew. They had large families that became prosperous on the farms and by selling products in towns. Lowland congregations were comprised almost entirely of Dutch refugees, while inland colonies contained some Moravians, Germans and Swiss. They constantly bought more farmland. The land would be leased for decades and eventuate in ownership. Their settlements extended gradually further and further upriver to Marienwerder, Graudenz, Swetz and Culm.

We know that our earliest families found economic and religious sanctuary along the banks of the Vistula River in northern Poland where their communities flourished. Mennonites and our early ancestors remained in the region in the 1700s even after the annexation by Prussia during the partitions of Poland. The birth certificates of our ancestors whom we can trace by name, stated cities in Prussia as their place of birth, not Poland. The explanation is easy. In 1772, and again in 1793 and 1795, Poland was partitioned by Russia, Austria, and Prussia and the Kingdom of Poland ceased to exist for a time. Most of the Vistula River delta was annexed by the Kingdom of Prussia. Vistula delta Mennonites formed one of the largest Mennonite communities in Poland.

The Plautdietsch language

Mennonites who lived in the province of West Prussia became identifiable as Low-German speaking Mennonites because during their 200-plus years in Poland/Prussia they developed their own Germanic dialect, known as Plaut Dietsch, also known as Platt Deutsch in German, or Low-German in English.

In the Vistula River delta between the present-day Polish cities of Gdansk, Malbork and Elbing, Mennonites found that the dialects of Prussian Low German (Nether Prussian) were spoken. Nether means lower in position. Mennonites already spoke a netherlandic or Lowlands, Nether- Saxon Low German dialect. That subsequently gave way to the manners of speech of local dialect(s). Mennonites adopted words and pronunciations slightly new to them but native to Prussia. However, they retained some of their netherlandic vocabulary. Despite having left the Netherlands in the 1500s, the Low German dialect of Mennonites today, wherever it is heard, still contains netherlandic words not usually heard in other dialects.

The following are a few examples:
klautre, klautere, klauterern (to climb, clamber)
krakjt, kraikt, krek (exactly, tidy)
ladijch, ladig, ledig (empty)
mausse, massa (in mass, many)
porre(n), porren (to urge, to prod)
tachentijch, tachentig, tachtig (eighty)
tüss, t'hüs, thuis (at home)

Prussian low German words adopted into Mennonite Low German from their neighbors of the Vistula are the following:
Eatschocke, Eadschocke, Erdschocke (potatoes)
Kodda, Kodder (rag)
Kjlemp, Klemp (cow)
Klopps (meatballs, patties)
Schrug, Scharrugge (old horse)
Ssoagel, Tsoagel, Zoagel (tail)

I am familiar with the sounds of the words in both groups, so I know that our families, generation after generation sustained the influence of the ancestors times in Prussia.

***

Unending Pressures

Prussian native citizens became envious and resentful of these foreigners who spoke another language and practiced a questionable, even unacceptable religion. Opposing clergy were often agitating for banishment of Mennonites. Throughout the seventeenth century the Mennonites of Poland Prussia lived continually under the fear of banishment, but the threat was never rigidly carried out. An effort in 1642 to confiscate their lands was averted with the payment of an enormous 'ransom.' Again in 1676 attempts were made to exile the Mennonites and that was averted because city councils realized the value of these industrious foreigners.

It was merely a matter of time before the lifestyles, faith convictions and pacificism of the Mennonites conflicted with the highly militaristic Prussian government. The Prussian government made acquisition of land contingent upon military service or costly payments in support of military training. Since Mennonites could no longer acquire new property without surrendering their pacifism, many decided to leave Prussian territory. The Mennonites who settled in the Vistula delta in West Prussia lived there for about 250 years before departing.

Increasingly, Mennonites in Prussia were selling their farms and courageously leaving for a fresh start. By the beginning of the 1800's, the Prussian government understood the impact on the country's economy created by the loss of thousands of contributing citizens. To curtail the flow of emigrants, Prussia placed a 10% tax on all possessions of people choosing to leave the country. At the same time, Napoleon's army was advancing on Russia. That discouraged Mennonites from going to Russia. Nevertheless, people continued to leave Prussia. Between 1788 and 1820 one third of the Prussian Mennonites moved to southern Russia.

10 NEW RUSSIA - MENNONITE SETTLEMENT IN UKRAINE AND CRIMEA

ALL FIVE FAMILIES FEATURED IN THIS BOOK, LEFT PRUSSIA AND MOVED TO SOUTH RUSSIA. South Russia was the vast southern mostly uninhabited areas of Russia that would soon be optimistically termed New Russia.

South or New Russia, Later Known as Ukraine

It was largely uninhabited but not empty. Ukrainians were settled in the land in successive waves, occupying two governorates called Ekaterinoslav and Kherson. These communities held about 50,000 inhabitants by the mid-1700s, including 11,000 Zaporozhian Cossacks. The nomadic Nogai Tatars were the primary threat to these settlements until 12,000 of them were persuaded to become Russian citizens. It was tagged as New Russia because the incoming Prussian immigrants turned the areas into enviable productive agricultural farmland. Our families played a part in that conversion.

Catherine II, born Sophie of Anhalt-Zerbst on 2 May 1729, died on 17 November 1796. She was known as Catherine the Great, reigning empress of Russia from 1762 to 1796. In 1774, Catherine the Great's armies defeated the Ottoman Empire (colloquially known as Turkish Empire). The population of Crimea became independent of the Ottomans. The Crimea, as it was sometimes called, was the first Muslim territory to slip from the Sultan's suzerainty. Then in 1783, Catherine the Great annexed or incorporated the Crimea into the Russian Empire thereby increasing Russia's power in the Black Sea area. New Russia, all of it now included Ukraine and Crimea, and was becoming an attractive area for colonization. Throughout the rest of the 18th century and the beginning of the 19th century, Russia was determined to colonize this vast New South Russian territory. This was largely the impetus Catherine the Great.

(Crimea: The Crimean Tatar name of the peninsula is Qırım; Russian is Крым (Krym), and Ukrainian is Крим (Krym). The word Qırım is derived from the Turkic term qirum ("fosse, trench"), and from qori- ("to fence, to protect").

Russian Immigration Policy

On December 4, 1762, Catherine the Great (Catherine II) of Russia, issued a manifesto that invited foreign settlers from Western European countries to settle in the vast southern areas of Russia. A second Manifesto followed on July 22, 1763. The rights and privileges that were extended to prospective settlers were generous.

The 1763 Manifesto was announced in foreign countries through embassies and agents of a newly established Bureau of Guardianship of the Foreign Colonists. The Manifesto was advertised in newspapers in Denmark, Sweden, Austria, Holland, England, Scotland, Ireland, the German Free Cities, and in certain small German states. Most countries were relatively uncooperative because they were competing for colonists. Initially, the Manifesto was not aimed specifically at Mennonite people. Although they heard about this offer, Mennonites were initially hesitant, not wanting to antagonize Prussian authorities. Nevertheless, Russia successfully attracted a range of ethnic settlers, including non-Mennonite Germans, Moldavians, Bulgarians, Albanians, Armenians, Greeks, Serbs, Corsicans, and Swedes. By 1765-1766 one hundred non-Mennonite villages were established in the province of St. Petersburg and along the lower Volga River.

The 1763 Manifesto's Generous Conditions:

1. The right to settle in any part of the country and to pursue any occupation.
2. Free board and transportation from the Russian border to the

place of settlement, with travel money. Free living quarters for half a year, and "free, productive land in colonies and rural areas" (note 9).

3. Free and unrestricted practice of one's religion according to the precepts of one's church. To those who intend to establish colonies on uninhabited lands, the freedom to build and control their own churches, but not to establish monasteries. An oath of allegiance can be made "in accordance with one's religious rite."

4. The freedom to proselytize Russia's Muslims, "to win them over and make them subject to the Christian religion in a decent way," but "under no condition whatsoever to proselytize among other Christian subjects [i.e., Russian Orthodox], under pain of incurring the severest punishment of Our law."

5. Exemption from the payment of taxes for a varying period of time (depending upon the place of settlement and type of occupation) and freedom from billeting troops.

6. Ten-year, interest free loans for building dwellings and for purchasing livestock and equipment for agriculture and industry.

7. The right of local self-government for those who establish agricultural communities, "in such a way that the persons placed in authority by Us will not interfere with the internal affairs and institutions" [e.g., schools]. "In other respects, the colonists will be liable to Our civil laws. However, in the event that the people would wish to have a special guardian or even an officer with a detachment of disciplined soldiers for the sake of security and defense, this wish would also be granted."

8. The right to import free of duty family belongings as well as goods for sale up to a certain amount.

9. Exempt from military draft or the civil service in perpetuity. "Only after the lapse of the years of tax-exemption can they be required to provide labor service for the country."

10. Freedom to establish market days and annual market fairs tax free.

11. Freedom to emigrate, though obligated to remit a portion of the assets acquired in Russia.

12. The privileges shall be enjoyed not only by immigrants, but also their children and descendants.

13. Provision to negotiate for other privileges or conditions besides those already stated. "We shall not hesitate to resolve the matter in

such a way that the petitioner's confidence in Our love of justice will not be disappointed."

Eventually, and gradually, maybe inevitably, Mennonites responded and took the Empress at her word.

Recruitment of Mennonites and Emigration

The first encouraging reports about possibilities in Russia came to Prussian Mennonites from a small group of Hutterites (they also were Anabaptists) who fled Austria for New Russia in 1770. They settled successfully on an estate owned by Russian General, Baron Pyotr Rumyantzev. He was satisfied with them. Earlier, during the Seven Years War that ended in 1763, Rumyantzev had become impressed by Mennonite agricultural achievements that he observed in the Vistula Delta where the Russian Army withdrew for winter billeting. He and Georg von Trappe met some of these Mennonites and subsequently recommended to the Empress that the Mennonites be considered for a special contract on the Steppes of the New Russia.

In August 1786 an invitation was specifically extended to the Mennonites, and Georg von Trappe became the chief agent for their immigration into Russia. Von Trappe also went to Prussia and repeated publicly an invitation to all who were interested to meet him at the Russian embassy in Danzig. Mennonite interest was driven not only by the venture of settling a vast agricultural area, but also by the prospect of escaping the oppression in Prussia. Noteworthy in the special contract that Mennonites received, was a guarantee of complete religious freedom and unconditional exemption from military service. Mennonites were required to remain separate from Russian neighbours, keeping their affairs independent of others. This was acceptable to Mennonites who valued religious, educational, and economical freedom.

During Georg von Trappe's trip to Danzig, he met Jakob Höppner and his wife Sara Dueck. They rented a store, a cafe, and the Bohnsmark village inn in the Vistula Delta. Von Trappe was impressed with Höppner's service as proprietor of the inn and suggested that Jakob serve as a delegate when and if the time came for the Mennonites to explore the possibility of immigrating to South Russia. Eventually, Jakob along with Johann Bartsch and Jakob von Kampen (who later withdrew) were elected to serve as delegates.

These two emissaries, Jakob Höppner (1748 - 1826) and Johann Bartsch (1757 - 1821), were sent to Russia to inspect the land, explore immigration potential and to interview both Viceroy Potemkin and Tsarina Catherine II on May 13, 1787. Empress Catherine planned a tour of Crimea. She invited Höppner and Bartsch to join her and the royal entourage. The Empress wanted them to see the possibilities of Crimea as well. These men were the first Mennonites to visit Crimea in any official capacity. They travelled by horse and coach from Berislav to Perekoto, to Simferopol, to Sevastopol and Feodosiya. This meant that even though many years passed before Mennonites started a colony in Crimea, there was familiarity with the land and its possibilities. Jakob Höppner and Johann Bartsch were satisfied with their findings in Russia, and they negotiated necessary terms of agreement with the authorities in St. Petersburg.

Interjection: Crimea is of particular interest to me because my direct Unruh lineage came from Crimea. During my term as president of the Evangelical Free Churches of Canada, I travelled through Crimea emotionally aware that this was a location of my heritage. My paternal grandfather C.K. Unruh and his seven siblings were born there. So were his cousins, Abraham H. Unruh and Benjamin H. Unruh. They were all born in Temir – Bulat (Philippstal). Here is a quick treasure. There was a Bible School in the nearby village of Tschangraw from 1918 to 1924. Johann Wiens (1874 - 1951), Gerhard Reimer (1885 - 1970) and Abraham H. Unruh (1878 - 1961) taught in that school. One year after the school was closed by the communists around 1920, these same three men founded Winkler Bible School in Winkler, Manitoba, Canada, and A.H. Unruh served as president. After twenty years at Winkler, Abraham H. Unruh became first president of Mennonite Brethren Bible College (MBBC) where my daughter Cari later attended.

Mennonite Settlement
Chortitza and Molotschna Colonies
I mention these colonies because they were the first colonies built and settled by Mennonites in New Russia. The first eight families arrived by covered wagons in the dead of winter in 1788.

They arrived in the already established Russian town of Debrovna and remained there for several months. In that same year 228 more families left for Russia, followed by additional groups, a total of 462 families.

The first settlers had been promised 500 rubles by the Russian government, but many received that grant only 8 years later. In establishing a farming community, they faced hard conditions and severe challenges. These were the poorest of the Mennonites in Prussia, living in sod huts. Together they established Chortitza, also known as the Old Colony, because it was the first Mennonite settlement on the banks of the Chortitza River, in the province of Ekaterinoslav in the Ukraine. Despite the hardships, by 1800 AD the Chortitza Colony had grown into 15 separate villages with 89,100 acres of land. (Information from Benjamin Heinrich Unruh, p. 231, Die niederländisch-niederdeutschen Hintergründe der mennonitischen Ostwanderungen im Jahrhundert. Karlsruhe, 1955.)

Russia's Alexander I issued another Manifesto on February 20, 1804. A new wave of immigration came to Russia from Prussia where difficulties for Mennonites had increased. During the next three years, another 365 Mennonite families entered South Russia, and a few settled at the Chortitza settlement, but most moved on to settle in the province of Taurida on the Molotschnaya River. These colonists established the new Molotschna colony. It was 100 miles southeast of the Chortitza settlement. By 1835 there were 1200 families (6,000 people) in 60 villages in the Molotschna Colony. From those two original colonies, most of the daughter colonies developed. The total immigration of Mennonites from Danzig and Prussia to Russia during the years 1788-1870 was approximately 2,300 families, of whom approximately 462 families went to Chortitza, 1,200 to the Molotschna, and 500 to Samara; 80 families remained in Vilna, Poland, on their way to the Ukraine. By 1870 about 9000 individuals had immigrated to Russia, mostly to the Chortitza and Molotschna settlements which, with population increase, numbered about 45,000 people. Forty daughter colonies were established by 1914, occupying nearly 12,000 square kilometres (4,600 sq mi), with a total population of 100,000.

Synopsis of Mennonite History in South Russia (Ukraine)

Economics: When our earliest family members arrived in New Russian, some of them did initially settle in the Molotschna colony. Both Chortitza and Molotschna were large in number of villages and population. Other colonies generally contained fifteen to thirty families. Mennonites acquired substantial landholdings. They were model farmers. They prospered in Ukraine. Each family began with 175 acres of land as a grant from Russia. On this land they raised cattle, sheep, and crops for their households. Wheat was the principal crop for market along with fruit and vegetables, flax, tobacco, and mulberries for the silk industry. A granary served one or more villages. Each colony had common land for use by the poor as well as to raise funds for starting new colonies for the growing population. Available farmland became a serious problem. The Russian government allowed colonists to divide their farms in halves and quarters. In other cases, daughter colonies were formed as colonies themselves purchased land. They were respected for their fairness in business, and their agricultural techniques were transferable to Russian farmers. Villages developed flour milling enterprises as well the manufacture of agricultural machinery. Chortitza built the first foundry in 1860, and others followed because there was a heavy demand for mills and farm equipment, and tens of thousands of mowers and threshers and this created jobs. Mennonites shipped machinery throughout the Empire. Feed and flour mills were wind-powered at first and then were replaced by motor and steam driven mills. Customarily, Mennonites did not assimilate into Russian society because they intentionally maintained a cohesive society of their own. Moreover, tsarist authorities wanted to keep Mennonites isolated from other social groups. Their interaction with South Russians was primarily as the employers of farm labourers. most extensive interaction with Ukrainians was as employers of farm laborers. While farming was essential, many citizens were accomplished and educated with other skills. That explains the effectiveness of the next item.

Government: The Mennonite colonies functioned like a democratic state, enjoying freedoms beyond those of ordinary Russian peasants. Each village was self-governing with an elected mayor and a magistrate, its own school, road care and care of the underprivileged. Villages were grouped into districts. Chortitza villages formed one district. Molotschna was divided into two districts, Halbstadt and Gnadenfeld. A district superintendent (a Mennonite) oversaw a regional administrative bureau. Colonies cooperatively operated their own hospitals, a school for the deaf, an orphanage, a home for elderly citizens, an insurance program, and departments to deal with delinquents and other social problems. The Russian government intervened minimally in the early years and Mennonites stayed out of Russian politics and social movements prior to the Russian Revolution that lasted for 2 years, 4 months, 3 weeks and 4 days from January 22, 1905 to June 16, 1907. The revolutionaries were defeated and Nicholas II retained the throne, but this was merely a dress rehearsal for the Revolution of 2017, when the monarchy was abolished and the Tsar executed.

Education: At a time when compulsory education was unknown in Europe, the Mennonite colonies formed an elementary school in each village. Interestingly for us to note, even though Mennonite schools were established by each village, many parents kept their children at home to help with the immense workload and chores. School students learned practical skills such as reading and writing German and arithmetic. Each village elected its own teacher from the community. The teacher was typically a craftsperson or herder, untrained in teaching, who fit class time around his occupation. Most schools used the Bible and the Catechism as their school texts. Religion was included as was singing in many schools. Schoolhouses often doubled as a church building in the early years. Few regulations were imposed by Russian rulers upon Mennonites during these initial years in Russia.

In 1820 the Molotschna colony started a secondary school at Ohrloff, bringing a trained teacher from Prussia. The Central School was started in Chortitza in 1842. Over three thousand pupils attended the Central School with up to 8% of the colonists receiving a secondary education. A school of commerce was started in Halbstadt employing a faculty with full graduate education. Those who wanted to pursue post-secondary education attended universities in Switzerland, Germany as well as Russia.

Religion: Each village organized an autonomous congregation. They all agreed on fundamental Mennonite beliefs, and yet there were cultural and traditional differences between Frisian and Flemish Mennonite churches. One interesting observation is that Pastors of Flemish congregations read sermons from a book while seated at a table, whereas Frisian pastors stood while delivering the sermon, sometimes with reference to notes and sometimes extemporaneously. Many pastors were untrained, chosen from within the congregation, and since the pastor was an unpaid position, the candidate was often a wealthy landowner or a teacher. They had respect in the community. In those early decades, this was far from ideal, and the congregational spiritual acumen and practice suffered.

Excommunication was the form of Church discipline used with members who had committed sins and refused to repent and to seek forgiveness. More conservative congregations employed the practice of 'shunning' or 'avoidance,' thereby cutting business and social connections with an unrepentant person. However, a sunned person experienced dire trouble, church members were obligated to help.

Mennonite Life Took a Turn for the Worse

It was during the 1870s, relations between the Russian Empire and Germany went sour. This affected the daily lives, the economy, and the political fortunes of Mennonites too. In 1871, the codex or agreement under which they had come to colonize Ukraine was revoked. Specifically, they forfeited their administrative autonomy. No longer could they govern themselves within their villages and colonies. They were required to use the Russian language for school instruction. Colony anxiety rose as villagers feared that Russia was trying to assimilate Mennonites into secular and Russian society. They would lose their distinct culture and values. They were losing autonomy. From 1874 they were expected to perform military service, albeit in a non-combative manner. Mennonite leadership feared that the Russians would continue to withdraw privileges and would demand more and more from the Mennonites. Meanwhile they carefully obeyed laws, and they prayed for the government, and during the Crimean War donated food and cared for the health of as many as 5,000 men and women in their hospitals. Despite several attempts by Mennonite delegates to meet with the czar in 1971-1973, they met only officials and with no suitable resolution.

First and Successive Waves of Emigration

That was just the beginning but that was enough to provoke many Mennonites to emigrate to North America. Those from the Chortitza Colony (Khortytsia Island region) favored Canada, and those from the Molotschna Colony along the Molotschnaya River valley, preferred the United States. Others moved to more remote regions of the Russian Empire, like Siberia.

In 1873 a delegation of twelve was sent to explore North America, seeking large tracts of fertile farmland. This group consisted of Leonhard Sudermann and Jacob Buller of the Alexanderwohl congregation representing the Molotschna settlement; Tobias Unruh from Volhynia settlements; Andreas Schrag of the Swiss Volhynia congregations; Heinrich Wiebe, Jacob Peters and Cornelius Buhr from the Bergthal Colony; William Ewert from West Prussia; Cornelius Toews and David Klassen of the Kleine Gemeinde and Paul and Lorenz Tschetter representing the Hutterites. This group returned with positive reports of good land available in the United States and in Canada. The more conservative groups from Kleine Gemeinde, Bergthal and Chortitza, chose Canada, which promised privileges equal to those previously held in Russia and a large tract of land to reestablish colonies in Manitoba (East Reserve and West Reserve). The more liberal groups, those from Molotschna, and the Hutterites chose the United States. They sold their properties often at reduced values and toiled through the paperwork and paid high fees for passports. But they left. Tens of thousands of the most industrious farmers in Russia were planning to leave the country. Realizing this concern, Russia tried to dissuade Mennonite colonist from departure or created barriers. Nevertheless, between 1873-1883, of the total population of 45,000 Mennonites in South Russia, 10,000 went to the United States and 8,000 to Canada. That was the first wave of emigration.

Our five families were among those who came at that time.

These included the parents of A.A. Willems, of Marie Fast-Doerksen, of Isaac Doerksen, and of Katherine Loewen. And it included Cornelius K. Unruh's parents as well. These emphasized families arrived in the United States and by various life events, eventually came to Saskatchewan. And this is why, Eddie Unruh was born to Katherine Loewen and C.K. Unruh in the town of Hepburn.

***

With the Bolshevik Revolution of 1917, the Mennonite villages were repeatedly terrorized. One of the leaders was Nestor Machno, who had worked as a farm hand among the Mennonites. He held many grievances. His vigilantes plundered and destroyed many Mennonite villages. It was a dark time for the Mennonites. Many young Mennonite men abandoned non-resistance when they witnessed the cold-blooded murders of their parents and rape of their wives and sisters. One of the groups that was formed to take up arms against was called "die Selbstschutz", meaning 'self-protectors.' During World War I, many of the Mennonites who had remained in Russia lost their lives because of various illnesses, such as epidemic typhus. Many also had their homes plundered and some families were massacred by bandits. After this time of war, revolution, anarchy, and famine, approximately 25, 000 more Mennonites immigrated to North America in the 1920's. After World War II another 12, 000 Mennonite refugees were accepted in Canada and the United States.

***

During the revolutionary upheavals of 1917-1921, such as the Russian Revolution of 2017; and the Ukrainian-Soviet War, 1917-1921, minority groups like Mennonites suffered. Yet it was the rise of the Soviet regime that brought major tribulation. Mennonites who continued to live in Russia lost educational control. Their churches were closed. The essential core of their community was severed. During the 1920s nearly 20,000 more Mennonites emigrated from the Soviet Union to western Canada. Mennonite farmers remaining in Russia, then suffered enormous losses during the Soviet collectivization program. By 1930, and during Stalin's regime, 91% of individual rural family landholdings, livestock and other assets were taken by the State and became collectively owned and state-controlled farms. Destitute Mennonites experienced enduring famines. Mennonite religious leaders were imprisoned. Villagers were deported to Siberia as kulaks (peasants). During the terrors of the second World War, the advance of German troops eastward forced the evacuation of Mennonites to move to the east. Just as violently, the Soviet army advanced westward, pushing Mennonites survivors west. The villages and homes they left behind, the entire colonies were dismembered and were never rebuilt.

Some Mennonite refugees who found themselves in Germany after the war were resettled in North and South America. Benjamin H. Unruh's interchange with the Third Reich, and Hitler's key ministry leaders became so vital. He negotiated for the extraction of German speaking Russian Mennonites and permission to emigrate to North America. His proximity to the Nazi regime has come under increased criticism in recent years as new information has been provided. I will mention him again in chapter twelve.

11 MENNONITE HOMESTEADERS AND CANADIAN PRAIRIE LIFE

AFTER CENTURIES OF THRIVING IN SOUTH RUSSIA MENNONITES FACED ABRUPT CHANGES. Their peaceful homesteading was disrupted when Russia demanded religious conformity in 1874. Their autonomy diminished. Mennonite military and tax privileges were revoked. The Russian language became mandatory, and Mennonite teachers were replaced in colony schools. This was a heartbreaking catastrophe. Mennonites felt that they must leave their homes, farms, and villages. Villages grappled with the question of where to go next. Russian-German Protestant groups like Mennonites and Hutterites chose North America for emigration. Many chose Canada.

The Great Plains
Mennonites in Russia, who had originated in southern Germany, Switzerland, and the Netherlands in the 16th century, began migrating to the Great Plains in the 1870s. The term "Great Plains" refers to a vast flatland covering Central United States and Western Canada. In Canada, it includes the southern parts of Alberta, Saskatchewan, and Manitoba, while in the United States, it spans most of Kansas, Nebraska, North Dakota, and South Dakota, along with parts of other states.

Canadian and U.S. officials, along with railroad companies, encouraged their settlement. Other factors contributing to this boom included Treaty agreements, the Dominion Lands Act of 1872 offering free homesteads, the North-West Mounted Police ensuring safety, and the construction of a transcontinental railroad. The Dominion Lands Act allowed individuals to claim up to 160 acres of land for a $10 fee, but with several stringent requirements. Settlers had to build a home, cultivate part of the land, and reside on the property for at least six months annually for the initial three years. Intensive advertising and international immigration agencies attracted settlers. A massive immigration wave to the Canadian West transformed the region from 1867 to 1914. It was to be expected that this would shape distinct ethno-cultural communities and diverse industries across Manitoba, Saskatchewan, and Alberta.

Reserves in Manitoba and Overpopulation

Manitoba became the primary settlement area in Canada. By a Canadian Order in Council in 1876, 500,000 acres in two different reserves in Manitoba were set aside for the exclusive use by Mennonites from Russia. That acreage capacity was 6% of Manitoba's total land area. "Reserve" was the name given to a compact tract of land set aside by the Canadian government for a certain number of years for exclusive occupation by a homogeneous group of settlers, to be divided according to their own plans. The two reserves were referred to as the East Reserve and the West Reserve. The Mennonite delegates from South Russia were eager to receive such land.

On March 3, 1873, the East Reserve was established within the newly constituted province of Manitoba. It was comprised of eight townships. It was located east of the Red River, with its northern boundary 20 miles southeast of Winnipeg and south of the new Lake Superior-to-Fort Garry Dawson Road just opening during those years. Its southern boundary was 20 miles north of the United States border. Its total acreage was 185,000 or 290 square miles.

The first contingents of settlers began to arrive in July and August in 1874. They, along with all others following them that autumn, headed for the East Reserve of eight townships of bush, swamp, and some dry prairie land. At least eight trans-Atlantic trips are known to have brought a total of 1533 men, women, and children from Russia to Canada in the same year. With few exceptions all these families made their way to the twenty-one village communities of the "East Reserve" before winter came in 1874. The seven thousand Russian Mennonites who arrived in the

1870-1880 period may have constituted the largest single newcomer group to enter Manitoba.

The West Reserve was established in 1875-1876 by settlers from the steppes of South Russia. It lay just north of the International Border, and between Emerson on the Red River and Mountain City near the Pembina Hills. Its open prairie land mass consisting of 17 townships, 500 acres or 612 square miles, was two and one-half times as large as the East Reserve. It turned out to be some of the best farmland in the whole province of Manitoba.

Back in the East Reserve it soon became evident that the territory had a shallow stony soil texture in many parts and suffered from excessive moisture. Hundreds of families from the East Reserve moved to the West Reserve. Conservative Mennonites of the Furstenland and Bergthal colonies moved to the West Reserve into the Morden and Winkler area of Manitoba. Within ten years there were 6000 residents living in 70 villages on the West Reserve. By 1893 these Manitoba "reserves" East and West, were overpopulated. There was no more available land in Manitoba, migration began to Alberta and Saskatchewan. I will focus on Saskatchewan.

Back to the question of why anyone would want to live on a reserve, the answer becomes clear when you know the priorities of this community. Within these villages and throughout the entire reserves, the Russian Mennonite occupants treasured their church traditions and placed a high value on unity, togetherness, mutual caregiving, and seclusion from outside society. In fact, they guarded themselves from the non-Mennonite culture and were determined to be independent of groups and agencies that might endanger their established societal mores and philosophy of living.

Rapid Development in Saskatchewan

Saskatchewan was the next province to settle Mennonites. The overpopulation of the Manitoba reserves led to the relocation of hundreds of Mennonite families from Manitoba to the Rosthern and Swift Current areas of Saskatchewan in 1893 and 1902 respectively. The first five families from Manitoba arrived near Rosthern, between Hague and Osler, 50 miles north of Saskatoon. The initial nucleus of this settlement came into existence in 1891–94 with the settling by immigrants of the Rosenort Gemeinde

(Church). This church later affiliated with the General Conference Mennonites from West Prussia, and Russia.

This was known as Rosthern and Saskatchewan Valley Settlement. It developed very quickly into a major bloc settlement of twenty villages that resembled the pattern established in South Russia. It then further progressed in several stages between 1895 and 1918, originally covering at least forty-two townships. Some families crossed the South Saskatchewan River to the area that is now Aberdeen and lived on separate farms rather than on reserve. Mennonites came from Minnesota, Nebraska, and the Dakotas and settled near Langham, Dalmeny, and up to Mennon and Hepburn. Many of these were Mennonite Brethren, whose churches were situated in Hepburn and Dalmeny. Mennonites also settled across the North Saskatchewan River from Waldheim, Langham, and Borden. A greater party from Kansas and Oklahoma settled near Drake about 100 miles southeast of Saskatoon. As time went on colonies of all sizes were established in the northern parts of Saskatchewan, near Meadow Lake, Carrot River, Lost River, and other places. Larger settlements were established near Herschel, Fiske, Kindersley, and Superb (Ebenfeld congregation) when the immigrants from Russia came in the 1920's. Colonies were also established in Hanley and Dundurn, south of Saskatoon. When the Bergthaler Church, which was a milder branch of the Old Colony Church, became dissatisfied in the 1920s with the Saskatchewan government requirement that the English language be used in their school system, the Bergthalers immigrated to Mexico and Paraguay.

A second, even more extensive Mennonite Settlement developed around Swift Current and Herbert, then spread northeastward to include the Vermillion Hills region. This vast settlement had its origins in two rather different Mennonite colonies established immediately east and south of Swift Current. First to arrive were Sommerfelder Mennonites from Manitoba, who settled in the Main Centre-Gouldtown area north of Herbert in 1900. They were soon joined by General Conference Mennonites and Mennonite Brethren, settling around Herbert in 1903–05. Within a couple of years at least 100 Mennonite families had settled there, most from Russian-German Mennonite colonies in the United States.

There were many smaller Mennonite concentrations widely scattered throughout the prairie portion of the province. Soon the adjoining districts of Eigenheim, Laird, and Waldheim were settled and some of those settlers came directly from Russia. Other immigrants came from Prussia and settled in the Tiefengrund district, which is only a few miles north of Laird. The southern part of Saskatchewan also received Mennonite settlers. Besides the Old Colony Mennonite settlement near Swift Current, other settlers located at Herbert, between Regina and Swift Current and surrounding districts. In Herbert and in Swift Current there are both Mennonite Brethren and General Conference Mennonite congregations.

Being Mennonite
The multiplicity of Mennonite origins in Europe means that the Mennonites of the Great Plains are by no means a homogeneous group, having brought with them differing traditions and emphases in their faith. The various Mennonite strains do, however, have many practices in common, including adult baptism, separation from the larger culture, simple living, and pacifism. Traditionally, pacifism has meant not complying with conscription (conscientious objection) and not supporting militarism. This pacifistic stance has often put them at odds with the state and non-Mennonites in general, both in Europe and in North America. Today, support for community-based nonviolent campaigns and conflict mediation agencies have become the primary outlet for these pacifist beliefs. Battles over conscription are increasingly rare. In fact, because of the publicized efforts of the Mennonite relief agencies, such as Mennonite Central Committee, service, rather than strident pacifism, became the group's defining trait in the latter half of the twentieth century. Alternative service in place of bearing arms proved acceptable in Canada.

Homesteading Defined by Tireless Labour
Homesteading in 1800s Canada's western provinces was a pivotal chapter in the nation's history, driven by the Dominion Lands Act of 1872. This legislation granted individuals aged 18 or older, the opportunity to acquire up to 160 acres of land for a mere $10 registration fee. Settlers construct their dwellings, cleared and

cultivated the land apportioned to them and built a life. Life in these untamed territories was marked by harsh winters and unrelenting challenges. Homesteaders faced the formidable task of manually clearing land for farming. Trees, a precious resource, were never wasted. When they needed to be removed, not a single tree was squandered. Trees served multiple purposes—providing tent frameworks, construction materials for homes and barns, and essential fuel for warmth and sustenance.

The prairies' unforgiving winters necessitated sturdy structures for survival. Many early homesteads were constructed using sod, a practical and cost-effective choice. Settlers often collaborated in this effort, cutting layers of grass, soil and roots into strips and stacking them like bricks to create walls, sometimes two or three feet thick. These sod homes provided refuge, offering warmth in winter and coolness in summer. Lumber played a role in doors and window frames, while canvas or greased paper covered window openings, as glass remained a luxury. Floors, often hard-packed earth, were topped with rugs, and roofs were comprised of boards or logs covered with layers of sod and hay, though they sometimes leaked during fierce rains and could collapse in the spring thaw.

In regions with an abundance of trees, settlers crafted log buildings that displayed their meticulous craftsmanship. Logs, carefully cut and trimmed, were interlocked to create solid structures, which were plastered inside and out with mud and whitewashed with a lye solution derived from wood ashes. As building materials became more accessible and affordable, frame homes resembling modern abodes began to emerge, complete with studs, lumber, and tarpaper.

Homesteaders contended with limited and unreliable water sources. Some embarked on perilous journeys in search of water, while the threat of wildlife, including bears, wolves, and cougars, loomed over crops and livestock, necessitating protective measures like fencing. Basic amenities were scarce in these pioneer communities, with candle wicks providing illumination and homemade wooden-soled slippers, fur coats, mittens, socks, and clothing offering warmth. Bread was baked outdoors in a special oven heated with flax straw and badger brush, and meat came from the farm's own animals. Life in these early settlements was defined by tireless labor.

Access to medical care was a significant challenge, with doctors and dentists often located fifty miles away. In response, the community relied on local bonesetters and midwives for assistance. These early settlements fostered a profound sense of unity and solidarity, forging close-knit communities. Residents were fiercely independent, guarding against external influences that could threaten their long-standing customs and beliefs. Their social and religious values placed a premium on communal well-being, emphasizing the importance of togetherness and the preservation of cherished traditions. Homesteading demanded unwavering determination, relentless effort, and self-sufficiency, shaping the course of Canada's history and the development of its western regions.

Settler Colonialism

The period of prairie homesteading (1880-1910) in Saskatchewan reveals a complex narrative regarding indigenous people. Mennonite stories, public education, and official records often overlooked the displacement of indigenous communities, but honesty and common sense compel me to acknowledge their prior presence. The Canadian government marginalized indigenous peoples by portraying settlers as valiant land conquerors, and it's essential to recognize this displacement. Indigenous communities were uprooted to make way for immigrant settlers, reflecting the government's settler colonialism approach. To accommodate newcomers after Confederation in 1867, the government 'obtained' or 'seized' indigenous lands. The aggressive promotion of prairie settlement, coupled with railway companies advertising fertile wheatfields and affordable train tickets, played a pivotal role. The Indian Act (1876) and Dominion Lands Act (1872) aimed to control land for settlers, while Indigenous nations signed the Numbered Treaties (1871-1877), ceding their lands to the Crown. This process was evident not only in Manitoba but also in Alberta and Saskatchewan. Immigrant homesteaders transformed the Saskatchewan landscape into ploughed fields, roads, fences, communities, churches, and cemeteries, shaping the land and its history. In recent decades, 'Truth and Reconciliation' has become a significant topic of public discourse, leading to federal and provincial efforts at reparation.

12 THE UNRUH NAME AND LINEAGE

ERIC CLAPTON'S FOUR-YEAR-OLD SON CONOR, TRAGICALLY PASSED AWAY ON MARCH 20, 1991. Following months of disabling sorrow, Clapton wrote a delicate ballad called 'Tears in Heaven.' Some lyrics are, "Would you know my name, If I saw you in heaven? Would it be the same if I saw you in heaven?" Clapton's musical questions resonated with me, prompting empathetic thoughts about my ancestors whose stories I have come to know. Our ancestors were responsible, hard-working folk. Their lives were marked by profound hardship, including untimely deaths of children, mothers dying in childbirth, rampant diseases, and limited access to medical care. Many lived in poverty, eking out a living as farmers. Even when they became landowners, their wellbeing and security depended upon powerful indifferent people. Despite education and scholarly achievements, they were not immune to the malevolent ruthlessness of the Bolsheviks and Stalinists. Their faith in God was a comfort to them. They did the best that they could do, leaving behind a legacy.

As their hard lives wound down, did they wonder whether anyone would remember them? They brought lives into the world, and soon their own time was over. As they had done with their own predecessors, their loved ones would place markers over their gravesites. But would anyone remember their names after a decade or two? Perhaps. However, after two, four, six, eight centuries? The answer is no. Many early family members have faded into obscurity, known only because they parented someone whose descendants at last, lived at a time and place where record keeping was deemed of importance.

I endeavour to remember them all, specially the unknown ones, to unearth their names, and to record their life stories. This way, more of our clan can become acquainted with the narrative they brought to us. In this chapter and the next I will delve into three aspects, the Unruh family name, the lineage leading directly to my brothers and me, and the enduring legacy of faith bequeathed to us by devout ancestors spanning eleven generations that I can track.

***

UNRUH, THE WORD, AND THE NAME
When properly pronounced, the "Unruh" form sounds like "Unroo," with soft but primary emphasis on the first syllable.
Our family name appears in several modified forms, Unrow, Unrowe, Unru, UnRuh, von Unruh, Unrau, Unrauen, Unruhe, Unruth, Unruch, Unrauch, Unrush, Unrouh, Unrruh, Unruuh, Unry, Eunruch, Onrouw and others. Variants occurred intentionally, or from inaccurate record keeping, or even illiteracy. Whether all Unruhs came from the same originator is not known. If they did, then my money is on that person's surname being 'Unruh.' (Laugh out loud)

Meaning.
Can there be meaning in the name Unruh? Some German words resemble our surname. The term 'unruoch' means careless or negligent. From Middle High German and Middle Low German words like 'unrouwe', and 'unrawa' speak of unrest and disturbance. They could suggest a restless person, even a quarrelsome, confrontational person. I suppose I should feel some discomfort about this, but I don't. On one hand I discount that a name dictates a person's temperament or behaviour, and on the other hand, I acknowledge that patience has not been my strong suit. I've done some weird stuff. Mildly stated, my brother Murray and I have assertive, confident temperaments. Our youngest brother Neale has a gentle, deferential disposition making him easier to live with. At least, that's what he tells me, ha ha. Mercifully, the unrest implied in our surname has experienced resolution in a way consistent with a quotation from St. Augustine, "You have made us for yourself, O Lord, and our hearts are restless until they rest in you."

For obvious self-regarding reasons, the meaning that I prefer for my surname comes from the German word *Unruh*. The *Unruh* is the balance wheel of a mechanical watch and a clock. The wheel in connection with a spring, regulates the pace or beat of a timepiece. The normal pace of time or the pace of history, is tied to the constant movement or "unrest" of the balance wheel, the *Unruh*. Pace, progress, movement, time measurement are inconceivable without the existence of the balance wheel (the *Unruh*). The predictable unrest ensures that everything keeps the pace and thereby remains in motion. One could call the balance wheel and the spiral spring, the actual heart of the clock. I'm going with that.

Derivation of the Name.

The origin of the name Unruh likely isn't a mere nickname but rather a habitational name linked to the place where the first bearer lived. Unruh might indicate someone from "Unrow," a coastal hamlet in Mecklenburg-Western Pomerania, situated on the Baltic Sea. Pomerania, known as such since 1000 AD, derives its name from the Slavic 'po more,' meaning "land by the sea." This region, with a tundra landscape formed by retreating glaciers and the Vistula River, is often referred to as the Low Countries due to its proximity to or slight elevation above sea level. The Low Countries, or Benelux countries, encompassed Belgium, the Netherlands, Luxembourg, parts of northern France, and western Germany, with shifting borders due to historical conflicts.

Unruh, traces its roots to this broad Pomeranian area, which was called Prussia during the birth of my earliest recorded Unruh ancestor. Herbert Wiebe's research dates the first appearance of the name to 1568 in various communities like Schönsee, Przechovka, Jeziorka, Konopath, Kazun, Tragheimerweide, and Thiensdorf. Our people most certainly were around then. At this point I simply cannot get beyond the earliest date I have in the mid 1600s. Our early ancestors were listed as Prussian-born, but the lack of data makes it possible that their predecessors hailed from northern Germany or the Netherlands. The Unruh, Fast, Loewen, Doerksen, and Willems families all share a common origin in northern Europe along the North Sea and the Baltic Sea's tundra region, along the Vistula River. Known as Weischel in German and Wisla in Polish, the Vistula River is Poland's longest river, passing through major cities like Kraków, Sandomierz, Warsaw, Plock, Wloclawek, Toruń, Bydgoszcz, Swiecie, Grudziądz, Tczew, and Gdańsk.

Disclaimer.

It troubles me that my research and now my remarks depend upon information recorded about men in the families but seldom about women. In the next chapter when I share with you the stories of faith within our family histories, it will again focus upon males. That is the available data. Yet, this is distinctly distorted and inaccurate. When the lives of God's people were snatched from them in times of persecution, women, wives, and daughters, died in faith. When men died early or by accident, women carried on, nurturing their children. Earlier, I told you that my Dad witnessed his mother daily going to the barn, to kneel in straw and pray. If that discipline was expected of each Christian, Dad felt he could not conform. That became Dad's honest but lame excuse for postponing his own surrender to Christ. Grandma's example also makes it clear, that women throughout the generations, walked by faith as devotedly and powerfully as the men. Wherever information is available, I draw attention to the women in our lineage.

UNRUH: THE LINEAGE

Neale, Murray and I, and our families, have an **unnamed progenitor** for our ancestral story and his surname was Unrau not Unruh. That may come as a shock. I resisted the probability for a long time. Twenty years ago, Frank Kasdorf, a friend in Manitoba developed a genealogical history for me. He did it as a favour to me. He had found that his lineage and mine had a distant connection. This led to his conclusion that my earliest ancestor of record was an Unrau rather than Unruh. I thought he was wrong. Further, I have playfully contended with friends named Unrau, as to whose name was the original form.

I traced our lineage directly to a man without a given name. I will call him the Progenitor, that is, the earliest recorded ancestor of a biological family group of descendants. In the Unruh line, ours is someone called **(unknown) Unrau (106809)** and his spouse:

(name unknown) (#1189653). They had three children, two with recorded given names and one without. And of course, it is that second one, the no-name Unrau guy who is in our immediate ancestral line that leads to our dad, Edward Richard Unruh. Take my word for it. This guy lived a great distance from Hepburn. Crazy to think about, but I am one of his grandsons, eight generations removed. So are Murray and Neale. He is our great, great, great, great, great, great, great, great grandfather.

Relationship Chart #1 from our progenitor to 3 brothers, Ron, Murray, Neale. The relationship comes via our great, great grandfather, great grandfather, grandfather, and father Cornelius K. Unruh, to his son, our father Edward Richard Unruh, and then to us, Dad's 3 sons.

1.   ? Unrau, (#106809) b. approx. 1633, progenitor
2.   ? Unrau, (#106810) b. approx. 1663, child
3.   Heinrich Unrau, (#106812), b. approx. b. 1693, grandchild
4.   Hinrich Unrau, (#106814), b. approx. 1723, great-grandchild
5.   Martin Unruh, (#165971), b. approx. 1753, 2Great-grandchild,
6.   Benjamin Martin Unruh, (#165973), b. 1783, Brenkenhofswalde, Brandenburg, Prussia, 3G-grandchild
7.   **Kornelius B. Unruh, (#165980)** b. 11 Nov 1820, Sofievvka, Volhynia, 4G-grandchild,
8.   **Kornelius K. Unruh, (#341800),** b. 17 Mar 1843, Waldheim, Molotschna, South Russia, 5G-grandchild
9.   **Cornelius K. Unruh, (#341804),** b. 20 Apr 1873, Temir Bulat, Crimea, South Russia, 6G-grandchild
10. **Edward Richard Unruh, (#484759),** b. 8 Mar 1915, Hepburn, Saskatchewan, 7G-grandchild
11. * Ronald James Unruh, (#606630), b. 1942, Hepburn, Saskatchewan, 8G-grandchild
     * Murray Dennis Unruh, (#606629), b. 1947, St. Catharines, Ontario, 8G-grandchild
     * Neale Bryan Unruh, (#606628), b. 1953, St. Catharines, Ontario, 8G-grandchild

Reminder: I include the *GRanDMA OnLine* database numbers for the ancestral names. This is a highly beneficial site that currently has genealogical information for 1,527,152 Mennonite and Hutterite individuals who can be traced to Prussia (now Poland) and South Russia (now Ukraine). For $20 you can subscribe to this database to continue your study.

In the next chapter I develop the spiritual legacy of the Unruh family story. That contains detailed accounts of individuals whose lives of service can inspire us. This chapter is focused on the lineage of the Unruh paternal line. I have placed in **bold letters** all of our key ancestors.

***

I begin with the progenitor, the **(unknown) Unrau (#106809)** and his spouse: (name unknown) (#1189653) who had 3 children. The children were: 1 Andreas, 2 Unknown, and 3 Abraham. With each of these men, I provide their children's names and relevant data.

1. Andreas Unrau, (#81469), was married twice. His first wife (unnamed) was described as from 'die Andre Kandt' (the other side), meaning she was not Mennonite. For that reason, Andreas' church excommunicated him, and he was separated from the church congregation for 50 years until wife #1 died. In 1715 in Przechowka, Schwetz, Prussia, Andreas married Liske Richert (a Mennonite) who was born in 1685. There were no children in the second marriage.

2. _?_ **Unrau, (#106810).** He is important to us. He married (unnamed wife) and they had three sons, 1 Hein, (#70366). 2 **Heinrich (#106812)**, and 3 Abraham (#106811). Heinrich's birth year is unrecorded, but his children's dates have been registered, leading me to think that the birth years of his wife and himself may be between 1648-1658. He, the unknown dude, and his son Heinrich (#106812) are forerunners in our lineage.

3. Abraham Unrau, (#106811). He is the third son of the progenitor, unknown Unrau (#106809) and his spouse, name unknown (#1189653). No further information is recorded about Abraham (#106811).

Recap: I have shown you the three sons born to our earliest Unrau of record, **(unknown) Unrau (#106809)**. His sons were 1 Andreas, 2 Unknown **(#106810).**, and 3 Abraham. I then highlighted the second son, **Unknown Unrau, (#106810)**, who traces to us. He had three sons.

1 Hein Unrau, (#70366), was born August 24, 1678, in Deutsch Konopat, Schwetz, Prussia; He died on April 19, 1719. <u>Hein was an Aeltester, a church elder or bishop.</u> *Ältester*, *Oudste*, and *Leeraar* were used interchangeably. He and his wife Sarke Jantzen, (#132876) had one child, Peter Unrau (#39743) born October 8, 1705, in Deutsch Konopat, Schwetz, Prussia; Died: February 1764, Przechowka, Schwetz, Prussia.

2 Heinrich Unrau, (#106812)). Heinrich was married to name unknown, (#480947). We are fortunate to have the given names for three of their four children, 1 Name unknown, 2 Abraham, 3 Liske, and 4 **Hinrich (#106814).** Family details for each son follow. Heinrich is important to us.

1. ? Unrau, (#87005). Nothing is known.
2. Abraham Unrau, (#106815) born about 1695. He was married three times. Don't jump to conclusions. The first two ladies died early deaths from natural causes. No information is provided about wife number one (#494227) or wife number two, Liscke Isaaks (#1523764). His third wife was Maricke Noefcken, (#106816) whom he married about 1728, in Przechowka, Schwetz, Prussia. Maricke was a Lutheran and later in Holland she was accepted as a member of Abraham's Mennonite congregation. Abraham was <u>a church elder, and he was ordained as minister</u> on July 16, 1719, by Elder H.B. Hulshoff.
He and Maricke had three daughters.
    1. Ancke (#58515) born in Przechowka, Schwetz, Prussia.
    2. Maricke (#33794) born 1731, in Przechovka, Schwetz, Prussia. Died December 22, 1758.
    3. Sarcke (#33853) born May 1, 1748, in Przechowka, Schwetz, Prussia. She died on April 24, 1807, Sady, Masovia, Poland.

3. Liscke Unrauen (#106817). No information was available. (Note: daughters were given a surname with a 'en' suffix. It was a common practice differentiating surnames of women from male siblings. It is still practiced in some localities in Europe. As was the case with names in our story, old church registries display this variant.)

4. **Hinrich Unrau, (#106814) married (name unknown) (#480931)** and they had twelve children. You would have thought that a mother of twelve would get honourable mention. Nope! No record. Look at the **twelfth child, Martin.**

    1. Hinrich Unrau (#100351). He and Unknown wife (#330778) had seven children.
    2. Liscke Unrauen (#47880). She married Ratzlaff, Peter (#47768) in 1727.
    3. Hans Unrau (#106821) born 25 January 1731. He married Liscke Schmiten, (#106789) and they had one son, Daniel Unrau (#106834) born 1 January, 1782, in Jeziorka, Schwetz, Prussia.
    4. Maricke Unrau (#106655) born about 1731. She married Benjamin Wedel (#106654)
    5. Abraham Unrau (#42317). In 1783, before he declared his faith in baptism, he was called to be a soldier by his Imperial Majesty of Prussia. He married Ancke Becker (#32094) who was born 25 April 1725, in Beckersitz, Schwetz, Prussia. They had five children.
    6. David Unrau (#106824) born April 1751. Church Records state that his first marriage was in Brenkenhoffswalde, but it doesn't say to whom. He had 4 children, 2 boys and 2 girls, but no names or other information is provided.
    7. Hein Unrau (#106638). <u>He was a deacon in the Neumark Church</u>. He was married twice, first to an unnamed woman, and then to Trincke Ratzlaff (#47872). Records show 4 children of Hein Unrau and Trincke Ratzlaff but give no names or other information.
    8. Jeorgen Unrau (#106716). He married Ancke Cornelsen (#106715). His children are unrecorded.

9. Peter Unrau (#106820). No information.
10. Efcke Unrauen (#106822) Daughters have a different surname. See footnote for an explanation. No information.
11. Trudcke Unrauen (#106823), no information.
12. **Martin Unruh (#165971).** Notice the spelling of the surname. **This twelfth child** is an integral member of our lineage. He is our <u>great, great, great, great, great grandfather.</u>

3 Hans Unrau (#267401) is the third son of Unknown Unrau, (#106810). Hans was married to spouse unknown to us (#273704), but known to him (smile), because they had four children. No information is available apart from the birthdates of three of the four.

1. Sarcke Unrauen, (#106818)
2. Hans Unrau, (#100103) born 7 February 1720
3. Efcke Unrau, (#32059) born 23 January 1724
4. Liscke Unrau, (#32743) born 2 March 1726

Now back to Martin **Unruh (#165971),** the twelfth child of **Hinrich Unrau's, (#106814).** I have noticed as you have, that the spelling of Martin's <u>surname has changed, from **Unrau to Unruh**</u>. All his siblings were recorded with the surname Unrau. The name 'Unruh' appears only in Martin's case. There is no explanation that I can find. Yet it is his surname that has been passed down to us. I repeat, Martin<u> was great, great, great, great grandfather </u>to my Dad's three sons, Ronnie, Murray, and Nealie, yep, us, me, and my bros.

Martin Unruh (#165971) was married, and his wife's name is unrecorded **(#165972).** Martin Unruh and his wife had only one child, a son whom they named **Benjamin Martin Unruh, (#165973),** who was born in 1783 in Brenkenhofswalde, Brandenburg, Prussia, and he died in 1835.

Benjamin Martin Unruh (#165973), and his wife Elisabeth Buller (#165974) had six children. Finally, we have a female spousal name. Note child number 5 Kornelius B. Unruh. But we won't ignore child 4, <u>Benjamin B</u>, because his descendants made a mark in world history. In chapter 13, the Legacy chapter, I'll share with you the extensive list of Christian leaders in that stream. For the moment, I will stick to the lineage that links directly to our generations.

Benjamin Martin's and Elizabeth Buller's six children were:

1. Maria Unruh (#165975) born in 1812, Brenkenhofswalde, Brandenburg, Prussia.
2. Elisabeth Unruh (#165976) born in 1814, Brenkenhofswalde, Brandenburg, Prussia.
3. Susanna Unruh (#165977) born in 1816, Brenkenhofswalde, Brandenburg, Prussia.
4. <u>Benjamin B. Unruh</u> (#165978) 10 November 1818, Sofievvka, Volhynia. He died on June 21, 1907, in Tokultschak, Crimea, South Russia. That is disputed by his own grandson, the prominent B.H. Unruh, who stated that he died in 1882 in Temir Bulat, Crimea. Another source gives a death year as 2005.
5. **Kornelius B. Unruh (#165980) born on 11 November 1820, Sofievvka, Volhynia**.
6. Tobias Unruh (#103897) born 8 January 1822, Volhynia.

According to the memoirs of son Tobias (#103897), this family immigrated from Brandenburg to Volhynia around 1816 and settled on the estate of count Olifar, near the town of Soviofka (Sofievvka) in Volhynia. Volhynia was located in the northwest of present-day Ukraine, bordering Belarus in the north, and Poland in the west. During the next twenty years the family moved twice, finally settling in South Russia, in the Waldheim village in the Molotschna colony. Benjamin Martin Unruh passed away in 1835.

I am focusing on child #5 with respect to a direct lineage link to my generation.

Kornelius B. Unruh (#165980) is Neale's, Murray's, and my paternal **great, great grandfather**. Like #4, his brother Benjamin B. Unruh, Kornelius was given the middle name Benjamin, in honour of his father. He was born on November 11, 1820, in Sofievvka, Volhynia. From his birth information we know that Volhynia was part of or close to the Vistula Delta of Poland which at the time was under Prussian control. So, he was registered as Prussian born. Later, as Prussia removed Mennonite privileges and imposed taxes upon them, pressuring Mennonites to integrate and to conform, their lives and religious practice became difficult. Kornelius B was among the thousands who chose to emigrate to South or New Russia to homestead under the auspices of Russian Empress Catherine II. The generous terms of her Manifesto granted Mennonites many liberties for their faith convictions and lifestyles. All of Kornelius B.'s children were born in New Russia (modern Ukraine). He died June 1879 in Crimea, South Russia.

Kornelius B. (#165980) married Maria Buller (#165983). She was born September 11, 1820, and they were married in 1841. They had five children. Notice the first born, **Kornelius K.** and his sister who was the second born child, **Helena (#86297)**. I will show you how these two people are keys in my father's lineage, and ours. Here are Kornelius B's and Maria Buller's five children.

1. **Kornelius K. Unruh (#341800)** born March 17, 1843, Waldheim, Molotschna, South Russia; died 1893. Kornelius K. Unruh was <u>dad's grandfather and my **great grandfather**</u>.

2. **Helena Unruh (#86297)** born March 5, 1849, Waldheim, Molotschna, South Russia; died: March 22, 1910, Hillsboro, Kansas. She turns out to be <u>my **great grandmother**.</u> Why? Because she had a daughter named Katharina who married her brother Kornelius K's son, Cornelius K. A fascinating story is coming in a paragraph or two.

3. Katharina Unruh (#213685) born February 28, 1856, Molotschna Colony, South Russia; died: May 24, 1936, Kazakhstan.

4. Anna K. Unruh (#341815) born January 28, 1858, Waldheim, Molotschna, South Russia; died: March 1925, Hepburn, Saskatchewan.

5. Heinrich K. Unruh (#341816) born October 21, 1864, Bruderfeld, Crimea, South Russia; died: March 15, 1932, Hepburn, Saskatchewan.

Kornelius K. Unruh married **Aganetha Kroeker** (#341801) on December 5, 1867, in Schwesterthal, Crimea, South Russia. She was born on May 16, 1848, in Lindenau, Molotschna, South Russia. KK's sister Helena was 'aunt' to his eight children. Here are those children.

1. Aganetha K. Unruh (#341802) born September 11, 1870, in Schwesterthal, Crimea, South Russia. She died on October 20, 1955, in Abbotsford, British Columbia.
2. **Cornelius K. Unruh** (#341804) born April 20, 1873, in Temir Bulat, Crimea, South Russia. He is **my paternal grandfather**, my dad's dad. He died May 16, 1959, in Vineland, Ontario.
3. Peter K. Unruh (#341806) born May 1, 1875, in Temir Bulat, Crimea, South Russia. No further information. Date of death is unknown.
4. Maria K. Unruh (#341807) born September 25, 1879, in Temir Bulat, Crimea, South Russia. No further information.
5. Anna Unruh (#510511) born September 12,1882, in Temir Bulat, Crimea, South Russia. We can assume that she died at a young age, since another child was born and given her name.
6. Katharina K. Unruh (#341808) born July 26, 1885, in Temir Bulat, Crimea, South Russia. She died on August 27, 1913, in Pascha-Tschokmak, Crimea, South Russia.
7. Martin K. Unruh (#148938) born December 30, 1886, in Temir Bulat, Crimea, South Russia. Martin died on February 26, 1975, in Abbotsford, British Columbia.
8. Anna K. Unruh (#341809) born 1890. No information available.

Seven of the eight children were born in Temir Bulat, Crimea, which became the family's permanent home. Only Aganetha, the first child, was born in another Crimean village of Schwesterthal. You have noticed that Aganetha and her mother, Aganetha Kroeker, have the same given name. It was a common practice for one daughter to be given her mother's name. (Among the Russian Mennonites there were certain cycles and traditions according to which the same names would be repeated in the family. The oldest son would be named after the father or grandfather, and the oldest daughter after the mother or grandmother.)

I am looking back for a moment.

Helena Unruh (#86297) was the second child of Kornelius B. (#165980) and Maria Buller (#165983). Her older brother was **(#341800) Kornelius K.**

    Helena married **Jacob Loewen (86296)** who was born August 23, 1842, in Hierschau, Molotschna, South Russia. His date of death is recorded as February 2, 1931, in Hillsboro, Kansas. They were married on October 28, 1866, in Bruderfeld, Crimea, South Russia. They had eleven children. Kornelius K. was 'uncle' to all of Helen's children. It is **child number 4, Katharina Loewen,** who is essential to the Unruhs. Katharina was Kornelius K's niece. Kornelius K's son Cornelius K. was Helena's nephew, and he was a first cousin to all of Aunt Helena's children and that included Katharina. Did you hear that? Stay tuned.

Helena's children were:

1. Jacob J. Loewen (#279910), was born on September 26, 1867, in Bruderfeld, Crimea, South Russia; and he died July 31, 1934. He married Katharina Loewen (#25479), and they had eleven children. Be careful here. Jacob had a sister who was also named Katharina (#341805). Jacob and his wife lived in South Dakota until 1905 when they moved briefly to Saskatchewan before moving back to the USA and settling in Hillsboro Kansas.

2. Maria Loewen, (#34026), born on December 30, 1870, in Crimea, South Russia. She married Johann Kunkel (#32202), and they had nine children. She died on April 23, 1960, in Freeman, South Dakota.

3. Helena Loewen, (#28983), was born June 26, 1872, Bruderfeld, Crimea, South Russia. Yes, she was given her mother's first name. After the deaths of two husbands, she married a third time. Johann Schafer (#940121) died at age 26. At 29 she married 44-year-old Franz Tessman #28854. He died at age 63 and Helena married 58-year-old Peter J. Nachtigal (#76002). She died on July 15, 1955, Reedley, California.

4. **Katharina Loewen, (#341805) was born on February 26, 1874, in Bruderfeld, Crimea, South Russia. She died on the 14th of December 1957, in St. Catharines, Ontario. She is my paternal grandmother, my dad's mother.**

5. Cornelius J. Loewen, (#279913), was born on September 24, 1875, in Marion, North Dakota. He married Maria Guenther,(#14542). He died on March 8, 1936, in Abbotsford, British Columbia.

6. Heinrich J. M. Loewen, (#14541), was born on March 29, 1878, in Parker, South Dakota. He married Maria L. Guenther,(#14542). He died on November 14, 1959, in Shafter, California. He lived 81 years.

8. Isaac Loewen, (#1058532), was born on the 6th of November 1879, in Dakota Territory. He died as an infant.

9. Anna Loewen, (#483401) was born on the 4th of April 1881, Parker, South Dakota. She died on June 4, 1957, in Los Angeles, California. She was married twice, first to Henry D. Peters (#483012), who died suddenly, and she was only 20 when she married Abram Strauss (#483402).

10. Aganetha "Nettie" Loewen, (#32708), was born May 14, 1883. She died on June 16, 1918, in Hepburn, Saskatchewan, at age 35.

11. Abram J. Loewen, (#372121), was born on June 13, 1886. Married twice, first to Anna Kopp and then to Justina Gossen (#102920). He died December 23, 1962, in Twinsburg, Ohio at 76 years of age.

12. Sarah Loewen, (#131108), was born on 25th of September 1886, Parker, South Dakota. She died on June 24, 1973, in Saskatoon, Saskatchewan, 87 years old.

Summary: Kornelius K. Unruh (#341800) and **Helena Unruh (#86297)** were siblings, brother and sister. **Kornelius K's** son, **Cornelius K. Unruh (#341804)** and **Helena Unruh Loewen's** daughter, **Katharina Loewen (#341805),** were first cousins. They knew each other and saw one another occasionally as children in Temir Bulat, Crimea. Katharina emigrated to the United States with her family. Cornelius had already emigrated with his older sister Aganetha and her husband, but now he was alone and working in the United States. Cornelius's parents and some siblings remained in Crimea. It is reasonable to assume that he located where his Aunt Helena and her family lived in South Dakota. Aunt Helena would have wanted to make sure that he was taken care of. It was then that Cornelius and Katharina met as adults, fell in love, and they married. So, Helena's nephew Cornelius K. was now her son-in-law. As a boy and as a young man, C.K. could not have imagined such a scenario, that his Aunt Helena would become his mother-in-law. And Katharina's Uncle Kornelius K., although he was still in the old country, South Russia, was now her father-in-law.

What this meant for my own father, **Edward Richard Unruh (484759)** was that his grand-aunt Helena was also his grandmother. Aunt Helena was his mom's mother. I truthfully do not know whether my Dad knew this, but I also doubt that he did.

Kornelius B. Unruh (#165980),

Kornelius K. Unruh (#341800)	Sibling	**Helena Unruh Loewen** (#86297)
Cornelius K. Unruh (#341804)	1st Cousins Spouses	**Katharina Loewen** (#341805)

Edward Richard Unruh (484759)

Grandma Katharina Loewen (#341805) and Grandpa Cornelius K. Unruh (#341804) were married in Hillsboro, Kansas, on December 2, 1894. Katharina gave birth to seven children. The first two daughters died as children.

1. Hannie Unruh, (#647468) born 16 June 1895. She died at birth or soon after.
2. Susanna Unruh, (#647469) born 3 April 1897. She died at 10 months of age, 8 February 1898.
3. Anna Unruh, (#11342) born 16 March 1899, Parker, South Dakota. Annie, as she was known, was baptized on August 9, 1914, in Hepburn, Saskatchewan. On December 15, 1918, she married Gerhard (George) G. Friesen (#9988), in Hepburn, Saskatchewan. George was born 9 January 1892, in Henderson, Nebraska. Aunt Annie died 12 June, 1948. George died 22 September 1961, Dalmeny, Saskatchewan. They had no children.
4. Cornelius C. "Neale" Unruh, (#484763), was born on November 27, 1903, in Hepburn, Saskatchewan. He was baptized on September 7, 1924. Neale married Aganetha

(Agnes) Hiebert (#484760) who was born on September 24, 1906, at Rural Municipality of Rhineland, Manitoba. Their wedding took place on September 24, 1926, at Plum Coulee, Manitoba. One child was born to them, a daughter. Verna Catherine Unruh, (#1073833). She was born April 30, 1927. She married Joseph Carl Closs (#1073834), who was born January 31, 1928, in Renfrew, Ontario. Carl died January 23, 2007 at the age of 78 at Devon, Alberta.

They had four children, two sons and two daughters.

1. Ian George Closs (#1482303), born on August 13, 1949. He married Eileen.
   They have a daughter (#1482304) named Christina Closs, born January 27, 2007. Christina has a son named Jared Closs Reidel.
2. Randolph
3. Kathleen, married to Martin Walroth.
   Son Kyle
4. Corinne was born on October 27, 1970 in Grande Cache, Alberta. She married Jon Silworsky.

5. Harry Charles Unruh, (#484762), was born on June 16, 1908, in Hague, Saskatchewan. On October 7, 1936, Harry married Ann Peters (#484758) in the MB Church in Hepburn. She had been born on January 13, 1910. Harry and Anne had no children. Harry died of rheumatic fever on December 7, 1948, at the age of 40.

6. **Edward Richard Unruh,** (#484759). Dad was born on the 8th of March 1915, in Hepburn, Saskatchewan. He married Tena Martha Doerksen (#484757), who was born on June 4, 1919, in Wolf Point, Montana. Their wedding took place in Saskatoon, on June 12, 1941.
   1. **Ronald James Unruh,** (#606630), b. 1942, Hepburn, Saskatchewan. He married Christine Frances Langlois, who was born July 23, 1943 in Droxford UK. Their wedding was August 12, 1967 in Calvary Church, St. Catharines.
   2. **Murray Dennis Unruh,** (#606629), b. 1947, St. Catharines, Ontario. Murray married Diane Dibbley

on May 30, 1970 in Wheatley, ON. Diane was born on January 28, 1950 in Coatsworth, ON.
3. **Neale Bryan Unruh,** (#606628), born on October 12, 1953, in St. Catharines, Ontario. Neale married Kathy Smale on Sept 4, 1982 at Richview Baptist Church, in Toronto ON. Kathy was born August 3, 1957 in Ingersoll, ON.

11 GENERATION RELATIONSHIP CHART

Our 11-generation Relationship Chart traces the lineage from the progenitor, an Unknown Unrau (#106809), to the families of three siblings, Ronald James Unruh, Murray Dennis Unruh, and Neale Bryan Unruh.

Fascinatingly, it is not just one family stream but **3 RELATIONSHIP STREAMS** by which this unknown Unrau can be traced to us and our current generations. Here's the explanation.

1. The first stream is from our progenitor through our grandfather Cornelius K. Unruh to his son, our father Edward Richard Unruh, and then to us.
2. The second stream is from our progenitor through our grandmother, Katharina Loewen to her son, our father Edward Richard Unruh, and then to us.
3. A third stream is from our progenitor through our maternal grandfather Isaac Doerksen to his daughter Tena Martha Doerksen, our mother, and then to us.

Generation Relationship Chart 1 of 3 from the progenitor to 3 Unruh brothers, Ron, Murray, Neale <u>via Great grandfather, grandfather, and father.</u>

1. ? Unrau, b. approx. 1633, (#106809) progenitor
2. ? Unrau, b. approx. 1663, (#106810) child
3. Heinrich Unrau, b. approx. b. 1693, (#106812), grandchild
4. Hinrich Unrau, b. approx. 1723, (#106814), great-grandchild
5. Martin Unruh, b. approx. 1753, (#165971), 2Great-grandchild,
6. Benjamin Martin Unruh, b. 1783, Brenkenhofswalde, Brandenburg, Prussia, (#165973), 3G-grandchild
7. Kornelius B. Unruh, b. 11 NOV 1820, Sofievvka,

Volhynia, 4G-grandchild, (#165980)

8. **Kornelius K. Unruh**, b. 17 MAR 1843, Waldheim, Molotschna, South Russia, (#341800), 5G-grandchild
9. **Cornelius K. Unruh**, b. 20 APR 1873, Temir Bulat, Crimea, South Russia, (#341804), 6G-grandchild
10. **Edward Richard Unruh**, b. 8 MAR 1915, Hepburn, Saskatchewan, (#484759), 7G-grandchild
11. * Ronald James Unruh, b. 1942, Hepburn, Saskatchewan, (#606630), 8G-grandchild
    * Murray Dennis Unruh, b. 1947, St. Catharines, Ontario, (#606629), 8G-grandchild
    * Neale Bryan Unruh, b. 1953, St. Catharines, Ontario, (#606628), 8G-grandchild

Generation Relationship Chart 2 of 3 from the progenitor to 3 Unruh brothers via great grandmother, grandmother, and mother.
1. ? Unrau, b. approx. 1633, (#106809) progenitor
2. ? Unrau, b. approx. 1663, (#106810) child
3. Heinrich Unrau, b. approx. b. 1693, (#106812), grandchild
4. Hinrich Unrau, b. approx. 1723, (#106814), great-grandchild
5. Martin Unruh, b. approx. 1753, (#165971), 2Great-grandchild
6. Benjamin Martin Unruh, b. 1783, Brenkenhofswalde, Brandenburg, Prussia, (#165973), 3G-grandchild
7. Kornelius B. Unruh, b. 11 NOV 1820, Sofievvka, Volhynia, 4G-grandchild, (#165980)
8. **Helena Unruh**, b. 5 MAR 1849, Waldheim, Molotschna, South Russia, (#86297), 5G-grandchild
9. **Katharina Loewen**, b. 26 FEB 1874, Bruderfeld, Crimea, South Russia, (#341805), 6G-grandchild
10. **Edward Richard Unruh**, b. 8 MAR 1915, Hepburn, Saskatchewan, (#484759), 7G-grandchild
11. * Ronald James Unruh, b. 1942, Hepburn, Saskatchewan, (#606630), 8G-grandchild
    * Murray Dennis Unruh, b. 1947, St. Catharines, Ontario, (#606629), 8G-grandchild
    * Neale Bryan Unruh, b. 1953, St. Catharines, Ontario, (#606628), 8G-grandchild

Generation Relationship **Chart, 3 of 3** from Progenitor to Ronald,

Murray, and Neale via maternal great grandfather, maternal grandfather, and mother.

1. ? Unrau, b. approx. 1633, (#106809) progenitor,
2. ? Unrau, b. approx. 1663, (#106810) child
3. Hans Unrau, b. approx. 1690, (#267401), grandchild ,
4. Liscke Unrau, b. 2 MAR 1726, (#32743), great-grandchild
5. Jacob Cornelsen, b. 26 JAN 1752, Klein Konopat, Schwetz, Prussia, (#3699), 2G-grandchild
6. Martin Jacob Cornelsen, b. 4 MAR 1787, Terespolno, Prussia, (#33801), 3G-grandchild
7. Catarina Cornelsen, b. Abt 1822, Alexanderwohl, Molotschna, South Russia, (#60296), 4G-grandchild
8. **Jacob Doerksen,** b. 14 SEP 1851, Waldheim, Molotschna, South Russia, (#353284), 5G-grandchild
9. **Isaac R. Doerksen**, b. 9 AUG 1891, Russia, (#353288), 6G-grandchild
10. **Tena Martha Doerksen,** b. 4 JUN 1919, Mountain Lake, Minnesota, (#484757), 7G-grandchild.
11. * Ronald James Unruh (#606630), b. 1942, Hepburn, Saskatchewan, 8G-grandchild.
    * Murray Dennis Unruh, (#606629), b. 1947, St. Catharines, Ontario, 8G-grandchild.
    * Neale Bryan Unruh (#606628), b. 1953, St. Catharines, Ontario, 8G-grandchild

7 GENERATIONS, a detailed Lineage

MARTIN UNRUH (#165971) had one child; a son named Benjamin Martin Unruh. Although our bloodline traces to a progenitor with the name Unrau, Martin is the first we know about, who carried the Unruh spelling. This lineage list primarily cites name and birth date and location.

LINEAGE OF BENJAMIN MARTIN UNRUH (#165973)

Here are names of his six children, three daughters and then three sons. No information exists about the three daughters. With each of the three sons, children 4,5, and 6, I list them in order of birth and under each son I list their children and birth dates. With bold font, I draw attention to our lineage that begins with Benjamin

Martin, then fifth child Kornelius B. Unruh, a grandchild named Kornelius K.

Benjamin Martin Unruh (#165973) and Spouse: Elisabeth Buller (#165974)

6 Children:

1 Maria Unruh, (#165975) About 1812, Brenkenhofswalde, Brandenburg, Prussia

2 Elisabeth Unruh, (#165976) About 1814, Brenkenhofswalde, Brandenburg, Prussia

3 Susanna Unruh, (#165977) About 1816, Brenkenhofswalde, Brandenburg, Prussia

4 Benjamin B. Unruh, (#165978) 10 November 1818, Sofievvka, Volhynia

5 Kornelius B. Unruh, (#165980) 11 November 1820 married Maria Buller (#165983) 1841

6 Tobias Unruh, (#103897) married Katharina Sperling (#103898) 10 May, 1844

Benjamin B. Unruh (#165978), the fourth child of Benjamin Martin was born November 10, 1818, in Sofievvka, Volhynia; married Maria Kunkel (#165979) born 6 January, 1828, Volhynia.

7 children and their children:

1 Heinrich Benjamin Unruh, (#133579) married Elisabeth Wall (#133580). They had 11 children.

1 Heinrich H. Unruh, (#133581) 7 October 1868, Schwesterthal, Crimea, South Russia

2 Unruh, Gerhard Heinrich (#313207) 28 March 1870, Marienruh, Crimea, South Russia

3 Unruh, Maria (#127366) 13 November 1871, Temir Bulat, Crimea, South Russia

4 Unruh, Cornelius H. (#133588) 8 April 1873, Temir Bulat, Crimea, South Russia

5 Unruh Katharina, (#108497) 15 March 1875, Temir Bulat, Crimea, South Russia

6 _?_Unruh, (#671086)

7 Elisabeth Unruh, (#133596) 11 July 1876, Temir Bulat, Crimea, South Russia

8 Abraham H. Unruh, (#213418) 5 April 1878, Temir Bulat, Crimea, South Russia

9 Anna Unruh, (#313210) 15 December 1879, Temir Bulat, Crimea, South Russia
10 Benjamin Heinrich Unruh, (#133597) 4 September 1881, Temir Bulat, Crimea
11 Peter Unruh, (#313211) 28 March 1883, Temir Bulat, Crimea, South Russia

2 Kornelius Benjamin Unruh, (#133606) 1849, Waldheim, Molotschna, South Russia
1 Kornelius Unruh, (#133608) Orloff, Molotschna, South Russia
2 Fritz Unruh, (#133609) Orloff, Molotschna, South Russia
3 Anna Unruh, (#484788) Orloff, Molotschna, South Russia

3 Peter B. Unruh, (#133610) 10 July 1857, married Maria Thiessen 1884
1 Maria Unruh, (#133612) 1885, Chrischona, Switzerland
2 Katharina Unruh, (#133613) 13 June 1886, Hochfeld, Alexandrovsk, Michailo-Lukashevo Volost, Ekaterinoslav, South Russia
3 Jacob Unruh, (#133614) 1888, Hochfeld, Yazykovo, South Russia
4 Louise Unruh, (#20738) 16 November 1889, Hochfeld, Alexandrovsk, Michailo-Lukashevo Volost, Ekaterinoslav, South Russia
5 Helena Unruh, (#133615) 7 April 1891, Tashchenak, Taurida, South Russia
6 Peter P. Unruh, (#133616) 1 September 1892, Tashchenak, Taurida, Crimea
7 Heinrich P Unruh, (#133617) 15 March 1894, Tashchenak, Taurida, Crimea
8 Margaret Unruh, (#133618) 8 July 1896, Tashchenak, Taurida, South Russia
9 Johannes Unruh, (#133619)1898, Ta shchenak, Taurida, South Russia
10 Anna Unruh, (#133620) 4 December 1899, Crimea, South Russia
11 Cornelius P. Unruh, (#133621)13 January 1902, Ohrloff, Molotschna, South Russia

12 Agnes Unruh, (#133622)23 July 1904, Orloff, Molotschna, South Russia

13 Martha Unruh, (#133623) 1 May 1906, Ohrloff, Molotschna, South Russia

4 Unruh, Anna B (#484796) 13 September, 186213 and Johann J. Wiebe (#484781)

11 Children:

1 Johann J. Wiebe, (#484787) 15 May, 18848

2 Philip John Wiebe, (#364186) 23 August, 1885, Dyurmen, Crimea, South Russia

3 Aganetha J. Wiebe, (#484774) 17 July, 18921

4 Cornelius J. Wiebe, (#484775)

5 Maria J. Wiebe, (#484777)

6 Heinrich J. Wiebe, (#484779)

7 Lena (Wiebe, #484785)

8 Susie J. Wiebe, (#484764)

9 Peter J. Wiebe, (#484768)

10 Lena J. Wiebe, (#484770)

11 Liese J. Wiebe, (#484772)

5 Unruh, Elisabeth B (#531673) and Heinrich Isaak, Married: 20 October 1885

2 Children:

1 Maria Isaak, (#532653) 21 September 1886, Johannesruh, Crimea

2 Helena Isaak, (#532654) 16 December 1895, Johannesruh, Crimea

6 Unruh, Maria B (#510541) married Hermann Penner (#510542) 26 April 1888

3 Children:

1 Maria Penner, (#510540) 30 June 1895, Schoental, Crimea, South Russia

2 Anna Penner, (#1031563) 2 August 1898, Schoental, Crimea, South Russia

3 Benjamin Herman Penner, (#1031570) 19 January 1901, Schoental, Crimea

7 Unruh, Abraham B. (#484795) married Katharina Stobbe (#510521) 3 March 1894

7 Children:

1 Paulina Unruh, (#510520) 10 January 1895, Johannesruh, Crimea

2 Abraham Unruh, (#510519) 19 February 1897, Johannesruh, Crimea

3 Maria Unruh, (#510518) 10 February 1900, Johannesruh, Crimea

4 Katharina Unruh, (#510517) 15 June 1902, Johannesruh

5 Augusta Unruh, (#510516) 17 July 1904, Johannesruh, Crimea

6 Anna Unruh, (#510515) 10 April 1906, Johannesruh, Crimea

7 Kornelius Unruh, (#510514) 23 November 1909, Johannesruh, Crimea

The lineage of Benjamin Martin's 5th Child Kornelius B. Unruh

5 Kornelius B. Unruh (#165980) 11 November 1820 married Maria Buller (#165983) 1841. **Highlighted because he is my great, great grandfather.**

Five Children: Child #1 **Kornelius K**. and Child #2 **Helena K** are noted in bold font because each of them had a child. His son Cornelius K, and Helena's daughter Katharina, married one another. They are Grandma and Grandpa Unruh to Ron, Murray, and Neale.

1 Kornelius K. Unruh (#341800) 17 March 1843, married Aganetha Kroeker (#341801)

8 Children:

1 Aganetha K. Unruh, (#341802) 11 September 1870, Schwesterthal, Crimea

2 Cornelius K. Unruh, (#341804) 20 April 1873, Temir Bulat, Crimea

3 Peter K. Unruh, (#341806) 1 May 1875, Temir Bulat, Crimea

4 Maria K. Unruh, (#341807) 25 September 1879, Temir Bulat, Crimea

5 Anna Unruh, (#510511)1 12 September 1882, Temir Bulat, Crimea

6 Katharina K. Unruh, (#341808) 26 July 1885, Temir Bulat, Crimea

7 Martin K Unruh, (#148938) 30 December 1886, Temir Bulat, Crimea

8 Anna K Unruh, (#341809) 1890

2 **Helena K Unruh, (#86297)** 5 March 1849 married Jacob Loewen (#86296) 28 Oct 1866

11 Children:

1 Jacob J. Loewen, (#279910) 26 September 1867, Bruderfeld, Crimea

2 Maria Loewen, (#34026) 30 December 1870, Crimea

3 Helena Loewen, (#28983) 26 June 1872, Bruderfeld, Crimea

4 Katharina Loewen, (#341805), February, 26, 1874, Bruderfeld, Crimea

5 Cornelius J. Loewen, (#279913) 24 September 1875, Marion, North Dakota

6 Heinrich J. M. Loewen, (#14541) 29 March 1878, Parker, South Dakota

7 Isaac Loewen, (#1058532) 6 November 1879, Dakota Territory

8 Anna Loewen, (#483401) 4 April 1881, Parker, South Dakota

9 Aganetha "Nettie" Loewen, (#32708) 14 May 1883

10 Abram J. Loewen, (#372121) 13 June 1886

11 Sarah Loewen, (#131108) 25 September 1886, Parker, South Dakota

3 Katharina K Unruh, (#213685) married David Warkentin (#341799) 1879.

3 Children:

1 Johann D. Warkentin, (#341812)1 28 February 1881, Karassan, Crimea

2 Cornelius D Warkentin, (#341813) 2 February 1883, Karassan, Crimea

3 Phillip D. Warkentin, (#341814) 9 December,1885, Karassan, Crimea

4 Unruh, Anna K. (#341815) married Nikolai Kroeker (#341817) 3 March 1881

10 Children:

1 Maria Kroeker, (#647421) 12 December, 18815,6,8

2 Klaas K. Kroeker, (#341818) 20 April 1884, Temir Bulat, Crimea

3 Katharina "Tena" Kroeker, (#31198)2 25 December 1886, South Russia

4 Anna Kroeker, (#341820) 22 March 1888, Russia

5 Anna Kroeker, (#647425) 22 May 1888

6 Cornelius Kroeker, (#647426) 30 July 1890

7 Helena Kroeker, (#341819) 24 February 1895, Parker, South Dakota

8 Heinrich Kroeker, (#647428) 16 April 1897

9 Mathilda Kroeker, (#647429) 24 August 1901

10 Abraham Kroeker, (#647430) 21 June 1903

5 Unruh, Heinrich K. (#341816) 21 October 1864 married Judith (Ida) Gossen, 1886

12 Children:

1 Heinrich Unruh, (#341823) 4 July 1887, Crimea, South Russia

2 Heinrich Unruh, (#341824) 10 May 1888, Crimea, South Russia

3 Judith "Ida" Unruh, (#341825) 20 January 1890, Crimea, South Russia,

4 Katharina Unruh, (#341826) 9 September 1891, Crimea, South Russia

5 George H. Unruh, (#341827) 1 March 1893, Crimea, South Russia

6 Cornelius H. Unruh, (#79067) 15 June 1895, South Dakota

7 Helena (Unruh, #341828) 24 March 1897, Parker, South Dakota

8 Anna Unruh, (#78990) 22 January 1899, North Dakota

9 Heinrich Unruh, (#341829) 9 September 1900, Harvey, North Dakota

10 Maria H. Unruh, (#341830) 11 April 1904, North Dakota

11 Jacob Unruh, (#212903) 23 March 1906, Hepburn, Saskatchewan

12 Johnny H. Unruh, (#341831) 28 April 1908, Saskatchewan

The lineage of Benjamin Martin's 6th and last Child, Tobias

Unruh.

6 Tobias Unruh, (#103897) married Katharina Sperling (#103898) 10 May, 1844.

10 Children:

1 Helena Unruh, (#265237) 13 January 1845, Waldheim, Molotschna, South Russia

2 Johann Unruh, (#57550) 11 November 1847, Waldheim, Molotschna

3 Peter Unruh, (#265238) 26 May 1851, Hierschau, Molotschna

4 Katharina Unruh, (#265239) 6 August 1854, Hierschau, Molotschna

5 Cornelius T. Unruh, (#103899) 19 September 1857, Hierschau, Molotschna

6 Anna Unruh, (#265240) 4 November 1859, Hierschau, Molotschna

7 Heinrich T. Unruh, (#103900) 27 July 1861, Hierschau, Molotschna, South Russia

8 Tobias T. Unruh, (#103901) 11 May 1863, Bruderfeld, Crimea, South Russia

9 Maria T. Unruh, (#103902) 15 October 1865, Bruderfeld, Crimea

10 Aganetha Unruh, (#103903) 12 March 1868, Bruderfeld, Crimea

Condensed generational List, 7 generations of 12 that we know.

In this list the relationships after individual names refers to their relationship to Ron, Murray, and Neale.

Martin Unruh (#165971) great great great great grandpa
  Benjamin Martin Unruh (#165973) great great great grandpa
    Kornelius B. Unruh, (#165980) great great grandpa
      Kornelius K. Unruh (#341800) great grandpa
        Cornelius K. Unruh (#341804) grandpa
          Edward Richard Unruh, dad
            1. Ronald James Unruh (#606630)
            2. Murray Dennis Unruh (#606629)
            3. Neale Bryan Unruh (#606628)

Helena K. Unruh (#86297) great grandma

Katharina (Unruh) Loewen (#341805) grandma
Edward Richard Unruh, dad
    1. Ronald James Unruh (#606630)
    2. Murray Dennis Unruh (#606629)
    3. Neale Bryan Unruh (#606628)

13 UNRUH THE CHRISTIAN LEGACY

THIS COMPREHENSIVE FAMILY HISTORY REFLECTS THE
COMPLEX INTERPLAY OF PERSONAL, AND FAMILY AND
HISTORICAL FACTORS. This chapter offers a rich tapestry of
stories across generations that have inspired me for the past thirty
years. The names from the preceding chapter will appear again, but
here I recount their lives. I describe their contributions, struggles,
and their enduring impact as parents, as community members, as
friends, businesspersons, educators, ministers, and missionaries.
This family's legacy is more durable than a monetary account. It
encompasses a diverse array of elements that include faith in God,
service to God, and a commitment to spiritual learning and living.
The names, their children, their lives, and achievements constitute
the legacy. As in the previous chapter, I have highlighted the
names specific to our direct lineage.

***

I will begin with this man.
Benjamin Martin Unruh (#165973) was <u>a minister of the
Brenkenhoffswalde church</u> in West Prussia. His wife was Elisabeth
Buller (#165974), and she was born February 11, 1783, in
Franzthal, Brandenburg, Prussia. They had six children, first three
daughters and then three sons, **1** Maria, **2** Elizabeth, **3** Susanna, **4**
Benjamin B., **5 Kornelius B**. (#165980), and **6** Tobias B.
Information about women in genealogical research is typically
scarce. This is unfortunate. Any family story is incomplete. This
glaring omission is explained by male-dominated record-keeping,

and historical legal and cultural norms. Upon marriage, women typically ceded their rights and property to their husbands, who assumed the roles of guardians, representatives, and sole decision-makers in matters such as property transactions and, in some instances, voting and family affairs. I cannot supply what cannot be found. I share your sense of loss or frustration. Benjamin Martin Unruh's and Elisabeth Buller's three daughters were:

1. Maria Unruh married a man with the surname Kunkel (#348959). No other information.
2. Elizabeth Unruh married a man with the surname Sperling (#348958). No information.
3. Susanna Unruh. No information exists.

Benjamin Martin's 3 sons. I present them in the order of their births, Benjamin B, Kornelius B and Tobias B. According to cultural practice, each son carried the name of his father, 'Benjamin, as his middle name. I begin with the extensive legacy of the fourth child who was the first son. Here are his children and grandchildren.

4. Benjamin B. Unruh (#165978). Call him BB.

Benjamin did not pursue a formal role as an educator or preacher. Nevertheless, it is evident that his household served as a virtual seminary, and he assumed the role of a spiritual guide for his children. Notably, his seven children and their descendants emerged as prominent and influential figures. This family narrative stands as a compelling and illustrative testament to their collective legacy. Each of Benjamin B's seven children, namely Heinrich, Kornelius, Peter, Anna, Elizabeth, Maria, and Abraham, are my first cousins separated by three generations. Here they are in order.

BB's Son 1, Heinrich Benjamin Unruh (#133579) (1847-1883). Call him HB.

Not only was Heinrich B. a church minister; he was also the patriarch of a remarkable family heavily invested in Christian ministry. Born on May 24, 1847, in Waldheim, Molotschna settlement, South Russia, he relocated to Schwestertal in Crimea during his childhood with his parents. On January 4, 1868, he wed Elisabeth Wall (1846-1922) in Temir Bulat, Crimea, and their first child, Heinrich H. (#133581), was born on October 7, 1868, in Schwestertal. Subsequently, they moved to Temir-Bulat in the Eupatoria (Yevpatoriya) district of Crimea, where they raised ten children, nine of whom survived to adulthood.

Remarkably, at the age of 25 in 1874, Heinrich B. was chosen as the minister by the Karassan congregation in Simferopol District, Crimea. He distinguished himself as one of the first ministers in Crimea to preach without written sermons, emphasizing personal conversion before baptism. Tragically, Heinrich B. passed away from sunstroke at the age of 36 on October 17, 1883, in Temir-Bulat, where he was laid to rest. Left to raise her children alone, Elisabeth continued to maintain a household deeply rooted in the Word of God and prayer, instilling in her children a profound commitment to service.

The enduring legacy of the Unruh family radiates through the lives of Elizabeth Wall's and Heinrich B. Unruh's five surviving sons, each of whom wholeheartedly dedicated himself to Christ and to service. Their collective impact, particularly exemplified by Abraham H. and Benjamin H., serves as a testament to the values instilled within their family home.

HB's Son #1, **Heinrich Heinrich** (1868-1912) (#133581).

Heinrich H. Unruh, born on October 4, 1868, in Temir-Bulat (Philippstal), Crimea, was a pioneering missionary and educator. After graduating from the Hamburg Baptist Theological Seminary in 1899, he married fellow seminary student Anna Peters. They were ordained as missionaries by the Spat Mennonite Brethren Church on August 27, 1899, and embarked on a mission to India's Nalgonda district, sponsored jointly by the Mennonite Brethren of Russia and the American Baptist Missionary Union. Despite challenges in obtaining permits and local persecution, they successfully established the Jangaon mission station, which included a church with 200 members and several affiliate stations. Still today, the Unruhpura Centenary Baptist Church reveres this missionary. The church bears his name. Recently, a Clinic is named in his honour. The church has an enormous enthusiastic congregation. It has a Facebook page.

(https://www.facebook.com/p/Unruhpura-Centenary-Baptist-Church-Jangoan-100064411766715/).

Heinrich Heinrich and Anna had seven children, six of whom reached adulthood. Tragically, at 44 years of age, Heinrich succumbed to typhus on October 23, 1912, in Jangaon, India. Anna briefly remained in India before returning to Russia in 1913 with her surviving children. She passed away on October 13, 1921, in Ohrloff, Molotschna. Ultimately, all six surviving children immigrated to Canada and settled in British Columbia, leaving a legacy of unwavering faith and dedication to their mission.

HB's Son #2. **Gerhard Heinrich** (#313207)
At age 19, he was baptized on 16 September, 1889, in Spat, Crimea, South Russia. He was a Mennonite Brethren pastor in Waldheim, Molotschna, Russia and then pastor of Mennonite Brethren Church in Steinbach, Manitoba. He married Helena Voth (#313205). They had thirteen children.

HB's Son #3. **Cornelius Heinrich** (133588)
He was a missionary to India. He married Martha Johannes Woltman (#133589). Three sons were born in India and one in Germany. The first two died at birth. Cornelius retired in Kitchener, Ontario. Two sons, Cornelius and Henry were students at Acadia U in Nova Scotia. One became a teacher and the other a pastor. After Cornelius H's death, his widow moved to the United States.

HB's Son #4. **Abraham Heinrich Unruh** (1878-1961). His name is highlighted because of his importance to me and to the MB Church globally. I have admired him since I first read about him thirty years ago. My great grandfather, Kornelius K. Unruh, was his uncle. My grandfather Cornelius K. Unruh and Abraham H. were cousins and friends.

Better known as Abraham H. Unruh and even A.H. Unruh. His life is a chronicle of ministry and education. His life journey spanned two continents and left an indelible mark on Russian and Canadian Mennonite Brethren communities, profoundly influencing generations of church leaders. Whether he was called Abraham H. Unruh or simply A.H., he stands as a towering figure in the history of the Mennonite Brethren Church, renowned for his remarkable contributions to both ministry and education.

Early Life and Education.

Abraham's story began in Temir-Bulat, Crimea, South Russia, where he was born on April 5, 1878, to Heinrich Benjamin Unruh and Elisabeth Wall. However, tragedy struck him at the age of five. His father passed away, leaving a family of ten children. Since the Unruh's were poor, Abraham and his younger brother Benjamin were separated from the rest of the family. They were required to live with my great grandfather, their uncle Kornelius K., in the Molotschna colony. They both found refuge there. Uncle Kornelius K. was good to them, spent time with each of them, nurtured them as he did his own children. They grew up in this home and were particularly close to two of K.K.'s sons who were of similar age, (my grandpa) Cornelius K age 10, and Peter K age 8.

Abraham's formal education commenced at the age of twelve when he enrolled in secondary school in Ohrloff. His quest for knowledge extended beyond the classroom as he pursued teacher training in Simferopol and further honed his skills at Perekop. At the age of seventeen, he earned his teaching certificate. He immediately began teaching at the elementary school in Menlertschik. In his own time, he was delving into the Bible, and into apologetics and theological texts. His spiritual life journey deepened and culminated in his decision to fully commit his life to Christ. On June 21, 1896, he professed his faith by being baptized in the Mennonite Church in Spat. His faith continued to grow. During these years his life took a significant turn when he met and married Katharina Toews, affectionately known as 'Tina.' They were married on September 19, 1900, in Menlertschik. Their union was a testament to love and faith. In Menlertschik Abraham taught for eight years, 1895-1903, fostering the intellectual growth of his students. After his tenure in Menlertschik, Abraham taught at the Barvenkovo elementary school and Kommerzschule (business school) from 1903 to 1915. In 1904, at the age of 26, he was ordained to the ministry. All these cities were in South Russia.

Turmoil and Red Cross Service.

The world was turbulent as the First World War raged on. Like other Mennonite men, Abraham chose an alternate path of service during the war by joining the Russian Red Cross from 1915 to 1917. However, instead of serving on hospital trains as he expected, his orders took him away from the battlefields. He was stationed in an office in Odessa. Following the war and Abraham's two years of Red Cross service, 1915-17, he and his family moved back to Barvenkovo. However, the country was sinking into anarchy with the Russian Revolution and anti-German sentiment was running high. Faced with rising hostility, the Unruh family decided to leave Barvenkovo and return to Crimea, where Abraham took on the role of principal at the Zentralschule (secondary school) in Karassan for two years.

Spiritual Emergence and Ministry.

These were tumultuous years that were marked by personal growth and professional development. Abraham's spiritual life flourished. His insightful biblical exposition skills and his dedicated service to the church gained recognition. This led to his ordination as a minister. In Tschongraw, Johann Wiens, a returned missionary from India, had established a Bible school, and he extended an invitation to Abraham to join the faculty. This institution attracted students from across Russia, offering vital theological training. Regrettably, after several fruitful years, 1920-1925, the Soviets enforced the closure of the school.

Emigration to Canada.

The political and economic instability in Russia forced the Unruh family to make a life-changing decision. In 1925, they emigrated to Canada aboard the S. S. Minnedosa and arrived 11 January, 1925, in Saint John, New Brunswick. The boarded a train and they settled in Winkler, Manitoba. Within his first year in Winkler, Abraham, still inspired by his experiences at Tschongraw, initiated the beginning of a Bible school. The school was established for the purpose of teaching the Bible, to prepare young people for missionary work and church leadership. Its name was initially Mennonite Bible School Peniel. The name Peniel was based on Genesis 32:26, *"I will not let you go, unless you bless me."* Joined by fellow Tschongraw teachers, Gerhard Reimer and Johann G. Wiens, Abraham led the Winkler Bible Institute for an impressive nineteen years from 1925 to 1942. The institution played a crucial role, shaping and training pastors and missionaries across Canada and the United States. Even during these years, preached in Mennonite communities both in Canada and the United States, and edited a small paper titled Die Antwort (The Answer).

A New Educational Institution.

In response to the educational needs of the Mennonite Brethren Church in Canada, the Canadian Mennonite Brethren Conference established Mennonite Brethren Bible College (later known as Concord College) in Winnipeg in 1944. At the age of sixty-seven, Abraham Unruh, was called upon to serve as its inaugural president. This institution would go on to have a profound and lasting influence on Mennonite Brethren churches, producing pastors, missionaries, Bible teachers, musicians, and other dedicated church workers. My daughter, Cari (Unruh) Locken attended this college from 1988-1992, graduating with a BA in Religious Studies and a BA in Music jointly granted by MBBC and the University of Winnipeg.

A Remarkable Personality.

With his tall stature and corpulent figure, his smartly trimmed beard and mustache, he had a patriarchal persona. He was pleasingly human and humble and enjoyed a delightful sense of humour. Such a wonderful combination of traits. Blessed with a strong and compelling voice, he was focused on effective communication. His lectures and sermons were methodically organized and easily comprehended. He was a dedicated reader. He had a deep and balanced theological knowledge even though he never attended seminary. During Abraham's productive years he displayed rigorous work habits and limitless energy, sustaining a full teaching load, preaching on most Sundays, and leading or speaking at Bible conferences throughout North America. Unsurprisingly, he was granted a Th.B. degree (1937) by Tabor College, Hillsboro, Kansas, and a D.D. degree (1938) by Bethel College, North Newton, Kansas.

Contributions to the Church.

Beyond his teaching and preaching, Abraham actively engaged in Conference boards, serving as the moderator of the Canadian

Conference. He made significant contributions to Sunday school education, producing a wealth of Sunday school material. He was a prolific author during his ministry years. His magnum opus, '*Die Geschichte der Mennoniten Bruedergemeinde* ('the "History of the Mennonite Brethren Church,') is a testament to his determination to preserve the rich heritage of the Mennonite Brethren. During his years of ministry Abraham wrote numerous books. Some of his other titles are:

1. Die Mennonitische Bibelschule in Tschongraw; (The Mennonite Bible School at Tschongraw.)
2. Eine Einleitung für die Lehrer der Sontagsschule; (An Introduction for the Sunday School Teachers).
3. Leitfaden für den Religionsunterricht; (Guide to Religious Education).
4. Nikodemus, (Nicodemus).
5. Gottes Wort als Wegweiser fuer die Gemeindezucht; (God's Word as Guide to Church Discipline).
6. Des Herrn Mahnung an die Gemeinde der Endzeit; (The Lord's Admonition to the Church of the End Times).
7. Der ewige Sohn Gottes; (The Eternal Son of God).
8. Der Prophet Jesaja; (The Prophet Isaiah).

Later Years and Legacy.

Abraham Unruh and his wife retired to Chilliwack, British Columbia. He experienced health challenges such as diabetes and diminishing eyesight. His enthusiasm for God's work was ongoing. Abraham hoped to attend the 1960 centennial celebration of the Mennonite Brethren Church held in Reedley, California, but God had other plans. On January 6, 1960, he preached his final sermon at Clearbrook MB Church, in Abbotsford, B.C. It was entitled, "We Beheld His Glory" (John 1:14). As he began his sermon on Sunday January 15, 1961, he went into a diabetic shock and a coma and passed away a few days later at the age of eighty-two. His funeral was held in the Mennonite Educational Institute (MEI) auditorium in Clearbrook, (Abbotsford) BC, and he was buried in Chilliwack.

Abraham H. Unruh's death marked the end of an era, symbolizing the transition from a generation that had grown up in Russia to the emergence of Canadian-born Mennonite Brethren leaders. Unruh was a spiritual statesman among his people. His legacy lived on in the hearts of the countless individuals he inspired and mentored. Abraham H. Unruh's life is a testament to steadfast faith, persistent dedication, and enduring impact—an exemplary journey that forever enriched the Mennonite Brethren Church on two continents.

Abraham H. and Katharina had eight children:

1. Liese Unruh (#1373287) born 4 October 1901, Barvenkovo, Kharkov province in Northeast (Ukraine), South Russia. She died at two years of age.

2. Abraham A. (#213420) born 20 October 1903, Barvenkovo. He sometimes used the name Abram. Abram married Annie J. Enns of Winkler on 21 October 1926. Abram and Annie had five children: Peggy (m. Walter Regehr), Kathryn (m. Robert Des Roches), Helen (m. Oscar Epp), Louise (m. George Block), and Donald (m. Margie Unruh). Having attended high school and polytechnical school at Simferopol, Crimea, Russia, Abram migrated to Canada with his parents in 1925, where he attended Winkler Bible School for four years, Ontario Bible College for one year, and Tabor College (BA, Th.B.). Unruh taught at Dalmeny Bible School for four years and Winkler Bible School for one year before being ordained in 1935 by Mennonite Brethren and appointed as a missionary to India, where he served for 32 years from 1935 to 1967. In India he served mainly in Gadwal and Wanaparty with shorter terms at Nagarkurnool and Shamshabad. His entire missionary ministry of evangelism and nurture was dominated by an overarching concern for the development of an indigenous church and training its leadership, as seen in his establishing of elders' institutes. In 1975, following the death of Annie Unruh (1972) he married Mrs. Agatha Friesen (nee Klassen) of Waldheim, Saskatchewan, who died on 31 August 1983. Abram Unruh died in Manitoba on 7 September 1988.

3. Cornelius (#1373288) born 14 October 1905, in Barvenkovo. Died at 4 years of age. His death and the death of their first child Liese, were considered tragedies, yet Katharina and Abraham testified that their faith in the Lord had been strengthened.

4. Johann (#405457) 20 June 1908, Barvenkovo. He was a carpenter and died in Toronto in 2002 at age 94.
5. Katherine A. "Katie" (#138165) born 20 June 1910, in Barvenkovo. She grew up and married Abram Henry Redekop. They moved to Ontario in 1946 and attended Fairview Mennonite Brethren Church in St. Catharines. He died in 1961 and she died in St. Catharines in 1993. Both are buried in Victoria Lawn Cemetery. They had three daughters and a son.
6. Victor (#405460) born 27 September 1914, in Barvenkovo. Victor died during WWII at the age of 30. He was a Pilot Officer in RCAF. He is buried Bretteville-Sur-Laize Canadian War Cemetery, Calvados, France.
7. Heinrich (#405459) born 8 February 1917, in Barvenkovo. Heinrich was a medical doctor practicing in Kamloops, B.C. He died at age 71 in 1988.
8. Lydia (#405461) born 10 February 1920, in Karassan, Crimea. She married Nicolai (Nick) Friesen. They moved to Chilliwack, BC in 1945 from Coaldale, AB.

HB's Son #5. **Benjamin Heinrich (#133597)** (1881-1959).

Benjamin H. lived a life that became a complex legacy of leadership and controversy. He was an exceptional Russian Mennonite educator, prolific author, and emigration facilitator, widely celebrated by Mennonites. Under different circumstances, he would have spent his entire career in the classroom and behind a church pulpit. Instead, his heart for Mennonites and their heritage, together with the timing of chaotic world events in the 1920s and 1930s, called him to action. Most North and South American Mennonites cannot tell their family immigration stories without appreciatively mentioning Benjamin H. Unruh. What most Mennonite accounts for decades failed to mention was Benjamin's affinity for Nazi nationalism.

Communism in Russia destroyed the Mennonite colony life. Deprivation and famine threatened their existence. Russian and Germany were enemies. German Mennonites wanted to be relocated. Benjamin responded to their call to help.
However, in Germany, Unruh displayed an early and fervent admiration for Adolf Hitler, maintaining a favorable view of him

until the war's conclusion. Remarkably, during the war, Heinrich Himmler even referred to Unruh as the "Moses of the Mennonites. "Recent revelations of his connections with Third Reich leaders and sympathy for German nationalism and Hitler have surfaced. My brief account merely introduces his complex life.

Benjamin H. Unruh was a second cousin of both my grandfather C.K. and my grandma Katharina. Of course, that means that B.H. was my dad's second cousin once removed and my second cousin twice removed, or two generations removed. Bloodline will not alter my objectivity. Only in the past twenty years have candid books and articles documented the truth. Benjamin demonstrates that a dedicated Christian with an altruistic passion to aide other people, must still think critically when assessing world events and ideologies. This is an absorbing story.

Early Life and Education.

He was born on September 17, 1881, three years after his brother Abraham H. Unruh. Following the untimely death of their father Heinrich B. Unruh, Abraham and Benjamin were sent to live with their uncle Kornelius B. Unruh. Kornelius B., a prominent Mennonite educator in Russia, nurtured their intellectual and spiritual growth, and recognized Benjamin's exceptional talents. In 1899, at 18, Benjamin was baptized and joined the MB Church at Spat, likely influenced by Kornelius B. Thanks to Kornelius B's connections, three affluent Molotschna district Mennonite families granted Benjamin a scholarship for graduate and doctoral studies in theology and history in Basel, Switzerland, from 1900 to 1907. His educational environment in Basel blurred the current German nationalism and European colonialism with his Christian ideals and the growth of God's kingdom. Despite Basel's influence of socialist-leaning Swiss Reformed figures, Unruh remained untouched by their values and continued his path. This academic foundation provided him with a career and was instrumental in his later work.

Marriage and Teaching Career.

He pursued a teaching career in Russia, specializing in Russian language and literature at Karlsruhe Technische Hochschule (Karlsruhe Technical University) and teaching

German and Religion at Halbstadt Kommerzschule (Halbstadt Business School). He also authored Bibelkunde (Bible Studies) for Mennonite schools in Russia. There was an occasion when Unruh was speaking in Basel in 1908. The meeting was attended by Vladimir Lenin during his Swiss exile. That earned Benjamin a sincere response from Lenin regarding the German colonists' contributions to Russian life.

As a student living on the Swiss-German border, Benjamin H. Unruh became entwined with South German Mennonites through marriage. In 1908 at the age of 27, Benjamin married Frieda Hege, a German from Loewenstein, Baden-Württemberg. Frieda Hege was born 1 January 1880, in Loewenstein, Baden-Württemberg, Germany. She died 28 December 1946, at Karlsruhe, Baden-Württemberg, Germany. She was a daughter of Elder Christian Hege of Breitenau.

During the years 1908-1918, Frieda bore eight children: Rudolph, Martha, Hans, Heinrich, Liesel (married to Horst Quiring), Olga, Maria, and Fritz (died during World War II). By 1918 there was growing unease in Russia and in Germany. Benjamin was 37 years old.

On the 17 March, 1948, Bayern, Germany, two years after Frieda's death, Benjamin married Paula Hotel who was born 2 November 1911. She was a daughter of Elder Johannes Hotel of Batzenhof near Durlach. She died on 19 February 1998, in Germany. They had no children.

Immigration and Leadership.

In 1920, Benjamin H. Unruh's life took a transformative turn when he was selected by Russian Mennonites to join the Russlandmennonitische Studienkommission (Russia Mennonite Study Commission). His deep understanding of Anabaptist-Mennonite principles, coupled with his oratory skills, earned him respect among Mennonites and Mennonite Brethren. This commission tasked him with exploring emigration possibilities abroad. Little did he know the profound impact this mission would have on his life. After spending most of 1920 in western Europe and North America, his passion for relocating refugees grew immensely. Consequently, he made the pivotal decision to leave Russia permanently and settle in Karlsruhe, Germany. In Germany

Benjamin H. became widely known and respected.

While living in Germany in the 1920s, Unruh became a dedicated advocate for famine-stricken Mennonites in South Russia. He was an able speaker and preacher and was a well-known figure at Mennonite conferences in Germany. He was never an ordained preacher primarily because he refused ordination unless all Mennonite branches in Russia agreed to his ordination. A prolific author, he wrote regular articles in the German press, history books about the Mennonite pilgrimage through the centuries and about specific Christian leaders. He also wrote scholarly material such as 'Die niederlandisch-niederdeutschen Hintergründe der mennonitischen Ostwanderungen' (The Dutch-Low German Background Of The Mennonite Eastward Migrations).

His unwavering commitment led to his instrumental role in the early history of the Mennonite Central Committee (MCC). He served as a commissioner for the Canadian Mennonite Board of Colonization from 1921 to 1925, guiding immigration to Canada. In 1929, collaborating with MCC, he orchestrated a rescue mission that saved thousands of Mennonites from Moscow, resettling them in Paraguay, Brazil, and Canada. His strong connections within German government agencies in Berlin turned his office in Karlsruhe into a vital hub for international Mennonite relief efforts. I cannot help but state my honest assessment. Unruh's work emphasized preserving Russian Mennonite culture while promoting German racial purity, a controversial stance aligning with National Socialism and Hitler. His influence in Canada, the United States, and Germany was profound. He raised funds to release and relocate countless Mennonite families from Soviet Russia. He advocated for special considerations during the Soviet Union's Great Famine (Holodomor) of 1932-1933; secured debt forgiveness for Mennonites in Paraguay and Brazil; and played an essential role in MCC's relief efforts in war-torn Poland and France in 1940. Unruh's legacy is marked by his remarkable accomplishments in the face of challenging circumstances. He also wrote 'Fügung und Fuhrung im Mennonitischen Welt-Hilfswerk 1920-1933' (Providence and leadership in the Mennonite World Relief Organization 1920-1933). He was granted the honorary Doctor of Theology at the University of Heidelberg in 1937.

Controversial Associations, Nazi Sympathies.
He's probably the most complicated personality in the entire
Russian Mennonite story. Unruh's contributions are unmatched.
His impact across various roles such as scholar, church leader,
eloquent speaker, immigration facilitator, and indispensable
genealogist is unparalleled. Yet it is noteworthy that in Germany,
Unruh displayed an early and fervent admiration for Adolf Hitler.
Hitler's political aspirations, framed as a Christian eschatological
hope, appealed to many, including German Mennonites like
Unruh. They endorsed a state that honored "positive Christianity"
while remaining blind to the totalitarian nature of the National
Socialist regime. German Mennonites, led by figures like Unruh,
saw themselves as contributing to the German Volk, with a
complementary role alongside the church. They viewed their
mission as preaching the Gospel in opposition to what they
horrifically labeled as "Judeo-Bolshevism." Remarkably, during
the war, Heinrich Himmler himself referred to Unruh as the
"Moses of the Mennonites!"

Legacy and the Contemporary Perception.
The life of Benjamin Heinrich Unruh is marked by a profound
paradox. On one hand, he made significant humanitarian
contributions to the Mennonite community by facilitating
immigration and relief efforts during tumultuous times. On the
other hand, his endorsement of Hitler's regime tarnishes his legacy.
Unruh's association with National Socialism serves as a poignant
reminder of how individuals driven by noble intentions can
become entangled with ideologies that contradict their deeply held
faith principles.

After World War II, MCC distanced itself from Unruh due to
his past Nazi sympathies, providing him with a modest pension.
Frieda Hege died on December 28, 1946, in Karlsruhe, Baden-
Wuerttemberg. On March 17, 1948, 67-year-old Benjamin married
38-year-old Paula Hotel. Benjamin died in a hospital in Mannheim,
Baden-Württemberg, Germany on 12 May 1959 at the age of 78.

Benjamin H. Unruh's and Freida Hege's children were:

1. Rudolph B. Unruh, born September 3, 1908, in Halbstadt, Molotschna, South Russia; died March 5, 1974, Karlsruhe, Baden-Wuerttemberg, Germany.
2. Martha B. Unruh, November 5, 1909, in Halbstadt, Molotschna, South Russia; died December 15, 1990, Karlsruhe, Baden-Wuerttemberg, Germany.
3. Hans B. Unruh, November 6, 1910, in Halbstadt, Molotschna, South Russia; died January 15, 1986, in Kaiserslautern, Rheinland-Pfalz, Germany. He was an opera singer in Germany.
4. Heinrich B. Unruh, November 7, 1911, in Karlsruhe, Baden-Wuerttemberg, Germany; died March 29, 2003, in Bruchsal, Baden-Wuerttemberg, German.
5. Elisabeth B. "Luise" Unruh, May 10, 1914, in Halbstadt, Molotschna, South Russia; died July 1, 1985, in Korntal, Baden-Wuerttemberg, Germany.
6. Olga Unruh, November 7, 1915, in Halbstadt, Molotschna, South Russia; died July 11, 1982, in Karlsruhe-Ruppurr, Baden-Wuerttemberg, Germany.
7. Maria Unruh, March 23, 1917, in Halbstadt, Molotschna, South Russia; no further information.
8. Friedrich "Fritz" B. Unruh, October 29, 1918, in Halbstadt, Molotschna, South Russia; died December 9, 1941, Kinykowo, Orel, Russia. He is believed to have died during war, WWII.

***

The preceding lengthy account concerned the family of Benjamin Martin Unruh's Child No. 4, Benjamin B. Unruh. Now I can tell you about Child No. 5, the second son, **Kornelius Benjamin Unruh.** He was none other than my great, great grandfather.

5. Kornelius Benjamin Unruh (#165980)
My great, great, grandfather. My Dad's great grandfather.

My father knew his great grandfather's name but knew nothing about his life and that he was an outstanding educator. Dad had no access to such information, and genealogy was not a table topic in prairie homes. You will enjoy reading about Kornelius B., great, great grandfather to Murray, Neale, me, and Verna (Uncle Neale's daughter).

Early Life and Education.

Kornelius B. Unruh was a dedicated Mennonite educator in Russia. He received his training at Halbstadt Zentralschule under Gustav Rempel. His passion for learning was evident from a young age. He began his teaching career at just seventeen years of age, on a wealthy family estate and later in a school in Blumenort, Molotschna. He had an insatiable thirst for knowledge, dedicating his free time and summers to private study in Ekaterinoslav, Kiev, and Odessa. Proficient in five languages, including Russian and French, and well-versed in modern educational methods, he introduced Russian at the Blumenort elementary school. In 1870, Kornelius B. Unruh returned to Halbstadt Zentralschule as a teacher, where he had once been a student. He then spent three years teaching in Moscow and Switzerland, including study at the Muristalden Protestant normal school in Bern, Switzerland. Later, he furthered his education in Russia, including a winter of private study in Moscow.

Marriage and Family.

Kornelius B. Unruh married Maria Buller (#165983) in 1841. They raised five children: **Kornelius K. (#341800), Helena (#86297)**, Katharina, Anna, and Heinrich. His family life was marked by love and dedication, and his children benefited from his passion for education and learning. This is the uncle who helped to raise his nephews, Abraham H., and Benjamin H. Unruh when their father, Benjamin B. Unruh died at an early age.
Educational Contributions.

Kornelius B. became principal of the Ohrloff Zentralschule, where he taught for 32 years. In co-operation with others, he helped to produce several textbooks for Mennonite schools, including the following: Biblische Geschichten für mennonitische Elementarschulen. Oberstufe (Halbstadt, 1902); Leitfaden zur Kirchen-geschichte für mennonitische Centralschulen in Russland (Neuhalbstadt, 1890); Leitfaden für den Religionsunterricht in den mennonitischen Centralschulen Russlands (Halbstadt, 1906); Kratkaya Nemetskaya Grammatika.

The English translation of those titles: 'Biblical Stories for Mennonite Elementary Schools'. upper school (Halbstadt, 1902); 'Guide to Church History for Mennonite Central Schools in Russia' (Neuhalbstadt, 1890); 'Guide for religious instruction in the Mennonite central schools of Russia' (Halbstadt, 1906); Kratkaya Nemetskaya Grammatika ... (a brief German grammar for elementary schools in Russia) (Berdyansk, 1898).
Ministerial Work.

K. B. Unruh was not only an exceptional educator but also a dedicated minister. In 1883, he was elected as the preaching minister of the Orloff Mennonite Church. Later, in 1905, he resigned from this role and founded a secondary school near Novo-Poltavka in the Kherson province. Afterward, he established a Bible school in Friedensfeld, within the Zagradovka Mennonite settlement. Zagradovka, sometimes spelled with an 's,' was located on the Ingulez River, 60 miles (100 km) northeast of Kherson. This extensive area of 60,000 acres was acquired by the Molotschna Mennonite Colony in 1871 to provide farmland for landless Mennonites, resulting in 16 villages established there between 1872 and 1883.

Unruh's Bible school served the residents of these villages and beyond, drawing students from distant colonies. Additionally, he taught Bible and German at the Zagradovka Zentralschule. Unfortunately, his health deteriorated due to his substantial weight (400 pounds), and he passed away at the age of 89 in 1910.
Here are Kornelius B's children, Kornelius K., Helena, Katharina, Anna, and Heinrich.

1. **Kornelius K. Unruh (#341800)** My Great Grandfather.
He was the firstborn child of Kornelius Benjamin and his wife Maria Buller. He was born March 17, 1843, in Waldheim, Molotschna, South Russia. He was my dad's grandfather and my great grandfather. He married Aganetha Kroeker (#341801) on

December 6, 1867, in Schwesterthal, Crimea. Kornelius K died in 1893 at the age of 50. Aganetha died in 1920 at the age of 78.

Aganetha bore eight children, Aganetha, **Cornelius K** (grandpa), Peter K, Maria, Anna, Katharina, Martin K, Anna K.

Aganetha's and Kornelius K's children were:
1. Aganetha K. Unruh, (341802)

That's right. Her mother Aganetha gave her the same name. She was born September 11, 1870, in Schwesterthal, Crimea. She was baptized on June 14, 1889. She married Heinrich (Henry) Kroeker, on November 19, 1889, in South Russia. Henry and Aganetha and her younger brother Kornelius K. emigrated to the United States. The Kroekers lived in Harvey, South Dakota for twelve years where six of their ten children were born. They were, Cornelius Kroeker, Heinrich, Aganetha, Johann, Anna, and Katharina. Because land was readily available in Saskatchewan, Canada, they moved their family to Saskatchewan in March 1903, as did her brother, our Grandpa Cornelius K.

Four more children, Peter, David, Wilhelm, and Martha were born in Canada. The last child Martha was born January 26, 1911, and five months later Martha's daddy, Heinrich (Henry) Kroeker died in Hepburn on June 8, 1911. Henry, Aganetha's husband, was only 44 years old. 41-year-old Aganetha meanwhile, had seven children living at home. Three years later, on January 25, 1914, Aganetha married widower, 54-year-old Jacob Priebe, himself the father of thirteen children. His wife Helena Enns had died in 1913, when five of his children were still of school age. Following Jacob's death in Hepburn in 1940, Aganetha moved to Abbotsford, B.C. where she lived until she passed away on October 20, 1955. The names of some of her grandchildren can be found using the GRanDMA Online website, but no other information is supplied.

2 My grandpa, **Cornelius K. Unruh (#341804).**

Kornelius K's second child was my Grandpa Unruh. He was born April 20, 1873, in Temir Bulat, Crimea. Temir Bulat was later called Razdalnoye, but now is Philipstal, Crimea. He was given the name Cornelius. His middle name, according to custom, was the same as his father's first name, Kornelius. So, he was Cornelius Kornelius. It's no wonder that much later, he was satisfied by the nickname "C.K." that was given to him by his friends. He was baptized at the age of 16, on June 21, 1889.

Immigrants

In 1893 at age 20, Cornelius K. Unruh emigrated from Russia to America with his older sister Aganetha (Agnes) and her husband (Henry Kroeker). Of Kornelius K's children, Aganetha (Agnes), C.K. and Martin Grandpa were the three Unruh siblings to emigrate from nationalistic South Russia. Martin emigrated at a later date than Aganetha and Cornelius K. The other four siblings, Peter, Maria, Katharina, Anna, and their parents remained and died in Russia.

Upon arrival in America, the three chose to live in Marion, South Dakota for three years. Wasting no time, on December 2, 1894, C.K. married Katharina Loewen of the Jacob and Helena (nee Unruh) Loewen family. In terms of immediate legacy, I must spend time here with Cornelius K. and Katharina Loewen who were our paternal grandparents, Murray's, Neale's, Verna's, and mine. Verna is the daughter of their son Cornelius, whom I knew as my uncle Neale.

They lived in a log cabin with a dirt floor which was regularly swept and kept smooth. Following the infant deaths of their first two children, daughters Hannie and Susanna, their first surviving child, a daughter, my aunt Annie (Anna), was born in 1899 in Marion, SD. The family of three moved to Harvey, North Dakota where they lived for four years.

Canada

Then came their move to Canada in 1903. At the age of 30, C.K. purchased a ¼ section of land, 160 acres, northeast of Hepburn, Saskatchewan for the price of $10.00. C.K.'s sister Aganetha (Agnes) and her husband Henry made the move north as well and homesteaded in Herbert, Saskatchewan. C.K. and Katharina had three more children born to them. They already had my aunt Annie, and now came uncle (Cornelius) Neale, uncle Harry, and my father Edward Richard. All three of C.K.'s and Katharina's sons were born on the Hepburn farm. My father Edward was born when C.K. was forty-two years old. Grandpa C.K. was 69 by the time I arrived in 1942.

Grandpa and grandma were believers and members of the MB church in Hepburn. Grandpa was an elder in the church. Their children remembered that family devotions at the house, consisting of Bible reading and prayer, were held daily after the supper hour.

Hepburn

CK was well known as a farmer, then a school board trustee, a Reeve, an active churchman, International Harvester agent, hardware store owner, an auctioneer, a hail adjuster for the province of Saskatchewan and later a helper in Harry's (his middle son) hardware store often delivering products to customers. He was one of five members of the original Mennonite Central Committee of Canada, and he sat on the committee that sponsored Russian Mennonites to emigrate to Canada, prior to and following WWII. In 1927 the Unruhs moved into town. They also took time to travel to South Dakota to visit Grandma (Loewen) Unruh's sister Marie (nee Unruh) Kunkel as well as her brother Jacob in Kansas. Four of their children predeceased them, Hannie 1895-1895, Susanna 1897-1998, Harry age 40 died in 1948 and Annie at the age of 49, also died in 1948.

C. K. and Katharina Unruh

Personal Recollections

Only a few personal recollections of Grandpa remain to me from my early years, but I do recall as a four-year-old in Hepburn, riding in a truck with Grandpa. Grandpa helped at the Hardware store that his son Harry owned. Grandpa and I were in a pickup truck to deliver a barrel of kerosene to a distant farm. 73-year-old Grandpa had hoisted the barrel and placed it on the bed of the truck and closed the gate. We drove to the Saskatchewan River where Grandpa drove the truck aboard a small ferry boat. Once on the other side Grandpa piloted the truck to the farm where he lifted the barrel and set it on the ground. On the way home, we stopped at a small store and Grandpa bought an ice cream cone for each of us. I remember his large hands with which he handed me my cone and with the other tussled my blond hair. I had no idea then about the story of my Grandpa's life.

Eight years is a long time to be separated from a grandparent. Mom, Dad, and I moved to Ontario when I was five in 1947. On only one occasion when Murray was five years old and I was ten, did my parents visit Hepburn again. In August 1955 Grandpa and Grandma sold all their belongings in Hepburn and moved across country, into a single bedroom in my parents' house at 531 Bunting Rd., in St. Catharines, Ontario. I was thirteen and I recall my surprise at grandpa's appearance. His upper body was bent over at the waist, and he walked with difficulty, with the visible shape of huge arthritic knees in the legs of his trousers. His hands trembled much of the time, even to feed himself. Grandma was diabetic and required a daily injection. Grandpa administered that syringe with his shaky hand. Grandma lived with us for sixteen months and died of a heart attack on December 14, 1957, at the age of 83. I pulled my pillow over my head to subdue the sound of the old man's agony as he cried, "Oh my Tina, my Tina!" Grandpa remained in our home for one more year before Mom and Dad moved him to a nursing facility in Vineland. I remember how he objected to this, chastening my Dad for doing something as horrible as this. Happily, within weeks however, he had made friends, all of whom could chatter together in Plautdeitsch. On May 16, 1959, C.K. passed away at age 86. I was 17 years old; Murray was 12 and Neale was 6 years of age. As I write, I have marked my 81st birthday. Yikes!

The Other Children

Following the births of Aganetha K and Cornelius K, six other children were born to Kornelius K. Four of the six remaining children are almost unknown because of insufficient ancestral data. Here is what we can know.

3. Peter K. Unruh was born on May 1, 1875, in Temir Bulat. No further information.
4. Maria K. Unruh was born on September 25, 1879, in Temir Bulat. No information.
5. Anna Unruh was born September 12, 1882, in Temir Bulat. She died in childhood. No further information.
6. Katharina K. Unruh was born on July 26, 1885, in Temir Bulat. She was named with her mother's first name and her dad's middle initial. She married Karl Kanke (#1090895), and they had five children all born in Crimea, Russia. Karle Jr. born in 1909, came to Canada and died here in 1997. Concerning Agneta, their second child, there is no information. Anna, the third child was born on April 19, 1910, in Crimea, South Russia, and she died in Amankaragay, Qostanay, Kazakhstan on May 10, 1984. A fourth child, Katharina K, was born 1 October, 1911, in Crimea and died in 2001. No other information is available. The fifth child, daughter Helene, left Ukraine for Poland in 1943 and immigrated to Canada after WWII, was married in Vancouver in 1953 to Heinrich (Henry) Heinrichs (#1015279). She died 25 July, 1996, in Vancouver, British Columbia.

Concerning the mom of these five, Katharina K. Unruh, no other information is available other than her date of death, August 27, 1913, in Pascha-Tschokmak, Crimea at the age of 28.

7. Martin K. Unruh (148938) was born on December 30, 1886, in Temir Bulat, Crimea. He was baptized in 1911 in Russia. On January 13, 1912, in Crimea, South Russia, Martin married Susannah Derksen (#148939). Five of their seven children, George, Agneta, Maria, Arthur, and Nicholas were born in Russia. Martin and his family emigrated to Canada in April 1925, settling in Morse, SK. Two more children, Agnes and

Waldemar Renaldo were born in SK.

I met Martin, this elderly man in 1974. Christine and our children travelled from Peterborough Canada to Langley, B.C. to attend an Associated Gospel Church national conference. Martin lived in Abbotsford. I visited Martin one day, but due to his infirmity, he required assistance from his daughter to communicate with me. She generously provided me with photocopies of relevant genealogy documents. My Aunt Agnes, Uncle Neale's wife who also lived in Abbotsford, had notified me about this man. My pursuit of ancestral information had already begun that long ago, almost fifty years.

8. Anna K. Unruh was born in 1890. This eighth child was given the name Anna, in honour of a deceased sister, child 5. No further information.

In Kornelius K's family of eight children, one died in childhood, and as I have already stated, only three of his seven surviving children emigrated to Canada. The others remained in Russia with him, and it is not surprising that records were not kept. The colonies were decimated by the departures of so many Mennonite families. There was so much unrest. Russia was recovering after the First World War. The Bolshevik Revolution changed governance forever in Russia. Soon Soviet control made the lives of Christians unbearable.

***

Kornelius B. Unruh's Remaining Children

After Kornelius K. Unruh was born, Maria Buller bore four more children, Helena, Katharina, Anna K., and Heinrich K.

2. **Helena Unruh (#86297)** was born March 5, 1849, Waldheim, Molotschna, South Russia. Helena married Jacob Loewen (86296) who was born August 23, 1842, in Hierschau, Molotschna, South Russia. Their wedding took place on October 28, 1866, in Bruderfeld, Crimea, South Russia. Jacob's date of death is recorded as February 2, 1931, in Hillsboro, Kansas. She died: March 22, 1910, Hillsboro, Kansas. Together they had eleven children. Her fourth child, she named **Katharina Loewen (#341805),** and she

was born on February 26, 1874, in Bruderfeld, Crimea, South Russia. More about Helena and Katharina in a page or two.

3. Katharina Unruh (#213685) born February 28, 1856, Molotschna Colony, South Russia; died: May 24, 1936, Kazakhstan. Yes, another Katharina, this one, Aunt of my grandma.

4. Anna K. Unruh (#341815) born January 28, 1858, Waldheim, Molotschna, South Russia; died: March 1925, Hepburn, Saskatchewan.

5. Heinrich K. Unruh (#341816) born October 21, 1864, Bruderfeld, Crimea, South Russia; died: March 15, 1932, Hepburn, Saskatchewan.

6. Peter B. Unruh (#133610).
After Heinrich B. Unruh and Kornelius B. Unruh, Peter was the third son in succession and sixth child born to Benjamin B. Unruh. Peter was <u>a teacher in Schoenau and Muensterberg. He attended the Crischona Bible School in Switzerland. He returned to the Molotschna, where he was a minister and teacher.</u>

Peter Unruh and Maria Thiessen had 13 children, 9 of whom survived, 2 sons and 7 daughters. Most of them came to Canada aboard the S.S. Minnedosa in 1924. Six of them settled in Kitchener/Waterloo, and one in Virgil. A daughter died in Kazakhstan, and a son was killed in a German paramilitary unit. Don't be surprised by this. Many Mennonite young men were conscripted, and many had been persuaded that Germany, their homeland was to be esteemed over Russia, even if under Nazi rule.

Peter's Fourth child, a daughter **Anna Unruh** (#484796), married Johann Wiebe and had 11 children. Of them, her first child was Johann Jr, who attended primary school in Schattenruh, Crimea, and the Zentralschule in Ohrloff, Molotschna Colony for 3 years. He then attended the school for teachers in Neu-Halbstadt, Molotschna Colony. <u>He was a teacher in Busau and also in Minlertschik, Crimea. He then became a church minister.</u> He was exiled to Solovki, Russia on April 6, 1930, but later returned to join his family who had been exiled to the Ural Region.

Child number five was **Elisabeth Unruh** (#531673) married to Heinrich Isaak, and they had two daughters. The daughters married and enjoyed families, and all lived their lives in Crimea, South Russia.

Child 6 was **Maria Unruh** (#510541). She married Hermann Penner and they had three children. Hermann and Maria died in Crimea, but all three children came to Canada, and made a life in Coaldale AB., marrying and having families.

Child 7, and the last child of Peter B. Unruh was **Abraham B. Unruh (#484795)**. He became an ordained minister in the Busau Church on Pentecost Day, May 12, 1915. He was introduced to the Busau Church by Peter Friedrichsen with the scripture from 2 Corinthians 5:20-6:10 (NIV) … *20 We are therefore Christ's ambassadors, as though God were making his appeal through us. We implore you on Christ's behalf: Be reconciled to God. 21 God made him who had no sin to be sin for us, so that in him we might become the righteousness of God. 6:1 As God's co-workers, we urge you not to receive God's grace in vain. 2 For he says, "In the time of my favor I heard you, and in the day of salvation I helped you." I tell you, now is the time of God's favor, now is the day of salvation. 3 We put no stumbling block in anyone's path, so that our ministry will not be discredited. 4 Rather, as servants of God we commend ourselves in every way: in great endurance; in troubles, hardships and distresses; 5 in beatings, imprisonments and riots; in hard work, sleepless nights and hunger; 6 in purity, understanding, patience and kindness; in the Holy Spirit and in sincere love; 7 in truthful speech and in the power of God; with weapons of righteousness in the right hand and in the left; 8 through glory and dishonor, bad report and good report; genuine, yet regarded as impostors; 9 known, yet regarded as unknown; dying, and yet we live on; beaten, and yet not killed; 10 sorrowful, yet always rejoicing; poor, yet making many rich; having nothing, and yet possessing everything.*

Peter B Unruh died at age 57 years, August 4, 1914 in Ohrloff, Molotschna. Maria died at the age of 65 years old. They lived in Taschtschenak Gut by Orloff, near Halbstadt. His tombstone was inscribed with the words: "Ich have dich Je un Je geliebr darum hab ich dich zu mir gezogen"; "I have loved you ever and ever that's why I drew you to me."

***

An essential look back for a moment.

As we know now, **Helena Unruh** (#86297) was the second child of Kornelius B. (#165980) and Maria Buller (#165983). Her older brother was (#341800) Kornelius K.

She married Jacob Loewen (86296) who was born August 23, 1842, in Hierschau, Molotschna, South Russia and his date of death is recorded as February 2, 1931, in Hillsboro, Kansas. Their wedding took place on October 28, 1866, in Bruderfeld, Crimea, South Russia. Together they had eleven children. Kornelius K. was 'uncle' to all of Helen's children. It is child number 4, Katharina Loewen, who is essential to the Unruhs. Katharina was Kornelius K's niece. Kornelius K's son Cornelius K. was Helen's nephew, and he was a first cousin to all of Aunt Helena's children and that included Katharina. Did you hear that?

Helena's children were:
1. Jacob J. Loewen (#279910), was born on September 26, 1867, in Bruderfeld, Crimea, South Russia; and he died July 31, 1934. He married Katharina Loewen (#25479), and they had eleven children. Be careful here. Jacob had a sister who was also named Katharina (#341805). Jacob and his wife lived in South Dakota until 1905 when they moved briefly to Saskatchewan before moving back to the USA and settling in Hillsboro Kansas.
2. Maria Loewen, (#34026), born on December 30, 1870, in Crimea, South Russia. She married Johann Kunkel (#32202), and they had nine children. She died on April 23, 1960, in Freeman, South Dakota.
3. Helena Loewen, (#28983), was born June 26, 1872, Bruderfeld, Crimea, South Russia. Yes, she was given her mother's first name. After the deaths of two husbands, she married a third time. Johann Schafer (#940121) died at age 26. At 29 she married 44-year-old Franz Tessman #28854. He died at age 63 and Helena married 58-year-old Peter J. Nachtigal

(#76002). She died on July 15, 1955, Reedley, California.

4. **Katharina Loewen,** (#341805) was born on February 26, 1874, in Bruderfeld, Crimea, South Russia. She died on the 14th of December 1957, in St. Catharines, Ontario. **Helena** turns out to be **my paternal great grandmother** because her daughter Katharina married Kornelius K's son, **Cornelius K., and they are my grandma and grandpa.** They are my dad, Edward's parents. This entire love story of my grandfather and grandmother Unruh is told in much detail in the preceding chapter 12.

5. Cornelius J. Loewen, (#279913), was born on September 24, 1875, in Marion, North Dakota. He married Maria Guenther, (#14542). He died on March 8, 1936, in Abbotsford, British Columbia.

6. Heinrich J. M. Loewen, (#14541), was born on March 29, 1878, in Parker, South Dakota. He married Maria L. Guenther, (#14542). He died on November 14, 1959, in Shafter, California. He lived 81 years.

7. Isaac Loewen, (#1058532), was born on the 6th of November 1879, in Dakota Territory. He died as an infant.

8. Anna Loewen, (#483401) was born on the 4th of April 1881, Parker, South Dakota. She died on June 4, 1957, in Los Angeles, California. She was married twice, first to Henry D. Peters (#483012), who died suddenly, and she was only 20 when she married Abram Strauss (#483402).

9. Aganetha "Nettie" Loewen, (#32708), was born May 14, 1883. She died on June 16, 1918, in Hepburn, Saskatchewan, at age 35.

10. Abram J. Loewen, (#372121), was born on June 13, 1886. Married twice, first to Anna Kopp and then to Justina Gossen (#102920). He died December 23, 1962, in Twinsburg, Ohio at 76 years of age.

11. Sarah Loewen, (#131108), was born on 25th of September 1886, Parker, South Dakota. She died on June 24, 1973, in Saskatoon, Saskatchewan, 87 years old.

Summary about C.K. and Katharina:

Kornelius K. Unruh (#341800) and Helena Unruh (#86297) were siblings, brother and sister. Their children were first cousins. Kornelius K's son, Cornelius K. Unruh (#341804) and Helena (Unruh) Loewen's daughter, Katharina Loewen (#341805), were first cousins. They knew each other and saw one another occasionally as children in Temir Bulat, Crimea. Katharina emigrated to the United States with her family. Cornelius had emigrated with his older sister Aganetha and her husband, but now he was alone and working in the United States. Cornelius's parents and some siblings remained in Crimea. It is reasonable to assume that he located where his Aunt Helena and her family lived in South Dakota. Aunt Helena would have wanted to make sure that he was taken care of. It was then that Cornelius and Katharina met as adults, fell in love, and they married. So, Helena's nephew Cornelius K. was now her son-in-law. As a boy and as a young man, C.K. could not have imagined such a scenario, that his Aunt Helena would become his mother-in-law. And Katharina's Uncle Kornelius, although he was still in the old country, South Russia, was now her father-in-law. What this meant for my own father, Edward Richard Unruh (484759) was that his grand-aunt Helena was also his grandmother. Aunt Helena was his mom's mother. I truthfully do not know whether my Dad knew this, but I also doubt that he did.

RELATIONSHIP Chart #2 clearly displays her descent from the same progenitor as C.K. In this chart, the line is traced to Edward Richard Unruh through his mother, Katharina (Unruh) Loewen.

1. ? Unrau, b. approx. 1633, (#106809) progenitor
2. ? Unrau, b. approx. 1663, (#106810) child
3. Heinrich Unrau, b. approx. b. 1693, (#106812), grandchild
4. Hinrich Unrau, b. approx. 1723, (#106814), great-grandchild
5. Martin Unrau, b. approx. 1753, (#165971), 2Great-grandchild
6. Benjamin Martin Unruh, (#165973), b. 1783, Brenkenhofswalde, Brandenburg, Prussia, 3G-grandchild
7. Kornelius B. Unruh, (#165980) b. 11 NOV 1820, Sofievvka, Volhynia, 4G-grandchild
8. Helena Unruh, (#86297), b. 5 MAR 1849, Waldheim,

Molotschna, South Russia, 5G-grandchild
9. Katharina Loewen, (#341805), b. 26 FEB 1874, Bruderfeld, Crimea, South Russia, 6G-grandchild
10. Edward Richard Unruh, (#484759), b. 8 MAR 1915, Hepburn, Saskatchewan, 7G-grandchild
11. *Ronald James Unruh, (#606630), b. 1942, Hepburn, Saskatchewan, 8G-grandchild
  * Murray Dennis Unruh, (#606629), b. 1947, St. Catharines, Ontario, 8G-grandchild
  * Neale Bryan Unruh, (#606628), b. 1953, St. Catharines, Ontario, 8G-grandchild

Grandma Katharina Loewen (#341805) and Grandpa Cornelius K. Unruh (#341804) were married in Hillsboro, Kansas, on 2 December, 1894. Katharina gave birth to seven children. The first two daughters died as children.
1. Hannie Unruh, (#647468) born 16 June 1895. She died at birth or soon after.
2. Susanna Unruh, (#647469) born 3 April 1897. She died at 10 months of age, 8 February 1898.
3. Anna Unruh, (#11342) born 16 March 1899, Parker, South Dakota. Annie, as she was known, was baptized on August 9, 1914, in Hepburn, Saskatchewan. On December 15, 1918, she married Gerhard (George) G. Friesen (#9988), in Hepburn, Saskatchewan. George was born 9 January 1892, in Henderson, Nebraska. Aunt Annie died 12 June, 1948. George died 22 September 1961, Dalmeny, Saskatchewan. They had no children. I knew Aunt Annie when I was a small boy, ages 1-5, before Mom, Dad and I moved to Ontario in 1947. Annie died during the next year.
4. Cornelius C. "Neale" Unruh, (#484763), was born on November 27, 1903, in Hepburn.
He was baptized on September 7, 1924. Neale married Aganetha (Agnes) Hiebert (#484760) who was born on September 24, 1906, at Rural Municipality of Rhineland, Manitoba. Their wedding took place on September 24, 1926, at Plum Coulee, Manitoba. One child was born to them, a daughter, whom they named Verna Catherine Unruh.
Verna Catherine Unruh, (#1073833). Married Joseph Carl

Closs (#1073834) on September 20, 1948. Carl was born January 31, 1928, in Renfrew, Ontario. Carl died January 23, 2007 at the age of 78 at Devon, Alberta. Verna and Carl had four children, two sons and two daughters, Ian, Randolph, Kathleen, and Corinne.

1 Ian George Closs (#1482303) born on August 13, 1949, in Chilliwack, BC, Canada. Ian married Eileen Florence Knox (daughter of Carlos John Knox and Evelyn May Pilbeam), on February 1, 1972 in Victoria, B.C. Eileen and Ian have two children, Christina, and Scott.

1 Christina Kathleen Jasmine Closs was born on July 19, 1973 in Victoria, B.C. Caroline married Ingrid Riedel on August 6, 2005 in Victoria, B.C. Christina and Ingrid have two sons. Rowen Thomas Closs-Reidel was born Feb 13, 2005 in Victoria. Jared Micah Closs-Riedel was born on Dec 16, 2007 in Victoria.

2 Scott Jason Patrick Closs was born on April 28, 1976 in Victoria. He and ? Unknown mother of the Cold Lake First Nations (Dene and Cree heritage), have one child, Neala Summer Lynn Janvier. Scott Jason Patrick Closs and Lynn Lidke, (who was born on Oct 17, 1981 in Surrey, B.C.) had a child, Hayley-Jane Carla Closs, born on January 25, 2009 in Surrey, B.C.

2 Randolph (Randy) Kevin Closs, born Sept 29, 1953 in Chilliwack, B.C.

3 Kathleen Agnes Mary Closs was born Oct 23, 1961 in Whitehorse, Yukon. She married Martin Walroth. They have one son. Kyle Martin Walroth born on Sept 9, 1998 in Calgary, Alberta.

4 Corinne Gayle Closs was born on October 27, 1970, in Grande Cache, Alberta. Another source says Wainright, Alberta. She married to Jon Silworsky. They have three children.

1. Nathan Nicholas Joseph Silworsky born Aug 10, 2004.
2. Makenna Catherine Agnes Silworsky born Nov 10, 2006.
3. Jon Walter Silworsky, born July 5, 1973 in Dauphin, Manitoba.

Verna is the daughter of my Uncle Neale. Verna is my first

cousin, my Uncle Neale's, and Aunt Agnes' only child. I was thrilled when, in 2021 a young lady named Christina contacted me inquiring information about the Unruhs because of her grandma (Verna Unruh) Closs. Her mother is Corrine, the daughter of Verna. Verna is 98 yrs old now (2023).

In 2022, I had a phone conversation with 96 yr old Verna who lived on her own, was very alert and savvy. It was interesting for me to think that she lived with Neale and Agnes until her own marriage, and in all the years with her parents she only knew her dad as a day job salesman and a nighttime musician with his own dance band, and as a smoker and a drinker. She had a couple of photos that showed him being baptized and enrolled in Bible School. Yet she knew nothing about that part of his life. She started all of this off with a question to me. "Are you religious or is your family religious." I was able to send her and her family, Neale's testimony of his faith and his later life. That truly completes his life story.

Neale and Agnes Unruh, wedding day & 40th Annivertsary

I met all four of my father's siblings. I knew Aunt Annie when I was a small boy, ages 1-5, before Mom, Dad and I moved to Ontario in 1947. Annie died during the next year. I have a faint recollection of Uncle Harry, but he is not someone that I recall without the aid of photographs. I regret that because I have learned what a gentle and good man he was. I met Uncle Neale twice when I was a boy. He and Aunt Agnes lived in British Columbia. I can recall that each Christmas for many years, Uncle Neale sent small gifts to Murray, Neale, and me. In June 1967 the three of us met him. Uncle Neale and Aunt Agnes drove across Canada from British Columbia to visit us at our Bunting Rd. home in St. Catharines. Neale was thirteen, Murray was nineteen, and I was about twenty-four years old. We were impressed with the enormous white Buick that he drove. The word we used to describe its luxury was 'swanky.'

***

Growing up in a prairie town and area populated by Mennonites does not ensure that all children find church appealing or that they will be people of faith. Neale and my dad Edward, eleven years apart in age, were both men whose commitment to Christ was postponed for some years. I have already told you my father's story, that when Murray and I were young, Dad attended Calvary Church with us. The truths of the Bible with which he was not unfamiliar became clear to him. At age 36 he placed his faith exclusively in Jesus Christ. He had always been a good man. Now he was a man with a convinced relationship with God. Here is my Uncle Neale's personal story, written by him. I have left is just as he wrote it.

My Uncle Neale's Testimony
"We do not stand in the world bearing witness to Christ but stand in Christ and bear witness to the world."

If someone had told me a few years ago that I would stand behind a holy pulpit and give a testimony of having accepted the Lord Jesus Christ as my own personal saviour, I would have laughed in their face. Yet here I am, and it is by the grace of God, and I thank him for that.

It is always a joy and pleasure to hear others give a testimony, specially when they can say, 'I was brought up in a christian home.' I can also say that I had a very good Christian father and mother.

Dad would read the Bible in the morning and thank God for the blessings and for food and would ask for guidance and direction for the coming day. In the evening we would all gather before bedtime. I had a sister and two brothers, and we would read the Word of God and Dad would often explain it to us. Then we would kneel down and each one of us would pray. I thank God for those early boyhood days. What I leaned hen has never left my memory and in later years they have served me well in finding my way back to the fold after living in a backslidden condition for over thirty years.

I was born and raised on a farm near a small town of Hepburn in Saskatchewan, thirty miles north of the city of Saskatoon. As a small boy I was not too worried about going to heaven, but I had a terrible fear of death and of going to hell. I was around ten years of age when one evening my sister Annie, who was a little older than me, and I were sitting together reading the newspaper. Mother was washing dishes in the far corner of the kitchen. Suddenly I heard a rumbling sound. It must have been in my imagination, but it seemed to get louder. I looked around but couldn't determine from where the sound was coming. Immediately I thought it must either be the Lord Jesus coming back again or the world was coming to an end. I got panicky and demanded that all of us get down on our knees and pray, thinking, hoping that in doing this, the Lord would hear me and still take me with him. Dad didn't understand my strange concern but said, "well, it is near the time for evening devotions so can't this wait until then?" I insisted that we kneel and pray right then, Mother sensing something profound had triggered this said, "Well, I guess we can pray now."

So, we knelt and prayed. During the prayer I noticed that the rumbling sound had stopped, and I was happy. After prayer we tried to resume our reading and I noticed the noise beginning again, but this time I was more discerning about the source of the sound. I noticed the Mother had a round-bottomed saucepan on top of the stove and as it heated, it was making all that noise. I went to my room upstairs, very annoyed with my stupidity.

The years that followed were not very exciting but did largely overcame my earlier fears, and at the age of 14 I thought I was pretty well grown up. I had started to smoke, which made me feel like a real BIG SHOT. My cousin was my age and had the same likes and dislikes as I did, and we were inseparable.

The following years were exciting. I learned how to dance, how to drink liqueur and where in my earlier years I had played violin in church at young peoples' meetings, I now turned my musical talents playing dance music. During this period, I became quite independent, although dad had always been very strict about going out at nights and staying out late. This did not worry me any longer. I knew that dad needed me to help on the farm and I had made it clear to him that I knew this, and consequently I took advantage of it.

My cousin and I would go to church now and then, not especially to listen to God but it made a nice meeting place and at the same time we had the opportunity to look over the crop of girls that was coming up. At the age of 19 I was attracted to a girl, and we saw each other as much as we could. Her name was Agnes.

In the early part of the summer of 1924 a good-looking well-built young man came into our community. That community was in real need of revival although I could not see it at the time. This preacher was in town for at least two weeks possibly three weeks. My cousin and I went to church pretty much every night, but it did not affect us too much, and if it had we likely would not have gone near the place. That I believe is how a sinner behaves when he is under conviction and does not know it.

At the meetings there were dozens of people who met the Lord for the first time by accepting Jesus as their Saviour. There were children aged 10,11 or12 years of age, and teenagers, and many young adults in their early 20s, and some older people. Looking back, I can see that it must've been a great time of blessing for parents of children and for older saints, giving them feelings of satisfaction and thanksgiving. The Holy Spirit was working everywhere.

One day I was told that my girlfriend Agnes had given her heart to the Lord. This had not been in my plans, and I thought it would soon pass. I thought she had done this because her friends did. Soon things would get back to normal I thought. I would have a talk with her and make her see things my way and we would carry on. However, our face-to-face meeting came sooner than I anticipated. One day I came to town for some machinery parts. I had the parts, and I was in a hurry. I got on my horse and headed home. As I came around a corner to the Main Rd., there she was. Agnes looked so happy with a wonderful smile. You can imagine that this took me by surprise, and I had no time to think what I wanted to say to her. It was awkward for both of us. I decided to let her start the conversation.

She didn't hesitate and said, "Neale, I suppose you have heard that I have found and accepted the Lord."

"Yes, I have heard," I said and before I could say anything else she continued.

"Neale, you know you have to do it sometime and why not now? Why not try it? It's wonderful and I would so much like you to come with me."

I had nothing more to say and believe me, my plans had gone very sour suddenly and I was on my way home. The trip home took much longer than usual. I found I was not in a hurry. I wanted to think. From that moment, I was under conviction, and it seemed as if the Holy Spirit was only working on me and no one else. I didn't realize it at the time, but I was told later that I was very quiet at the supper table. I was sure mom and dad knew what was going on, but they didn't say anything.

Mom and Dad went to church that night. I didn't want to go but after they left, it seemed as if I could not resist so I went to church too. The Bible text that night was the last three verses of Matthew 11. Verse 28 *"Come unto me all ye that labour and are heavy laden and I will give you rest. 29. Take my yoke upon you and learn of me: for I am meek and lowly in heart and you shall find rest unto your souls. 30. For my yoke is easy, and my burden is ligh*t."

I won't forget the sermon or the entire night. As usual the evangelist kept two rows of seats on both sides near the platform for the people who would come to the front to receive counselling and prayer. I was sitting in the balcony where all the tough guys usually sat. I was feeling sorry for the way that I was living, and I knew I had a choice to make. What was it going to be? The meeting ended and everyone was leaving. My cousin nudged me and said, "let's get out of here." I shook my head "no' and stayed seated. When my cousin saw my struggle, he left me. Moments later there were two fellows beside me, putting their arms around me and speaking to me. That was the first time in many years that I had prayed.

When I got home that night my parents were still awake, but I did not want to speak to them or have them talk to me. I went straight through the kitchen and up the stairs to my room. I could hear my parents talking well into the night and I was sure that they were praying for me. I did not sleep well that night.

The next day seemed to be a very long day. I couldn't concentrate on work. I had no appetite. I spent a lot of time in my room thinking and praying. One at a time I asked my Mom and Dad into my room. I knew that I had hurt them many times before. I asked for their forgiveness. Naturally they were only too glad to forgive me and to pray with me and for me. That night, as on other nights, I went to church again. In fact, I felt like nothing could hold me back but before I arrived at church, I went to make one call. I called on the owner of the confectionary store and I told him I came to ask his forgiveness and to pay him the thirty-five cents for chocolate bars I had stolen from his store. Bars were five cents in those days and although it doesn't seem like a lot, I believe it was the Lord testing me as to whether I would submit to His will. This owner told me that he was very glad I had made my spiritual decision, and he was sure the Lord was in this and would take care of me.

Now I was four blocks from the church, and suddenly it seemed that everything got brighter as if the entire sky was lit up. A voice inside me said, *"You have begged the Lord to forgive you. He does not want you to beg. Your sins are forgiven."* It was an awakening and I had peace inside me, and almost uncontrollable happiness. I will never forget that experience. Dad told us afterwards that when he saw me walking into church, he imagined the whole building got brighter.

In August of that year a baptism took place in the North Saskatchewan River when 63 people were baptized and I was one of them. Shortly after that I felt that God was calling me to serve him in some way. I had an uncle who was involved in missionary work in India. I thought there could be no better place for me that to work in foreign missions. I also knew that I lacked biblical knowledge, so I needed to prepare. I decided to go to Bible School in Herbert, Saskatchewan. Money was scarce but my mother and sister and many others made contributions and I left for school with enough money for tuition, room and board, books, and a one-way train fare. It was the first time I had ever left home.

I was a bit lonesome at first, but it did not take long before I fitted in. Naturally music helped me and soon I was organizing programs. There were strict school rules, the strictest of which was that a young man and a young woman must never be seen together by themselves inside any buildings or anywhere on the property. Believe me, I was on the carpet more than anyone else for breaking this rule, but I was skilled at making apologies and begging for mercy. It turned out to be a memorable winter. I was happy. It seemed that this education was what my heart yearned for.

Then it was spring and time for graduation but that also meant saying goodbye to friends and that was difficult. Nevertheless, I was looking forward to seeing family and friends back home. That turned out to be a great reunion. The young woman that I left behind was still waiting for me and we just picked up where we had left off.

It was a busy time of the farm as spring times usually are. I was very involved in farm work. I was very involved in church activity. I was asked to join the church choir. Everything seemed to be going well. Then sometime in the middle of the summer I began to feel that I no longer had a close relationship with God and yet I didn't think I was doing anything differently. It seemed to me that God was drawing away from me and this bothered me a lot. The feeling didn't change even if I prayed a lot. We had family devotions, and I had my own time as well. I attended church regularly. The fire I felt inside before disappeared, and soon I was living the kind of life I lived before. I resumed smoking and cursing, and I didn't care. I avoided Christian friends and that included my girlfriend. Yet she was determined to prevent me from throwing away everything that was good. I know now it wasn't God withdrawing from me, but me distancing myself from Him.

One evening one of Agnes' friends brought her to our family farm to speak to me. She pleaded and cried, asking me to turn back while it was still not too late. That didn't have an effect on me. My answer to Agnes was this. "This religion deal was not meant for me and if you do not like the way that I want to go, then we must part or dissolve our partnership." However, Agnes said she did not want to so, but that she would stick by me no matter what.

In March of 1926 Agnes and I were married. We lived on a

farm and our plans were to make big money and do big things. But life did not go according to our plans at least not fast enough for me. So, in the fall of 1929 we sold out and moved to B.C. We didn't know where to go but we had heard of Chilliwack and that is where we landed. It was the Great Depression and we settled in an unknown land, and we knew no one. I have both beautiful and sad memories of those years. This is the reason. Before long it became known that I could play dance music and soon I was playing as often as I could. Other work was scarce, and I had to do whatever I could to keep us going. I sometimes earned only seventy-five cents for four to five hours of playing music. However, as time went on, I did get steady work but kept on playing for dances. It was extra spending money. My bookings increased and I was finding it hard to do a day job and play at night as well. I needed a stimulant to get me through the day and to cheer me up and that was alcohol. That was only the beginning.

In 1937 I organized my own band, and I played violin, saxophone, and clarinet. Two years later in 1939 WWII broke out and when I was not accepted into the Armed Forces, I turned all my energy into entertainment. I played as many as five nights per week even while I worked during the day, and this was hard on me. When we couldn't get competent help at the day job, we had to do more ourselves and for more hours. Without noticing I began to drink more and more at all times. Even when I thought about it, I didn't care.

When the war ended and life settled down, everything slowed down including the demand for entertainment music. What didn't slow down was my drinking. And it didn't bother me because I thought I was in control. I thought that one day when I chose to do it, I would stop drinking completely. I seriously thought this was possible. But that day was far off. The effects of my drinking were felt in our home. It was like a cold dark cloud settling inside our home. The love and affection we enjoyed once was no longer there.

Only very slowly did it occur to me that I might have a drinking problem. Others with whom I associated had known this for a while and even talked to me about it. I discounted it, thinking I could stop drinking any time I chose. I even set dates when I intended to quit, dates I ignored. I kept making excuses, and I would work late, or play at dances or have a meeting and always arrive at home late at night and I was drinking. And each morning I would resume work with a headache and a hangover.

Then in early 1949 I talked it over with Agnes and I quit my job, and we rented our Chilliwack house to some people, and we moved to Prince George where a very good job was waiting for me. I also saw this as my opportunity to break away from my old habits and to make a new start. Agnes was hoping for the same thing, getting me away from old friends and environments. Perhaps there was a chance we could be happy again.

"How wrong I was. How wrong we both were. I was trying to run away from something that followed me. Typically, in the open social atmosphere of Prince George, when people wanted to get acquainted with me, they sized me up and then they offered me a drink. That suited me perfectly. I welcomed their warm greetings. I would take a drink and soon after that I felt no shame about having done so. I was back in the same habit.

In spring of 1952 my nervous system was so disturbed that if I didn't have a drink before going to work, I would begin to shake so badly that I could not think or write notes. Of course, I didn't associate it with drinking. I thought it was a health problem, so I went to Vancouver to a medical clinic to be checked out. After four days of tests, I was told in no uncertain terms that I should not touch alcohol again. Well, that didn't go over well with me, Mr. Big Shot. I knew I was a heavy drinker, but I also thought that I could handle more alcohol than other people. So, I didn't admit to myself that I had a problem.

I don't like talking about the following two years because of the heartache I caused. Agnes was working fulltime, and all my salary was spent on my drinking. At times I booked off work for three or four days to sober up and get over my sickness. I ate almost nothing, and drink became my food. I began not to care what might happen to me. Dear Agnes nursed me back to health over and over, time after time. I would make more excuses to my boss as to why I was not at work. My wife would check me in the morning before I went to work, how I looked and whether I was dressed appropriately. There were times when the pain, both physical and mental, the remorse, the shame and disgrace were enormous for me.

My mind got to the point where I was just unable to cope. I was tired. My nerves were torn to shreds. I couldn't sleep and when I would finally doze off, I would go into D.Ts (delirious tremors). I would awake with shock, and it seemed my heart would almost stop. I won't tell you about the visions that I had. Terrible. So, I would try to sleep again. Week after week this went on. Unless you have gone through this, you cannot understand this experience. I began to realize that the ones that I had been hurting for years were still with me pulling for me. They were doing everything that was possible to make me comfortable, to give me help.

Then came the time that I attended A.A. (Alcoholics Anonymous). At the first meeting I was too tired and too frustrated to benefit. I attended another meeting the following week. At this meeting I learned that I must revisit in my mind and heart where I was years earlier. In fact, I could not get away from God and I couldn't escape my need for his help. At the beginning of every meeting something was read, and I will quote it. *"Remember that we deal with alcohol. It's cunning. It's baffling and powerful. Without help it is too much for you. But there is one who has all power and that one is God. May you find him now."*

"I found myself back where I had left off thirty years earlier.
I began attending church again. My wife has never been a drinker. Agnes detested any kind of alcoholic drink. She never smoked. That being said, she was not that struck on the idea of me going to church, specially regularly, like every Sunday. But I knew that I couldn't survive without other Christians, and I kept going. I also prayed that she would soon come with me.

One wonderful Sunday morning she was getting herself ready and when I asked whether she was coming with me to church, she said, "Yes." For a while she came in the mornings but soon, she also came in the evenings with me. It has now been a few years since this started. Even the remorse of her own backslidden years has been removed from her conscience. Today she and I know that the LORD lives in our home, night, and day. Oh, how we thank God for this.

If I can be of any help to anyone who has a similar problem, don't be afraid to contact me. It's easier to come back to Christ when you are young. You don't have so much that you have to straighten out as I did with all my years of sin."

What a potent word from a changed man. I became the president of the Evangelical Free Churches of Canada in 2002. It was a surprise and a blessing to meet Pastor Tim Seim of Abbotsford Evangelical Free Church. He told me my Uncle Neale's story. That's the church where Uncle Neale became a Christian, at least where he finally said, "Lord, I'm yours." Uncle Neale and Aunt Agnes became members of the church. In time he became a song leader at church because he could keep a rhythm 'in time'. Of course, as only Tim can tell a story, Neale had only a handful of songs that he liked to lead so Tim was never able to request a song specific to his message if Neale was doing the leading. My Uncle Neale was once lost, but then in mercy, he was found.

***

HARRY was the middle son of C.K and Katharina.

Harry Charles Unruh, (#484762), was born on June 16, 1908, in Hague, Saskatchewan.

On October 7, 1936, Harry married Ann Peters (#484758) in the MB Church in Hepburn. She was born on January 13, 1910. Harry and Anne had no children. Harry was a dedicated Christian, whose reputation was defined by the life of Christ within him. Uncle Harry operated the Hardware Store in Hepburn and the RCMP commissioned Harry to be the Judge for small town crime and misdemeanours. Harry died December 7, 1948 at the age of 40. Harry died just 18 months after Dad and Mom had moved from Hepburn to Ontario. My dad was heartbroken at the news of Harry's death. He travelled alone by train from St. Catharines to attend Harry's funeral. Harry's death was a terrible blow to Ann that affected her for a long time. She eventually remarried and lived in Chilliwack, B.C. I have a faint recollection of Uncle Harry, aided by photographs. I have learned that he was a gentle and good man person. Mom and Dad told me about him. His greatest impact on me was through my father's story of Harry's last days in a Saskatoon hospital before he died. He shared his personal story of faith in Christ and his hope of heaven with anyone who was willing to listen. That thought stayed with me all through my childhood and youth. I can only imagine my father's and mother's sorrow when Dad's sister Annie died 6 months later on June 12, 1948. And June 12, is my parents' wedding anniversary.

C.K. Unruh's and Katharina Loewen's 3rd son was my Dad.

EDWARD Richard Unruh, (#484759). Dad was born on the 8th of March 1915, in Hepburn, Saskatchewan. He married Tena Martha Doerksen (#484757), who was born on June 4, 1919, in Wolf Point, Montana. Their wedding took place in Saskatoon, on June 12, 1941. Mom and Dad had us ... 3 sons. I am sure Mom wished at times for a daughter.

1. **Ronald James Unruh, (#606630),** b. 1942, Hepburn, Saskatchewan. Ron married Christine Frances Langlois (#1305027), on August 12, 1967 in Calvary Church, St. Catharines. Christine was born July 23, 1943 in Droxford, UK; emigrated to Canada 1957. Ron and Christine have two children.
   1. Carinne May (Unruh) Locken (#1493049), born Jan 14, 1969. Cari Married Timothy Grant Locken (#1119248), May 16, 1998, in Surrey, BC, Tim was born July 30, 1966, Germany.
      1. Kailyn May Locken (#1119252), born Sept 5, 2000, Edmonton, Alberta.
      2. Ryan Timothy Locken (#1119253), born June 26, 2002, Edmonton, Alberta
      3. Jayden James Locken (#1119254), born Nov 17, 2004, Edmonton, Alberta
   2. Ronald Jeffrey (Jeff) Unruh (#1493050), born February 21, 1970, Smiths Falls, Ontario. On July 18, 1999 in Surrey, B.C. Jeff married Gina Marie Mikkelson, born May 4, 1974 in Norway.
      1. Kale Mikkel James Unruh, born December 11, 2004, Surrey, BC
      2. Kadence (Kady) Marie Mae Unruh, born March 8, 2007, Surrey, BC

2. **Murray Dennis Unruh, (#606629),** born September 7, 1947, in

St. Catharines, Ontario. Murray married Gloria <u>Diane</u> Dibbley (#1305026) on May 30, 1970 in Wheatley, Ontario. Diane was born January 8, 1950, at Coatsworth, Ontario.

1. Elizabeth (Beth) Joy Unruh Woelk (#962509), born June 26, 1973 in Burlington, Ontario. On August 10, 1996 in St. Catharines, she married Eric Daniel Woelk, born May 4, 1969 in St. Catharines, Ontario.
   1. Selah Joy Unruh Woelk born July 24, 2002, in Grimsby, Ont.
   2. Karis Grace Unruh Woelk, born Sept 7, 2006 in Grimsby, Ont.
2. Matthew (Matt) (#1495729) born June 11, 1976 in St. Catharines Ont.; On May 12, 2001 in Vauxhall, AB, Matthew married Cristina Margaret Olfert, born Sept 7, 1978 in Tabor, Alberta.
   1. Aaralyn Hope Unruh, born January 26, 2006 in White Rock, B.C.
   2. Ellarie Claire Unruh, born April 19, 2008, in White Rock, B.C.
   3. Silas Murray Thomas Unruh, born July 14, 2010 in White Rock, B.C.
   4. Mia Carabelle Unruh, born February 20, 2013 in Grimsby, ON.
3. Andrew (Drew) (#1353967) born April 22, 1980, Swift Current, SK; Married Emily Susanne Thiessen born June 28, 1985 in St. Catharines; married Sept 15, 2017 at Stonewall Estates, Lincoln, ON.
   1. Genevieve (GG) Grey, born March 2, 2020.

3. **Neale Bryan Unruh, (#606628),** born October 12. 1953, St. Catharines, Ontario, married Kathy Smale, born on August 3, 1957 in Ingersoll, Ont. Married Sept 4, 1982 Richview Baptist Church Toronto Ontario.
   1. Amy Lyn Hollywood (nee Unruh) born November 14, 1984 in Hamilton Ont. She married Christopher Mark Hollywood, born June 13, 1978; married August 18, 2007.

The Legacy of Mom and Dad

Edward Richard Unruh earned a laborer's wage. Dad worked for over 40 years at Anthes Imperial that produced furnaces. For most of those years until he was 65, he was on an assembly line, up and down, screwing in metal parts. His work ethic was a commendable model for his three boys. He purchased a family home before he turned forty years of age. He took his family to a rented cottage for summer vacations. He took us for Sunday afternoon car rides. He sang with us. He yodeled. He loved our Mother. He was proud of his sons. When we married, his love for our brides gave them a strong sense of comfort in an extended family. He trusted in God, and he supported all three of us as we took on Christian service vocations. Dad was not a theologian, but he tried to understand scripture and he sought to live by its principles. Dad never took a leadership position at church. If he was asked to be on committees or boards, he declined. He knew his strengths and limitations. He enjoyed serving but the service had to be in the areas of his competence and comfort. Smart man. Private man. Honorable man.

My father died on March 1, 2008. He has been gone such a long time now. I have a thoughtful impression. I am the eldest of our sibling trio. I knew Dad when he was a younger man. I was his only child for the first five years. I knew him when my mother was young and dark-haired and slim. As time moved forward my experience of Dad included the way he related to each of my brothers in their infancy and boyhood and adolescence. I knew Dad when his 5-foot six-inch frame was strong. I knew him always as a good man, a gentle man, a gentleman.

My brothers Murray, five years junior to me, and Neale, eleven years younger than me, experienced Dad through the years when I was no longer around. I was the first son to leave home for college, and then I married and finally I was working in other cities. When both Murray and I were away from home, Neale had some years alone with Mom and Dad before he himself was married. In the last years, Murray and Diane, lived near Dad and Mom, and became exemplary caregivers to our aging senior parents. In the last years, Murray almost daily went for a chat and a coffee with my father, and I lived four provinces away. Diane assisted my mother when her care was beyond Dad's understanding. Words fail to express the admiration I have for Murray and Diane. They both served my father and mother and served us all in their loving care of my folks.

My father set a good example for me and my brothers. Like him, we have sought to be a conscientious workers, decent dads and loving and loyal husbands. I hope I am remembered as good man. I wish I could have lived perfectly in all respects for the sakes of others. Both Dad and I put our faith exclusively in Jesus Christ. I am not my father, yet occasionally my own walk, or gestures, my habits, and my whistle, evoke memories of my father.

Dad had a dry sense of humour and here is an anecdote. While she still lived with Dad before being moved to a full care facility, Mom exhibited symptoms of dementia. She was in the habit of packing belongings in boxes. Anything and everything could be packed or unpacked depending on the moment. Murray arrived one day, and Dad asked him whether he would like a coffee and bite to eat. Murray nodded yes, and Dad plugged in the kettle. It would be instant coffee. Murray went to the cutlery drawer for two spoons and two forks. The cutlery was gone. He asked Dad what was going on. Dad nonchalantly replied, "Oh, Tina must have packed them." Then he humorously added, "It really doesn't matter, she packed my teeth too."

For a couple of years Dad lived alone in his apartment, after Mom was in full care. Dad displayed that he was independent, courageous, patient, easy-going, tender-spirited, uncomplaining, and content. Then Mom died in November 2007. It was to be expected. Dad finally grew weary of loneliness. At the age of 93, Dad's heart and mind cooperated to let him leave on May 1, 2008. He had lived for six months without Mom (Tina).

This next story reveals the wonder of this marvellous man.

One year earlier, when Dad was 92, he was over the moon because he was going to a Christmas Dinner with his favourite girl. Mom had been in long-term care for one year while dad lived alone in an adjoining apartment facility. It was December and a Christmas Dinner Party was planned for residents. Dad had asked my brother Murray, "do you think it would be okay if I took Mom to the dinner?" Murray replied, "I don't see why not." Mom's meds were balanced, and she was feeling better than she had in a long time. Murray made the arrangements. The caring staff promised to have Mom's hair done and a lovely dress ready to wear. Mom could be seated in a wheel chair and if she grew weary during the evening, he could leave with her. Murray had Dad's suit dry cleaned, and Dad had a favourite tie to wear. Murray sensed Dad's excitement as the date grew nearer. Murray said he would accompany Dad to Mom's room to insure all was well. Dad was noticeably pumped about this evening. His face and his mood told Murray that Dad was going on a date, a special evening with his sweetheart. They took the elevator to the first floor and as they walked down the lengthy corridors, an enthusiastic Dad surprised Murray by breaking into song. The tune was unfamiliar to Murray as Dad sang heartily the words to 'Darktown Strutter's Ball,' a landmark 1917 recording by the Original Dixieland Jazz Band.

I'll be down to get you in a taxi, honey.
Pick you up 'bout half past eight
Oh, honey don't be late
I want to be there when the band starts playin'

Remember when we get there, honey
Two step, we're gonna have a ball
I'm gonna dance out of my shoes
When they play the Jelly Roll Blues
Tomorrow night at the Darktown Strutter's Ball

There were two more verses. Dad sang them all. Upon finishing it by the end of the corridor to Murray's utter shock, Dad jumped off the ground and clicked his heels together.

***

Mom celebrated 88 birthdays. Family was everything to her. We have missed her since 2007. The blurring of our memories occurs despite our desire to remember. Some of what I write here will be repetitious. It's okay with me.

What an interesting woman Mom was. Born to a homesteading couple in Montana, she lost her dad when she was two. She became part of a large, blended family headed by her mom and a stepfather. Her childhood and youth were spent in Waldheim and Hepburn. Opportunities did not abound on the prairies in the twenties and thirties, especially for a girl. Mom completed grade 9, and then felt compelled to find employment. She was industrious from the start, knowing how to sew, how to bake and to cook. She worked at service jobs for others. She married and then WWII came. The post war years in Hepburn began with mom and dad teaming to start and to run a Coffee Shop with a reputation for great pies. Finally, Mom and Dad moved to Ontario. Mom was busy with children and work-at-home projects, sewing for others. She was hired to sew costumes for the St. Catharines skating club. She cleaned other people's homes. She worked in Ruth Miller's restaurant as a waitress. She worked in her church, Calvary Church, always in the kitchen. It was what she knew best to do, and what she became known for. For several summers, she was head chef at Fair Havens Bible Conference grounds, serving hundreds of people three meals per day. In fact, over time, she operated her own Catering Business. Wealthy people hired Tina Unruh, and she prepared grand dinners for large gatherings. Her happiest employment was as Day-time Food Services provider for Ontario Paper head office. Having her designated parking spot was a big deal. She even prepared a cook book and sold 1,000 copies. In all these pursuits she was encouraged and assisted by the gentle man whom she had loved when she was a stunning young woman of 22. Sometimes it seemed that Ed had no greater ambition than to Tina succeed.

Mom's ultimate personal fulfillment was found as she worked with the local church women's group. She took on a leadership role and became recognized as a woman of integrity and of spirituality. She was elected eventually to the presidency of the entire southern Ontario region. Those responsibilities required her to read and to study the Bible and other books and she grew spiritually and intellectually. She had to lead meetings, give spiritual talks and presentations, and while humbled and sometimes terrified, she amazed herself that she could do this and that her leadership was valued.

In our parents' home throughout our childhoods, we had so many opportunities to meet people, listen to stories, and comprehend God's good news. Mom and Dad didn't go to workshops to learn how to parent. They knew nothing about intentional spiritual parenting. They didn't teach us the Bible. In their view, that's what the church did. Sunday School and Boys' Brigade and Youth Program were never activities we felt forced to attend. They were simply normal. We admired guys and girls a few years older for whom faith was vital. We chose to be involved rather than feeling constrained.

Mom's and Dad's constancy and authenticity most certainly affected their three sons. Each of us became involved in Christian service. Mom and Dad were satisfied that there was a happy and contented life. They were married for 66 years.

Grandchildren Have Memories of Ed and Tina.
Amy Unruh Hollywood wrote, "I remember glasses of cold coffee on the counters. I remember the smell of grandma baking bread. I remember Tic Tacs in grandma's purse and Sen-Sen in grandpa's pocket. I remember grandma's endless collection of Canadian Living magazines stacked in the magazine rack. The stack of books they kept just for me on the bookshelf at the end of the hallway (the scratch and sniff one was the best).

"I remember grandma's Avon products in the bathroom and how she smelled. Grandpa's whistling everywhere he went. I remember their pride at every grandchild's wedding and the joy at watching their family continue to grow.

"I remember Ed's quiet and gentle strength and how he was never afraid to let Tina shine. How much Tina did shine and how beloved she was by everyone. I remember their faithful service to God and the church and their joy that their example filtered down into future generations. I remember how well they loved all of us, in big and small ways."

Cari Unruh Locken wrote, "I remember being at FairHavens and visiting Grandma in the kitchen. She was always busy working and I thought it was amazing how she could make food for hundreds of people.

"I remember Grandpa always whistling a happy little tune. I remember Grandma & Grandpa looked classy and put together. I remember Grandpa's selection of pastel-coloured pants - a man not scared to wear pink! Grandma always looked so beautiful in her crocheted outfits and her hair!!... I loved her hair and when I was little, I dreamt that my hair would one day be white like hers.

"I remember Grandpa coming up behind me, putting his hands on my shoulders and gently rubbing my shoulders. A tender touch of affection meant so much to me. I remember how they loved their children and were so very proud of them, as well as their grandchildren.

"I remember how Grandma made SO much food for our family gatherings (including way too many jello salads!) I remember her amazing popcorn balls at Christmas and how we'd eat way too many of them. I remember, while on a camping trip, Grandma showing me how to make whipping cream without any electric device to whip. I thought she was a genius! I remember how happy they were and how much they loved each other."

Beth Unruh Woelk wrote, "I remember the paska bread Grandma mailed from Ontario to Saskatchewan for Easter. I remember Grandma's pickled peas. I remember Grandpa's roses.

"I remember gathering around the pool table for holiday feasts in the basement of Bunting road.

"I remember the awe and love in their eyes when they held their great-grandchildren."

Matt Unruh wrote, "I remember how Grandma's beautiful eyes squished when she smiled. I remember Grandma holding her grandkids faces for an uncomfortably long time as we said our goodbyes, soaking in our facial features. I didn't mind. It was love. It's hard not to associate memories of Grandma without the rich smells and tastes of feasting during the holiday seasons — what an amazing cook — I loved it all (except the pickled beets), but it was really special when she would make traditional Mennonite food like Wareniki.

"I remember Grandpa tickling and massaging my back for so long after a big meal and everyone was sitting chatting and laughing together. I remember Grandpa as a quiet but lovingly supportive man—he didn't need to say much to communicate his love. I remember being fascinated by the large tank shell(?) that would act as a door stop. I was enthralled by stories of Grandpa, a Mennonite by heritage, serving on his own volition in WWII. I remember Grandpa's pants worn well above his belly button. It made it look like he had long legs and short body. I remember Grandpa had a lead foot. He didn't drive like an old man.

"I remember the smell of Lavender in the bathroom and the feel of their bathroom carpet and padded toilet seat. I remember Grandpa liked to keep cactuses—that influenced me as a kid—I wanted a cactus too. I remember Grandma loved to keep beautiful China and take those out for teatime. It was always felt special."

14 A. A. WILLEMS

My Preamble

ABRAHAM A. WILLEMS IS THE PRIMARY SUBJECT OF THIS CHAPTER. A.A. is the appellation by which he was known to friends. A.A. is the biological grandfather of many of my cousins whose mom or dad were the progeny of Abraham and Marie. Those cousins are Deanna (Low) Morrow #1229862; Douglas Wayne Low #1229864; Kathryn McIlveen, #1501726; Kirsten McIlveen, #1501727; Anthony McIlveen; Dean Willems, #1164026; Pete Willems, #1164030; Andrea Klaring, #701377.

However, A.A. had no biological connection to these cousins: Jane Elaine (Doerksen) Jones #606633; and her brother Rodney Elroy Doerksen (deceased) #663454; or to my brothers Neale and Murray or to me, Ronald James Unruh. To the five of us, A.A. was our step-grandfather.

The explanation is simple. Jane's father Peter Doerksen and our mother Tina Doerksen were siblings. They were the children of Marie Fast and Isaac Doerksen. Isaac Doerksen was our biological grandfather. He died in 1920 when he was 29 years old. For Jane, Rodney, Murray, Neale and me, Isaac was the grandpa we never knew.

When Grandma Marie remarried it was to A. A. Willems. He had six children born by his first wife. Marie gave birth to five more children, Leslie, Gladys, Ruth, Esther and Rubina (Ruby). The offspring of those eleven children, and of Isaac's two children are cousins who called A.A. Willems, 'Grandpa.'

As grandchildren, some of us had the opportunity to spend personal kid time with Grandpa Willems. Doug Low says,

"Grandpa loved the Welland canal and would ask the sailors to toss him coins from the ships. I have a small handful of foreign coins that grandpa collected from passing vessels."

I recall Grandpa playing checkers with me. He always won. This frustrated me because I thought I knew how to play very well. Then came the day that I caught him cheating, a simple move of a checker to a place of advantage. He was an intimidating old dude. With fear I called him on it. He looked at me and broke out in silent smile. It was obvious to me then that his pleasure had been in fooling me. He didn't mind me catching on to him. That was a pleasure too.

Kathryn tells this story. "Grandma Willems came and stayed in our guest room in Oakville, Ontario. I would have been 5 years of age. I looked into the guest room and there was a glass of water at her bedside with something in it. As I got closer, I saw her teeth in the glass! I'd never seen that before & I had to ask my Mom about that strange sight."

Deanna Low Morrow shares three charming little girl memories.

"I hated Sundays growing up. The whole morning was spent at church, then home for lunch and a nap, then most Sundays Grandma came over for waffles which I hated (and now love because Art makes the most amazing waffles). I think we always had waffles because it was easy for my mom to make and easy for Grandma to eat. This seems uncharitable to my adult self, and I'd give anything to have Grandma over for waffles now!"

"I have a memory of Grandma babysitting me in their apartment and making fried chicken. I can still remember the ancient fork with a bone handle that she used. I actually looked for years at antique shops until I found a similar fork. That chicken was delicious by the way."

"When Grandma went to Tabor Manor initially, I visited her there sometimes. She would give me simple hand sewing projects to do. I was and still am not into handcrafts, so I did not enjoy it. I don't ever remember talking to her, as in just chatting. I can't recall her voice or any interaction we had. The good news is that a cart would come around in the afternoon with coffee and cookies and Grandma always let me take pfeffernuesse cookies – that was something special and a treat for me!"

***

I am grateful to my Uncle Les Willems and his sisters, my Aunt Ruth Willems Low, and Aunt Esther Willems McIlveen, for taking time with me through recent years to share with me their recollections and their written notes. Les passionately gathered genealogical data about his 'Willems' surname as well as for the maiden name of his mother Marie Fast. It was inevitable that I would benefit from Uncle Les' work. My mom was Les' brother (half-sibling). They had the same mom but different dads. Marie Fast was married to Isaac Doerksen when she gave birth to Peter and Tina (my mom). Doerksen is my mom's maiden name. After Isaac died, Marie married Abraham A. Willems. His wife had passed away two years earlier. A. A. and Marie had five children, Gladys, Les, Ruth, Esther and Rubina (Ruby).

What that means for me is that the Willems clan is not a direct link to my heritage. Yet Grandma Marie Doerksen Willems is a link. She was my mom's mom, my grandma, and she played an integral familial role in my childhood. So did her husband A. A. Willems and all the Willems children, the aunts and uncles and cousins, that are fascinatingly part of my life and my study in this book.

The following preface by Les Willems indicates that he wrote an original document that forms the substance of this chapter. I allowed myself the function of editing his preface material, verifying dates and names, and incorporating information from numerous other sources.

Ron Unruh

Les' Preface

Who were Marie Anne Fast and Abraham Willems? It has been my consuming passion to tell their story. There needs to be an account of their lives and events for the family members and all who yet will come into the world with a relationship by name or genetics,

Both Marie and Abraham were remarkable people who came from an impressive lineage. Telling their story will necessarily be broader than the biographies of two individuals. This lengthy heritage of people comes from a time in history when people developed from a culture and tradition that was based on a humble faith in a creator God and confidence in themselves. It was faith that withstood changing times and difficult experiences. Our family faced many difficulties. No matter how devastating the setbacks were, the family instinctively looked forward. My mother (Marie Doerksen Willems) resiliently reminded us that 'this too will pass.' It always did. I remember more laughter than I can recall tears.

Marie and Abraham were my parents. It was natural that I should feel a close bond to them. Their decisions and my career choices separated me from them during my mid-teens, and it astonishes me now that with the passage of years, I have acquired such avid interest in all facets of their lives.

My father was fond of notable quotations. He often repeated a Low German saying when we were parting after a visit. "Sän, denjk an wea du bes un vejät nich waut du bes." When translated it means, "Son, think of who you are and don't forget what you are."

Les Willems

***

Here then is the collaborative result of Uncle Les' first-hand knowledge and my researched information.

Ron Unruh

ABRAHAM A. WILLEMS AND FAMILY

Hey cousins, our Grandpa Abraham A. Willems was born on February 27, 1883 in Mountain Lake Township, Cottonwood County, Minnesota. The Willems clan arrived in Minnesota two generations before Abraham was born. He was one of twelve children born to Abraham S. Willems and Sarah Flaming. Ten of the children lived to achieve old age, two died in infancy. Among the ten was one set of twins, Anna and Bernard Willems, born on August 16, 1893. All but one child was born in Minnesota, USA. David, the youngest was born in Saskatchewan, Canada.

Abraham A. reminisced often about his childhood years in Minnesota with its abundance of lakes. He told of adventures and tragedies while white water rafting with friends.

Abraham chose to take his father's name for his middle initial

172

and during his adult years he was often called A. A., around town and even more affectionately, "Obraum," by his mother and his two wives. I'll explain the two wives as the story continues.

***

THREE GENERATIONS OF THE WILLEMS FAMILY

Gerhard And Katharina Willems

Lichtfelde was one of the many typical small Mennonite villages in the large Molotschna Colony on the steppes of South Russia. A steppe is an ecoregion characterized by grassland plains without trees. Katharina Rempel was born in Lichtfelde on March 3, 1823. Her family had left Prussia years before to live in South Russia in order to pursue freedoms and farmland. Katharina would become Abraham's grandmother.

Gerhard Willems was born on November 11, 1820, in Neudorf, Gross Werder, Prussia. As a young man Gerhard decided to join thousands of other Mennonite people migrating to South Russia. There in the Molotschna colony Gerhard met Katharina. They fell in love and were married and settled in Lichtenau, They began a family. One has to admire the stamina of women who bore so many children in those years. Katharina gave birth to sixteen children. Five of their children died in infancy or early childhood.

As their eldest children were becoming young adults, Gerhard and Katharina realized the limited opportunities that existed within the established colonies. Soon their children would desire farmland of their own but that was unavailable where they were. They learned that new territory was being opened in Crimea. In 1862 the Gerhard Willems family were among the many families that moved from Ukraine's mainland to Crimea in order to establish the Karassan colony. During their years in Karassan their last four children were born. The Willems were members of the Karassan church.

Only eight years later in 1870 Czar Alexander II ended the military exemption that had been approved to Mennonites as a lifetime grant. Petitions to the Czar resulted in an allowance of a ten-year window during which Mennonites would be permitted to relocate from Russia. One third of the total Mennonite population chose to leave Russia at that time. Gerhard and Katharina and his children were examining their options and how they could make such a momentous decision. What an enormous family choice. In these family discussions we can imagine how raw must have been the emotion. Where would they go? Could all of them go? Would all of them go? Who of them would go?

Shockingly and without notice, Katharina became very ill. She was so ill that she knew she could not recover. Thinking of all her children and their futures, she pressed her husband to prepare to leave the country. He agreed to her desire. She died when she was 52 years old on May 11, 1875 in Kutyuki, Crimea.

Here are the children about whom Katharina had maternal concern.

1. Gerhard, born 21 October, 1842; (died same day)
2. Gerhard Jr, born 17 January 1844, Lichtenau, Molotschna, died Apr 4, 1916 (72)
3. Anna, born 8 August 1845, South Russia; died Feb 17, 1932 (87)
4. Katharina, born 28 October 1846; died Feb 7, 1847 (3 mo)
5. Peter, born 9 January 1848, South Russia; died Dec 1, 1887 (39)
6. Heinrich, born 17 October 1849, South Russia; died Jan 6, 1928 (79)
7. Johann, born 25 April 1851, South Russia; died Jan 20, 1905 (54)
8. Bernhard, born 10 April 1853, South Russia; died Apr 12, 1912 (59)
9. Cornelius, born 5 February 1855, South Russia; died Aug 9, 1902 (47)
10. Katharina, born 7 October 1856, South Russia; died 1890 (34)
11. Abraham S., born 17 November 1858, South Russia; died Nov 13, 1945 (87)
12. Elizabeth, born 6 March 1860; died 1862 (2)
13. Elisabeth, born 31 March 1862, South Russia; died Aug 9, 1927 (65)
14. Jakob, born 15 March 1864; died 1864 (died same day)
15. Maria, born 6 August 1866, South Russia; died July 3,

1895 (29)
  16.   Margaretha, b. 17 September 1869; died 1917 (48)

One month after Katharina's death, Gerhard and ten of his children, five sons and five daughters left Crimea, South Russia. The only child who remained in Crimea was the eldest son named Gerhard Jr., and we do not know his reasons. The explanation might be as simple as the fact that he was married to Maria Kaethler, and they had two small daughters who were two and four years of age and they were settled and happily farming. So, they stayed in Crimea. Eventually Gerhard Jr., and Maria had nine children all of whom were born in Crimea between 1871 and 1885. Gerhard worked in Keneges, Crimea from 1871 until 24 Feb 1873. He then worked as a blacksmith in Karassan until 25 Feb 1874. He began working in Alexanderfeld (Kutyuki), Crimea on 26 Feb 1874. At the age of 72 on April 8, 1916, Gerhard Jr. died in Kutyuki, 41 years after his mother's death.

But what about Gerhard Sr.'s ten other offspring? Together with other Mennonite families, eleven Willems adults, their spouses and children boarded a train at Hochstadt at 7:00 a.m. June 17, 1875. They travelled through Karkow, Wollowchish, Austria, Hanover, Kassel, Achen to Amsterdam. At that point they exchanged rubles for American dollars and boarded the steamer named S.S. Nederland on June 26th. The S.S. Nederland sailed through some violent seas at times and arrived in Philadelphia, Pennsylvania on July 13, 1875. Two days later the family boarded a train that took them to Mountain Lake, Minnesota on the evening of July 18, 1875.

There had been other options than Minnesota. Railroad companies competed to attract settlers as the American Midwest began to open up. Kansas and Nebraska were attractive to Mennonites because of the moderate climate in comparison to the bitter winters in South Russia. Gerhard had learned of droughts and grasshopper plagues in those states during the two previous years. Perhaps that made the decision easy. Gerhard and his family would be pioneering a homestead in Minnesota, six miles southwest of Mountain Lake. They built a house and a barn with stakes driven into the ground and with ploughed sods placed between the poles, then plastering the entire surface inside and out with mud.

Then the land was broken using oxen teams and later horses. Other settlers did the same, and the community grew, and churches and schools were erected.

Gerhard lived there until 1899 when he moved to Saskatchewan and died one year later March 12, 1900, in Rosthern, Saskatchewan at the age of 79 years, 4 months and 1 day.

***

Abraham S. Willems (#5891)

In the preceding list of sixteen children, child number eleven is Abraham S. Willems. He is super important to us. He was our grandfather's father. To my Willems cousins I can say that Abraham S. Willems is 'your' great grandfather if your surname is Willems or your mom's surname was Willems. And A.A. Willems is your grandfather. However, for Jane, Neale, Murray, and me, A.A. Willems was our step grandfather.

Abraham S. was seventeen years old when he and his family arrived in Mountain Lake, Minnesota in 1875. The woman whom he would marry was Sarah Flaming, the daughter of Andreas and Maria (Voth) Flaming. She was their ninth child of a family of twelve children, 2 sons and 10 daughters. The Flamings immigrated to Minnesota in 1877, two years after the Willems family arrived.

The book entitled 'A Good Land' is a lovingly dedicated self-published book with the subtitle, 'The History of the Abraham S. Willems Family in Canada. 1899 – 1999.' It's a marvellous composite of family anecdotes and stories contributed by members of the ten Willems families that have spun from Abraham S. and Sarah Flaming. These individual family histories were compiled and edited by Norman W. Jantzen and printed privately.

Abraham S. worked along with his brothers at hard family farm labour, but actual money had to be found somewhere else. He landed a job with the railroad that paid him 75 cents per day. Rev. Heinrich Voth was a church builder, pastor, and evangelist. He organized the Mennonite Brethren Church in Minnesota as well as in Manitoba just north of the border. While Rev. Voth was in town during Easter services in 1880. Abraham S. was converted. It was true then as it can be today, that one can be a church attendee and be familiar with Christian faith and yet not have made a personal life commitment to Jesus Christ. The following year in January 1881, Sarah Flaming and Abraham S. were married. They settled on a tract of land and worked hard through the difficult conditions of those years.

Children of Abraham S. Willems and Sarah Flaming:

1 Willems, Gerhard A. (#57390) born 7 December, 1881, Mountain Lake, Minnesota; died 11 Mar 1976, Riverside, California

2 Willems, Abraham A. (#57391) born 27 February, 1883, Cottonwood County, Minnesota; died 21 Mar 1965, St. Catharines, Ontario; Married to Anna Wiens (#428072), 6 FEB 1908, Hepburn, Saskatchewan; Married to Maria P. Fast (#277288), 29 NOV 1923, Hepburn, Saskatchewan.

3 Willems, Heinrich A. (#665896) born 17 April, 1886, Mountain Lake, Minnesota; died 16 Jan 1971, Hepburn, Saskatchewan

4 Willems, Johann A. (#57764) born 16 October, 1887, Windom, Minnesota; died 6 Nov 1981, Waldheim, Saskatchewan

5 Willems, Bernhard "Ben" (#41959) born 23 May, 1889; died 27 Sep 1890

6 Willems, Sarah (#24988) born 7 May, 1891, Mountain Lake, Minnesota; died 20 Mar 1964, Waldheim, Saskatchewan.

7 Willems, Anna (#31633) born 16 August, 1893; died 23 Dec 1975.

8 Willems, Bernhard A. (#501565) born 16 August, 1893, Windom, Minnesota; died 20 Jun 1963, Waldheim, Saskatchewan.

9 Willems, Jacob F. (#432622) born 2 July, 1895, Windom, Minnesota; died 2 Jul 1976, Waldheim, Saskatchewan.

10 Willems, Isaac A. (#665893) born 7 November, 1896, Windom, Minnesota; died 1 Aug 1979, Saskatoon, Saskatchewan.

11 Willems, Katharina (#48152) born14 October, 1898; died 18 Oct 1898.

12 Willems, David A. (#111734) born 24 May, 1901; died 27 Jun 1988, Saskatoon, Saskatchewan.

A.S. Willems and eight sons
A.S., Gerhard, Abraham A., Heinrich, Johann, Bernhard A.,
Jacob, Isaac A., David A.

Abraham A. Willems, Grandfather

The book, 'A Good Land', contains a section entitled 'Family of Abraham A. Willems, that was written by Ruby Willems and Les Willems and submitted by Les Willems. It contains the following information.

***

It might be true to say that he became a self-made man. As a sixteen-year-old A. A. emigrated from Minnesota together with his parents, six brothers and two sisters, to Canada, and specifically to the Rosthern District of what was then called the British Northwest Territories and on September 1, 1905 became known as the Province of Saskatchewan. The family settled on land that overlooked the North Saskatchewan River, an area now known as Brotherfield.

Life on the prairies in the early 1900's was nothing if not exciting and adventuresome. A. A. told stories of his experiences on river ice, or swimming in the swift currents, or of expeditions to

Rosthern to obtain food and supplies, and the hazards of trips made during winter storms. He told of journeys via horseback and how he encountered packs of wolves.

Physical distances between friends seemed enormous. Social life revolved around church activities. For families in their area, during their first few years, church services were held in their own homes. Some Sundays became all day outings consisting of visits with neighbouring friends. In 1902 a new church building was erected, and the Brotherfield Mennonite Brethren Church became their home church. A. A. re-counted the devout faith of his parents and the rigid standards that were established for him and his siblings. He confessed that his conduct did not always meet with their approval, yet his mother was always supportive.

"Being an older son in a large family meant that Abraham A. had little opportunity for formal schooling. He was needed on the farm. He recounted tutoring sessions at his mother's knee."

('A Good Land, The History of the Abraham S. Willems Family in Canada, 1899-1999.'pg. 16).

A.A. liked to say that he was his mother's favourite, and that when the others told him he was a 'black sheep,' his mother came to his defense. When he was in his late teen years, school was not considered necessary for him any longer.

Through church functions, the Willems family became acquainted with the Jacob B. Wiens family. Rev. Jacob Wiens was the pastor of the Edenfeld M.B. Church. A. A. held Rev. Wiens in high esteem and doubtlessly was positively influenced by this saintly man. It was in 1906 that A. A. and two of his sisters, Anna and Sarah publicly professed their faith and were baptized in the North Saskatchewan River and they became members of the Brotherfield M.B. Church.

There were several attractive daughters in the Wiens family. In A.A.'s own words, he "set his 'hat' on the eldest and prettiest of the lot"! And A. A. said, "These were the years of my success." So, on February 6, 1908 Rev. Peter Nickel officiated the marriage of A. A. Willems and Anna Wiens in the Edenfeld M.B. Church. They then settled into their homestead home that was two miles west and one mile north of the Brotherfield Church. A. A. looked back on that time by saying that they immediately prospered in every way. On November 16, 1908 their baby boy Menno was born in Brotherfield. Their wheat crops yielded thirty bushels per acre that sold for $4.50 per bushel. On April 18, 1910, Lilly was born. Good fortune continued.

Abraham A. Willems and his wife Anna purchased a farm that was located one half mile directly south of the new village of Hepburn. They and their two children, Menno age three, and eighteen-month-old Lilly, moved into their new home. Their early years were prosperous. It seemed too good to be true. They had large and nearly new buildings and a house with lots of room for their family. Being near Hepburn meant they were close to a school, to stores and a post office and to an active church. The village was located on the Canadian National Railway line and Hepburn and area was flourishing. Best of all A. A. and Anna liked the people who lived there, such as the families of C.K. Unruh and Toby Schmidt. They had known these families and others from previous associations when they pioneered near Brotherfield and the Windom School District.

In autumn of that first year in Hepburn their daughter Rosie was born on October 19, 1911. Anna and A. A. established a relationship with a woman named Miss Baerg to negotiate a contract for nursing care. That became a relationship that lasted for three decades.

The years were filled with annual events, the seasonal planting of crops in spring and the harvests in fall. There were school picnics and kinderfest church conferences and the family of A. A. Willems grew. Edwin arrived On March 24, 1915. The Willems second child Lilly was six years old in 1916 when she became ill during a diphtheria epidemic. Lilly died that year on June 16th and was buried in the cemetery beside the Hepburn M.B. Church. Then on January 6, 1917 Annie was born and the family learned to understand new challenges because Annie was a Downs Syndrome child. Anna had given birth to six children, one of whom was deceased, and one of whom needed special care. It was a busy household and a busy farm that was doing well with the sale of crops.

Hepburn was incorporated in 1919 and it was bursting with

optimism and opportunity. In 1918 A. A. Willems moved his family to a new farm site, a large land base, a new house and barn and one of the longest granaries in what was sometimes referred to as 'the New West.' It was located 1.25 miles due East of Hepburn. A. A. Willems and family were embarking on their own trip into the decade of the 'Roaring Twenties.' No one knew what lay ahead. 1919 was the year that Gracie was born on February 14. Two years later, on March 15, 1921 Anna gave birth to Abram and life was wonderful. Seven children in total, one deceased, six of whom were full of life and possibilities, three sons, and three daughters.

It was 1921 and the family was experiencing what we all know in this world, that life is not comprised of only sunshine and smiles. No one could have imagined that mother Anna would die nine months after Abram was born. There was darkness and tears. On Dec 30, 1921 A.A.'s beloved Anna passed away from pneumonia and accompanying complications. She was thirty-nine years of age. She was ill for only a few weeks and could not recover. Her death was sudden and so very unexpected for this family. The family plunged to intense despair. A.A.'s grief was profound as was the anguish of all the children. It had lasting effects upon them all well into adulthood. Abram (Abe) never knew his mother. He was put into the care of the John Strauss family for the next two years.

The children recalled the days of grieving that followed their mother's passing. Menno was thirteen years old; Rose was ten. Ruth Low recounts, "Rose told me that the children often heard father weeping inconsolably in his seclusion in the barn. He could be heard crying out to God to show him a way out of his despair, to show him what to do with the children. He loved Anna deeply and he was never the same man again."

Time passed. Life carried on. Then one day father appeared dressed in his best and he announced to the children that he was going "to find us a new mama." That announcement would bring about a dramatic change that would create a new and larger family.

***

New Wife, New Mom

Arrangements were soon completed for a wedding between A. A. and his newly found bride, Maria Doerksen (nee Fast) of Dalmeny. Marie Fast Doerksen had been born in Marion, South Dakota on April 27, 1894 to parents Peter and Katherina Fast. Maria's parents now lived in Dalmeny, having moved to Canada some years earlier from Mountain Lake, Minnesota, where Marie's formative years were spent. Her parents had attempted to be pioneer farmers in Minnesota, but it was difficult to find good soil. Canada was open to immigrants so they thought they would give this a try.

Maria had loved life in Mountain Lake, Minnesota before moving to Montana to homestead with her brothers. It was in Montana that she met Isaac Doerksen who had come from Kansas to homestead in Montana. When her parents, Peter and Katherina heard that Isaac was extremely ill, they told Marie and Isaac to bring their small children, Peter, and Tina to Canada to live with them. This family of four moved from their homestead in Montana USA to Dalmeny, SK just a few months before Isaac died. Isaac died on June 13, 1920.

Maria was now a widow and a single parent of two children. If that was not burden enough, sometime following Isaac's death, Maria's parents, Peter, and Katherina decided to return to Mountain Lake, Minn., leaving Marie and her two small children. As a single mom, Marie found it necessary to work for others. People learned that she was a trained seamstress, so an arrangement began. She could care for her children and herself by moving from one family farm to another sewing clothing for the families in exchange for room and board. At one point Marie informed her parents that when she completed the current family sewing project she would also return to Mountain Lake. That didn't happen. It was during one of these reciprocal sewing ventures that she and A. A. Willems met. He thought she was very nice. She told her parents that she would stay in Canada. Her parents were astounded.

Abraham was forty years old, and Maria was twenty-nine. They were finding each other to be the answer to their prayers. A. A. had six children, and Maria would now be mother to her own two children and a stepmom to six more. A. A. and Maria were married on November 29, 1923 in the Hepburn M.B. Church in a ceremony officiated by Rev. Peter Friesen.

Yours, Mine, and Ours, All Together.

A new family chapter began. Abraham and Maria, his family and her family now began the process of building 'their family.' A Low German express was "deine, meine, and unse, oulus toupe' and that should sum it up ... 'yours, mine, and ours, all together.' Blending families did not come easily. The six Willems children born to Anna loved their momma very much, missed her greatly, and most certainly found it difficult to adjust to a new mom and two new siblings. Those six children were Menno who was fifteen years old, Rose was twelve, Edwin was eight, Annie was six, Grace was five and Abram was two years old. Marie's two were Peter aged seven and Tina five years old.

Gladys Marie was the first child to be born in this new marriage union, on October 14, 1924. Two months into the joy of Gladys' arrival came the saddening death of seven-year-old Annie on December 22, 1924 (7 years & 11 months old). She was buried in the Church cemetery where her sister Lilly was interred. Leslie was born on May 24, 1927. Ruthie (Ruth Alma) was born on August 21, 1931. When Ruth was born, Edwin, Abe, Peter, Grace, Gladys and Leslie were living on the farm. Esther Edna was born on March 28, 1933 and finally Ruby (Rubina Evangeline) on December 19, 1937. What a family, six Willems children, plus two Doerksen children, plus five more Willems! All of them were born in Hepburn, Saskatchewan.

The economy was buoyant and prosperous even though interest rates at the new bank in Hepburn was at 16%. Wheat sold for a high $4.50 per bushel. More automobiles began to appear on village streets. And A. A. Willems owned one of those new cars. In 1927 a new public school was built and there was a fresh enthusiasm for education among children and youth. The older school buildings were being used for a new Bible school, Bethany Bible School, that soon became one of the most influential institutions in a vast area. A.A. referred to this post-secondary facility as the most significant accomplishment of the Mennonite Brethren Church in Saskatchewan. A faith relationship with Jesus Christ was a family spiritual priority and the best that can be said is that "most of us had a relationship with Jesus," (Ruth Willems

Low).

The Dirty Thirties

The decade of the 1930's known famously as the 'dirty thirties' was epitomized by the drought in the Prairies of Canada even as it was in the United States. This was the period of the great depression. A. A. lamented that his eight-year-old son, Leslie, had still never seen what real rain was. Ruth Willems Low says, "All our clothes, coats, suits and dresses were constantly sewn by Mom. She helped to keep us alive."

During Abraham's twilight years in the 1960's he had many open conversations with his son Leslie, when he unburdened himself about what he believed were failures or disappointments in his past. He felt that his family began to unravel when the economy soured during the 1930's. When A. A. related these stories at the end of his life there was a flood of tears. He said, "My children misunderstood and nothing I could do would turn out right." He also said, "Now, those that remain, with the benefit of hindsight, hopefully will know the right story."

This would be a decade when A. A. took his family from the farm and moved some of them, the youngest five children, to Ontario, stayed for a couple of years and then moved briefly back to Saskatchewan, changed his mind again, and returned to Ontario. As Les recounted it later, he indicated that this period of years was still an unpopular topic among some remaining family members, including the older married children in Saskatchewan.

Recounting the 1930s

Ruth was born in August 1931 and the house with its limited space remained crowded. Rose was seldom at home because she was working in Waldheim, mostly at her Grandma's home. In 1932 Menno married Sarah Fadenricht of Hepburn and their wedding reception was held in the M.B. Church. Esther was born in 1933. While the family continued to grow numerically, the economic depression was deepening.

In 1935 however the decision was made, whether by common agreement or as is believed, by Pete's own choice, he moved to his maternal relatives in Minnesota. It does appear that the decision was discussed with Abraham and Marie, and they concluded as well that it was in Pete's best interest.

Pete, or Peter Doerksen was Jane's and Rodney's dad.

Jane (Doerksen) Jones shared a memory.

"I was told by Les that my dad Peter left the Willems' home and farm for a better life. I never understood what that really meant, though many years ago, Les and I talked for hours about our family, and he told me that he and my father were very close. He said he understood why my father left and that it was just time for him to move on. My understanding was that he came to Mountain Lake MN and stayed with a lovely, wealthy couple who owned the Balzer Manufacturing Co., in Mountain Lake. He was given a job. They all went to the Mennonite Brethren Church and that was where dad met my mother. Mom told me that it was 'love at first sight for both of them'" (Jane {Doerksen} Jones)

***

In 1936 Rose married Jacob Nickel of Dalmeny, Saskatchewan. She was twenty-five years old. The wedding reception was held at home under a large tent that was set up beside the house. This was the last major party event and expenditure that A. A. put on in Saskatchewan.

On December 19, 1937 Ruby (Rubina Evangeline) was born. This story is worth telling. A. A. celebrated by purchasing a Victrola gramophone. News of her birth was withheld from older children for a few hours, so the purchase of the Victrola caused a fuss. The children were wondering how and why Papa would do this when there was no money. A.A.'s response was, "It is Christmas." That didn't do much to solve their dismay when they had no other Christmas presents. But then, a large package arrived for the family; a Christmas gift from twenty-year-old Pete in Minnesota and it contained gifts for everyone.

In 1938 sickness entered the family home. Tuberculosis was the scourge of the day in Canada. Grace was diagnosed with tuberculosis. Grace was the first daughter to become ill and she was confined to bed most of the time. She did not improve so A.A. and Marie, drove her to a new hospital called a Sanatorium located in Saskatoon and dedicated specifically for tuberculosis patients. Grace was placed in isolation. She was twenty years old. There was no official medical quarantine imposed upon the family but as word spread, there was social ostracism, people avoiding any contact or exposure to the family. Family members seldom visited her, although mother Marie visited as often as she could.

At the same time rumours of war began to come from Europe. It was discussed what this might mean for the family if Canada entered the war. Conscriptions would most certainly require decisions by Willems young men. The young men learned what it meant to be conscientious objectors. It was wrong to engage in war and to take a life. Mennonite young men could not consider military service. It was firmly held that the family must maintain the faith of their forefathers and remain pacifist. Would all the boys agree? Were all the boys committed to the Mennonite ethic? Then war was declared by Canada against Germany.

War and More Tuberculosis

By 1940 only a few of A. A's and Marie's close friends continued to visit them, such was the understandable concern over Tuberculosis. More concerning now was the necessary discussion about the younger girls, Gladys, Ruth, and Esther also needing to go the Sanatorium (The San). Some friends advised against allowing this because it was speculated that patients going to the San were considered incurable and would never return home. Anguish was desperate in the Willems' Home. One after another, Gladys, Ruth, and Esther were admitted to the San. Ruth was almost nine years old when she was placed in care and Esther was almost eight years old. Marie visited the girls in Saskatoon when a neighbour would drive her to the hospital. "I'd say she came to visit us every six weeks. Dad never came. In exchange for the ride she was given, Mom would sew a dress for the driver's wife," (Ruth Willems Low). No explanation exists to shed light on A.A.'s decision not to visit the girls in the San. He is simply given grace on this matter because there are things we cannot ever know and should not presume.

It was 1941 and things became even more stressed. The dairy herd and the sheep were confiscated by authorities to be tested for T.B. They were found to be infected and the animals were subsequently destroyed. Nothing was left. The depression had taken material possessions and now the exodus began. Edwin at age twenty-six departed for Ontario to find work. Tina (my mom) was twenty-two and was living and working in Hepburn. Abe was twenty years old, and he was 'farmed out', a term referring to him working on other farms. For the entire summer he worked for farmers in Watrous, SK. And now came the defiance of the conscientious objection tenet, as Abe decided to enlist for military service, and he too departed for Ontario.

The Japanese attacked Pearl Harbour. It was the end of 1941.

The Prayer Vigils

What could be done about their distressed situation, with daughters in hospital, their married children, the young men at work, no income other than what little monies the oldest children might provide. Secluded behind the barn A. A. prayed and Marie did the same in the straw stack in the pasture. This they did for days and weeks. While they thought they were praying in secret, the children who remained at home were observing them nightly. Soon God would answer was the impression they all held tightly. When mom and dad were occupied with chores, it was eleven-year-old Leslie's responsibility to care for his three-year-old sister Rubina (Ruby). Marie, A. A., Ruby and Les were the only ones still living at home. Four daughters were in hospital. It is difficult to imagine how frightening and heart wrenching these times were.

In spring of 1942 God answered prayer. One by one the girls came home from the Sanatorium. Gladys first, then Ruth and then Esther, and they were free of the virus, but they were in recovery for many months from the lengthy process of treatment and isolation.

Ruth Willems Low describes this in the following account.

"A cure for T.B. in the form of a pill was found in 1949 but that was too late for us. Until then we were told that treatment consisted of lots of food, rest, and fresh air. I became very overweight and when I came home, the boys at home called me watermelon. I was warned that I would die if I didn't rest. Many people in Hepburn died. I struggled physically at home and stayed in bed most of the time and was carried downstairs for a long time. All of this was a heavy burden for a girl of eight years of age." (Ruth {Willems} Low)

Grace was not yet well enough to come home. She had been in

hospital for four years by this time.

School term was ended for the summer, and it was June. One evening at the supper table, with A. A., Marie, Gladys, Les, Esther, and Ruby, father made an announcement. It was astounding. "We are going to leave the farm and we will move to Ontario. We will make a new start." It happened just that quickly. Within weeks they were gone, A. A. and Marie and the youngest five.

Ruth wrote, "Dad and Mom, Esther and Ruby moved back to Ontario in 1942. I had left one year earlier to find a job. I lived for a while with Ed and Alma after spending the summer with Rose and Jake in B.C. working on fruit farms and helping Rose with her children."

What other choice was there really? Poverty, crop failure, grasshopper plague, drought and cows put down because they tested positive for Tuberculosis, forced the difficult decision to leave the farm, to leave the prairies and to move to Ontario. A.A., his wife Marie, and their five youngest children, Gladys, Leslie, Ruth, Esther, and Rubina made that move in June 1942. Menno and his family moved to A.A.'s farm to occupy it and tend it.

When the Willems family arrived in St. Catharines, they were fortunate to be able to settle into reasonable accommodation as tenants on the Forman's fruit farm. Leslie began to search for work.

Grace died in 1945 at the age of 26 from T.B in a Saskatoon, SK hospital. Her stepsister Ruth wrote about Grace.

"She was a beautiful young woman, the same age as her stepsister Tina (Doerksen) Unruh. We were living in St. Catharines when word came that Grace was ill and near the point of death. This must have been a most difficult time for Grace. At Dad's request, Mom boarded a train to make the trip west to be with Grace when she died. A book could be written about how this affected us. I was deeply wounded by my own experience with the illness and in hospital.

Ruth Willems Low.

15 LES WILLEMS: A Personal Account of My Formative Years

Ron's Preface

STANDING SIX FOOT FOUR INCHES TALL AND WITH AN IMPRESSIVELY DEEP VOICE, he was unlike anyone else in my small world. I was a boy when I met him. Les Willems was my mother Tina's half-brother, having the same mother, but a different father. He was my Uncle Les. I liked him and admired him. Uncle Les respected my dad and loved my mom. Mom and Dad enjoyed his visits to our home. So, did I.

This chapter contains Les' own words. It is a significant souvenir. His writing is a genuine, honest, unpolished, and personal story. That's what makes this a fun read. I have retained his entries, headings, and fragmented sentences just as Les wrote them in a booklet using his longhand cursive. Les' account is untouched apart from a few spelling and grammar corrections that I have made. There is a major dating error that I have chosen to explain rather than to correct.

The first journal entry is set in December 1938 in which Les announces the birth of his youngest sister Ruby. However, we know Ruby was born December 19, 1937. That presents a dilemma I choose not to solve. Should all succeeding dates be adjusted? I will leave the journal entries just as I found them. As 1938 started Gladys was 14 years old, Les was almost eleven, Ruth was 7 years of age, Esther was five and Ruby only one month old. Within nine months, on September 1, 1939, WW2 began in Europe when Nazi Germany invaded Poland. Tuberculosis was ravaging families at home in Saskatchewan. Soon Grace, Gladys, Ruth, and

Esther were all in a medical sanatorium in Saskatoon, far away from their home.

At the front of a Hilroy notebook Les recorded genealogical, biographical, and historical notes. At the back of that notebook Les started this journal. I do not know when he wrote this. Les' purpose for this journal is an enigma. My first thought was that this was a young boy's diary that marked prominent days and events. However, some statements and verb tenses persuade me that as an adult, Les was looking back at meaningful and cherished memories. Then there are also some entries that suggest to me that Les was writing this entire journal specifically for Ruby, his beloved kid sister, ten years younger than him. Finally, there is the curious addition of two statements, the first dated 1996 in which his failing eyesight made Les run out of steam to continue with his journal. The other statement marked 1997 when his eyesight had improved. This he made additional to his precious story.

Ron Unruh

My Formative Years, 1938-1952 by Leslie Willems

Dec. 19, 1938, 8:30 PM

Mom was with us kids decorating the Christmas tree and living room. There was a commotion between Mom and my older sisters. Abe was sleeping upstairs. They woke him up to hurry and fetch dad. He was mad as hell! Dad was attending a meeting in the church in town – something about the Christmas pageant.

Dad returned home and rushed Mom to town in the cutter. He used the 'fast team of horses' - they were in a hurry! It spoiled what had been such a fun evening. I had to go to bed.

Dec. 20 AM Tuesday

I had to wash in cold water and get ready for breakfast. Dad was there but where was Mother? We were told to sit down and be quiet. Gladys and Abe had a secret and made fun of me because I didn't know what it was. Gladys made faces!

Dad made an announcement. He was beaming. "You have a baby sister!"

I was full of questions but had to be quiet and wait. Dad read the Bible and prayed with us.

It was a Tuesday and I had to go to school. I was in grade 4.

After school we could go to see Mom in the hospital in town. At 4:10 PM I was shown my baby sister, Wow! I met Rubina Evangeline.

Dec. 21-23, 1938

Just prior to Christmas – Dad brought home a new second hand Victrola gramophone 'His Master's Voice' with a number of modern 78 speed records. My favourite is 'The Big Rock Candy Mountain.' There was consternation among the older siblings. How could he afford it when they needed new clothes and there was no money! It was rumoured he had paid $2.00 for it.
This purchase was to be kept a secret, a surprise for mother when she and Rubina would come home for Christmas.

Dec. 25

What a Christmas! A parcel arrived from Pete, a gift for everyone. I got a box of chocolates. Pete was in Mountain Lake, Minn. I had missed him so much but now he was 21 years old and able to afford such wonderful gifts. His absence was starting to pay off.

We got our shares of peanuts, some walnuts, some nigger toes (Brazil nuts), oranges, popcorn balls and all of this piled high on our plates that were set on the table in the place assigned to each family member on Christmas Eve. And a new baby sister! Rubina Evangeline. Could it get any better? (We never heard of Christmas stockings until much later).

A new red barn with six white horses and a sleigh. I heard Mom tell people that, "Dad built the barn himself." The question was, where did he get the horses and the sleigh? We had no money.

1939 First Half of the Year

Nothing too exciting to report. Glad to be in school now. Before, when Ruth and Esther were babies, I was at home and had to rock the cradle when they cried and keep them quiet. What a trying time that had been – I would sit and watch out of the window towards Hepburn, waiting for my older siblings to come home from school so that Gladys could relieve me from my tedium and then I could go outside and play. Why did she always loiter there so long? As I watched her come down the road, I could tell that she was deliberately walking slowly, although she would deny this to mother when I complained to no avail. But now it was Esther's turn until Ruth came home from school. My chores were to fill the firewood box and bring in the drinking water from the well and carry out the slop pail and feed it to the pigs, and to fill the boiler at the back of the stove with rainwater from the cistern and sometimes I would even spell Ruth off to rock Rubina Evangeline!

Last Half of the Year. F. J. Baerg, my schoolteacher announced that war had broken out in Europe. It was what father had long speculated. What would that mean, I wondered, but it did not affect Rubina Evangeline.

1940.

I was in grade 6 and getting into serious trouble in school. This would be my last year under F. J. Baerg if I passed my grade. My buddy Carl Schmor was in the same grade as me, and we were pretty sure F. J. would not want us for another year, but you could never be certain with that old bird!

What the hell is going on? It is happening again. Is it going to be like two decades ago? That was the period when there was so much sickness. Mom and dad were both widowed. Dad had buried two of our sisters. Most everybody else was near death!

Where is everybody? Menno is married and living in Brotherfield. Rosie is married, living near Dalmeny. Ed is living on the Sawatsky farm. Pete is in Mountain Lake. Tina is living in town. Abe is in Watrous for the summer. Grace has been in the sanatorium for a year now. Now Gladys, Ruth, and Esther are also in the sanatorium. Rubina and I are the only ones at home with Mom and Dad.

Dad told me, "Rubina is in your hands! You see that nothing happens to her or goes wrong!" I should've told him how scared I was. Rubina Evangeline was learning to walk.

1941.

I was in grade 7, Whoopee! This was Junior High and was held in the upper room of the school! Reuben Dyck the teacher, was quick to deal with me. On only the second or third day he caught me acting up. He told me to stand. Then he called to attention all the grade 7, 8 and 9 students. In a soft voice he told me that the students were adults and did not wish to be disturbed by a disorderly child. If I wished to stay with them, they would be glad to help me but if not, I could be sent back to the children's classroom. Could I behave like an adult, he asked. "Yes sir," I did not hesitate. I got the message. From second last in the class of 18 in grade 6, I moved up to third place in grade 7. One of my finest achievements. Reuben Dyck was by far the best teacher I ever had. Summer vacation from school.

Mom and dad infrequently made visits to the girls in the Saskatoon sanitarium. I remained at home with Ruby. She had learned to ride piggyback on me. Rubina would put her arms around my neck and her legs around my waist and hold on, freeing my arms to balance as we walked. I had to be responsible for her, so I dreaded these times alone with Rubina. But she must not know this. So, we went for long walks pretending we were going to visit relatives. It was just my excuse so we would not be alone in the scary empty house.

1941 continued.

Like all small children there were times when Rubina cried. But when Rubina and I were alone she never cried. I sensed that she knew of my fear of keeping her safe and that I loved her dearly.

When mom returned from a visit to the girls, she usually had very little to say. And for a few days after each of those visits dad was never around. I knew he wasn't far away because all the horses were accounted for. The atmosphere was emotional. One thing though, the verbal disputes between mom and dad that I recalled from earlier years had stopped now.

I became accustomed when I went to bed at night, to lie awake waiting to hear the squeak of the wire latch on the fence gate that was outside my window on the north side of the house. Mother would let herself through the gate and I knew she was on her way to the straw stacks in the meadow. I would always follow her just in case she needed help. But I kept back out of sight and sound so she would not be distracted. There she would prostrate herself in the straw and pour out her heart to God. She mentioned each one of her children by name, asking God to hold them in his hand, and to give her strength to accept His will. These were the only times that I ever heard my mother use the German language. For as long as my sisters were in the Sanatorium these prayer vigils continued. But I was not the only observer. I discovered that my father was always behind the barn listening.

1941 continued.

When the folks went for a visit to see the girls in the Sanatorium, I took Rubina for a walk. I was diligent to be at home when they returned until one day because of a prairie thunderstorm, we had to keep under cover in a bush a very long way from the house. When the storm finally ended, the folks had already returned home and found us missing. Their anxiety was considerable. When I got home, father was furious. My explanation of being in the bush rather than the house perplexed him. He said, "Maybe I have an idiot for a son!"

I didn't want to tell him there were spirits in the house when we were alone. He already had enough to worry about. But I think mother knew something was wrong, something disturbed me. She told me that next time Rubina and I could go along with them to the city. What a relief! I couldn't wait to see the four girls. On the next visit someone with a sedan had room for all of us, and Rubina and I went along.

What joy to see the girls but oh the grieving that ensued. I can't tell the full story here, and I don't know how it affected Rubina. She must have sensed the change in me, but she was so young. If she sensed the despair in me, would it impair her faith in God? Rubina Evangeline you must have faith!

1941 continued

The hell of 1941 is not over. Two major events where Satan triumphed. Abe came home to leave for good. He was leaving to enlist for military service. There was a heated exchange between Abe and Father in the barn. Then Abe came to the house. He retrieved the most precious gift our mother had ever received from him. It was a gas Aladdin lamp, a light that permitted her to see into the night. Mother had exceptional seamstress skills. This lamp permitted mother to sew clothes, drapes, and tablecloths for the whole community. For this she received compensation, and this was the only source of income for the family. The lamp had become her prized possession and father recognized its importance for the whole family.

Now Abe carried the lamp outside to the woodpile, placed it on the chopping block and proceeded to smash it with the axe. There was weeping and wailing. I stood and watched him as Abe walked down the road toward Hepburn and the train that would carry him east to Ontario. I loved my brother and could not understand what made him act this way. What I came to understand was that he had cut himself off from any ties, not only from my mother, but also much more seriously from my father. Dad was devastated. What did watching this do to you Rubina?

1941 and more.

The second calamity. Our parents were both American born. All of mother's relatives were in the United States. I was in school when the news flash came to us; the Japanese had struck Pearl Harbor. Canada would go to war. Christmas 1941, Rubina is four years old, and she has become so beautiful that she has eclipsed Shirley Temple! I am in grade 8 and learning from Reuben Dyck that it is possible to change the world around you.

I can't be a Mennonite. I am not a conscientious objector and I think they are two-faced. I told Mr. Dyck so.

1942.

In all the hell of 1941 there had been some happenings that had gone unappreciated by me. Tina got married on June 12, 1941. It started to sink in that I had a brother-in-law. He was Ed Unruh, and he was someone I held in high esteem.

Our brother Edwin had gone to Ontario and news from him was cheerful. Menno had moved to the Sawatsky farm and was close by in order to help us with our farm if we needed him. Gladys had come home from the sanatorium. There was news that Esther and Ruth were making good recovery. They could be home soon. This to me was miraculous after the rumours that we would never get the girls back. Rubina was no longer my sole responsibility because the girls would come home, and they could help.

1942 continued

Spring! Since the crops were in, I only missed a minimum of

absent days from school. Ruth and Esther are home! Rubina is experiencing sisters. I concentrated on my grade 8 year-end exams. Each student has a private interview with Mr. Dyck. Now it was my turn. I was very nervous, wondering how I had done. Why do private interviews?

Mr. Dyck started, "Les, I am proud of you. You have improved yourself so much over the past year and a half."
Wow! He gave me my report. It was the best I had ever done. At least I had something to be proud of and someone who was proud of me.

"Are you planning to continue into high school?" he asked.

"Yes," I replied, "I certainly am."

"That's good," he said, "but I will not be coming back to the school next term."

I was keenly disappointed. I hoped he would change his mind.

I was elated the day school was closed for the summer.

That day at suppertime came a momentous disclosure for my father. Plans were nearly completed. We would be moving to Ontario to try to make a new start.

It seemed too good to be true. Rubina had three sisters at home. And I had no concern about the farm.

1942 continued

The end of June and we were aboard the train on our way to Ontario. Menno with his family were moving onto our farm until father could determine what our future would be in Ontario. Rubina had a new doll and was oblivious to all cares as she played with Esther, and I only had to concentrate on my own future.

Needless to say, these were trying times in Ontario, while the family was bouncing from pillar to post before we got settled into a reasonable accommodation as tenants at Foreman's fruit farm.
In the meantime, I got exposed to the experience of being employed full-time at various jobs.

1942 continued

After work at Loblaws' groceries near the middle of August, I was making my way down St. Paul Street in St. Catharines. On my way home I ran into Mr. Reuben Dyck. We were both dumbfounded. I was dumbfounded at seeing him in a military uniform in St. Catharines. He was dumbfounded at finding me carrying a lunch bucket on the street in St. Catharines. "What was he doing in uniform?" I asked. His answer was that he knew he would soon have to respond to a draft call, and he considered it his duty to enlist. It was news to him to hear that our family had moved to Ontario.

What about my plans to continue my future schooling, He asked?

I had no definite answer for him. It was a good question I thought.

1942 continued … Mid-August

I had one of my Tête à Tête chats with mother that had become more frequent since our move east.

"Guess who I met yesterday? Reuben Dyck! "

Mother was amused, but then I said, "Mr. Dyck wanted to know what would happen about my going back to school now?"

"Oh Leslie!" Mom said sadly.

There was an ominous silence. Long story shortened. I got a permit from the Board of Education for an under aged juvenile to leave school while under 16 years of age. It was granted to me on two counts; 1. My help was needed to provide for a growing family! 2. My choice would be an asset to selective service to release older males for military service.

Done! Although I was dazed, I got a work permit for any apprenticeship program of my choice. This meant I was growing up. I would pay my wages to support the family, minus a small allowance that my mother worked out with my father's consent. My father had become disenchanted with my attitude, and he told me so. Well too bad about that. But to hell with the rest of the world. No one had the right to tell me what to do. Especially I would not go to a Mennonite church.

1943

After several job changes and tryouts with various apprenticeships, I had a chauffeur's license that was obtained through Selective Service. I was an under aged driver assisting the war effort. Then I began to apprentice for a glazier at Niagara Glass. My bond with Rubina was growing. I teased my sisters Esther and Ruthie too much. I don't know why. Gladys was too

involved with her church friends and had no time for me. It was
okay. She had had a pretty hard time with sickness. My father was
losing control of the family. Much worse, he was losing respect for
me. My rapport with mother was constant. But more and more she
expressed concern for my welfare.

1944

My work was going well. My self-confidence was growing. I
was becoming a hero for Rubina. Our relationship was becoming
intimate. She thought I was a dragon slayer. I showered her with
affection. I embezzled money at work. It afforded me a charge
account at Bacon's Confectionary just down the street from where
we lived on Welland Avenue in St. Catharines. To impress Rubina
with my acquired status I took her to Bacon's for treats and I
charged them. In later years Ruby was to tell me that she used to
go there a lot and get things charged to my account. Bill Bacon
knew that Ruby was my sister!

1944 continued

Before I go on with this accounting, let me establish one thing.
Dad, it was not, and it is not my fault that Rubina got lost! I'll
finish this when I stop grieving. Thank you for helping.

I'm back and I want to get on with this record. I'm reminded
of a favourite quotation that I have used in years past when
extreme trials brought my progress to a halt.

"I have been wounded, but not slain. I'll lay me down to rest a
while. And then I'll rise and fight again."

During the days of my reflection, I was introspective. This
period has been most helpful for me in finding answers to
important questions that I have had about some of the experiences
in my life.

Rubina, this is the year you started school. You are still my
pride and joy, but I have other cares now. Most important it is
becoming more difficult to do what's right. You're discovering me
in some very private practices. Late at night on the upper deck of
the veranda you came out when I was having a secret smoke. I let
you have a puff. You naughty girl. You knew that there were
nights when I was coming home drunk. Mother would divert
father's attention, but did he know anyway? Was I still your hero

Rubina Evangeline?

1945

What a momentous year! Mother went to see Grace who remained in the Sanatorium in Saskatoon. When mother returned to us in St. Catharines and told us of Gracie's death and the circumstances surrounding her passing, I was numb, and I felt guilty. Mother said Gracie's face lit up when she told Grace that my message to her was that I had accepted Jesus as my Savior. That was two-faced, dishonest. I should also have said, "I don't know if he has accepted me."

But Rubina, God performed miracles even in our family and Rubina you must have faith!

Midsummer and the day the sun stood still, or so it seemed. Mom, Dad, and all you girls boarded the bus to return to Saskatchewan to live. I remained behind, resolved that I could make it on my own. This happening would take a volume to describe.

Rubina, I thought of you as little as I possibly could to keep you out of my mind!

1946

The war had ended months before. There would be no need of me in the military. I was making new and important friends. I had a girlfriend, a real steady. The dragon slayer was having new conquests and was growing, at least in the image of his own mind.

1947

My existence had become very self-centered. I had no one to look after but myself. My earning power increased dramatically. I was flush with cash in my pockets when confronted with an opportunity to visit you. Why not? Then I must do it.

Late spring and I appeared on the doorstep of what had been grandpa's house in Waldheim! Wow! Two years of your absence and how you had grown Rubina, more beautiful than ever!

Nothing like a 19-year-old brother with cash to impress a nine-year-old sister!

No cares, we parted again and went on our merry ways. (Explanation: I travelled west to visit Dad, Mom and the girls who now lived on Grandpa Abraham S. Willems' farm in Waldheim.)

1948

The telling of our individual experiences would fill volumes, but we had few opportunities to be together.

1949

I am living in Kingston I have become my own man. I'm engaged to be married to a beautiful American girl, just like the one that married dear old dad.

I received the news that mom, dad, Ruth, Esther and Rubina have moved back to St. Kitts on the April Easter weekend. I took my betrothed to St. Kitts to meet my family. First thing I learned from you is that it's not Rubina but Ruby. That's what you called yourself. You made that clear. Ruby, she likes you! My Helen and Ruby are going to be friends.

1949 continued

June 18 wedding bells! Watertown, New York State. My mother, God bless her. She's the only one from my entire large family that made it to our wedding. I understand, I think. It's because of economics; well at least it's because of their priorities. Then Helen and I had opportunity to visit family during our honeymoon in Niagara Falls.

1950

Ruby, you paid us a visit in Kingston with one of your girlfriends. We had a good time. (Ruby is thirteen years old).
1951 Long weekend holidays.

Easter, Thanksgiving and Christmas continue to be times when we can visit and spend time together. We have re-established a close rapport, you, and me Ruby. During my big brother chats with you, I talked about the facts of life, the birds and the bees etc. and warned you about teenage boys. OK I think you're well informed and reasonably streetwise.

1952 - 1953

There was a hiatus in my career when Helen and I moved to St. Kitts, ostensibly to start a glass business. That never happened.

On New Year's Day 1952 I caught a bad cold that turned into pneumonia. It led into a short hell that lasted approximately three months until Helen and I moved to Niagara Falls. I was employed at Sir Adam Beck, in the underground tunnels of a generating plant. That helped. I discovered who I had become. We moved back to Kingston. I don't think I was much comfort for you Ruby. But oh, so important for me was that I established contact with my brother Edwin and found the respect I had lost for my father.

***

Uncle Les' last journal entry was dated 1953. This is the conclusion of Les's journal. In 1953 Ruby was 18 years old and Les was 29 years of age. Although Les' descriptions evoke more questions for us, what he has written enables us to better understand what those years were like for a large, not so easily blended family when work was scarce, and sickness threatened, and war was disruptive, and everyone was wondering how they might create a satisfying future.

At the end of his journal two more brief statements are written and they are dated Dec. 8, 1996, and Jan. 29, 1997. Les was 68 and 69 years of age when he wrote the final two statements. His beloved sister Ruby died a few weeks before Les wrote the 1996 comment. Here are those statements.

Dec. 8, 1996 – Why am I doing this? It has been how long? Days? Maybe weeks. I am in a trance. I can't go on. My sight is failing. I'll put this away for now."

Jan. 29, 1997 – Intermission is over. I'll continue Ruby's pursuit with some help. Contacted Ruth Knight on the phone. I'll call Karen Pascale. I can see again. What happened?"

This is my own conjecture. The reference to Ruby's 'pursuit' concerned the family information that Ruby was gathering either for her own purposes or for the A.A. Willems family article she was writing to be contained within the book entitled, 'A GOOD LAND' – The History of the A.S. Willems Family in Canada,

1899- 1999.' Willems Reunions were held in 1959, 1980 and 1997. The Willems have been very grateful for the legacies of previous generations.

Ruby died on October 28, 1996.

Les died October 29, 2010, fourteen years after the death of his beloved little sister.

16 MY BOYHOOD, YOUNG ADULTHOOD AND GOD'S CALL

BEFORE I BECAME A MAN, I WAS A BOY. My life is far from extraordinary, and it doesn't warrant an entire book. A chapter or two should suffice to encapsulate the events and express my gratitude for my 81-year journey. I still find it astonishing that the shy, easily embarrassed boy I once was would eventually become the pastor of four congregations and lead a denomination comprising 150 churches in Canada. My original career aspiration was in graphic art and fine art painting, so the only plausible explanation for my path is divine intervention. It was God, the One whom multiple generations of my family served, who influenced me and ultimately redirected my course. Upon retiring, I found fulfillment in painting portraits and landscapes, as well as in writing. Throughout my life, I have experienced a wide spectrum of emotions, including worry, embarrassment, exhilaration, confidence, pleasure, fear, sorrow, and contentment. In these final two chapters, I will tell you why I am grateful for the life I have lived.

EARLY CHILDHOOD IN HEPBURN 1942-1947

Tina Martha Doerksen and Edward Richard Unruh were married on June 12, 1941, at the ages of 22 and 26, respectively. I came into the world on September 13, 1942, just before my father enlisted in the Royal Canadian Air Force. Consider this: my parents had only been married for fourteen months before they found themselves separated by the demands of World War II, a challenging start to their marriage. My dad's military journey took him from Vancouver, BC, to Gananoque, ON, and eventually to Whitehorse, Yukon, all while the war raged on. I can recall that Dad visited during his furloughs, and I recall a gift or two from him. Surprisingly, his absence didn't leave a lasting mark on me. Then, in 1945, when the war finally concluded, Dad returned home to stay, and for me, it simply felt right.

In 1945, following the end of the World War Two, Dad and Mom opened and operated a coffee shop on Hepburn's Main Street. Dad also operated a gas station at the corner. No imagination was used in naming the streets and their names remain the same today. Main Street was the main street running East and West. At the west end of Main was Railway St., so called because, you guessed it – it runs north to south along with the train tracks. The parallel road on the other side of the tracks is called West Railway St. On the west side of the tracks is the grain elevator. My paternal Grandparents, Cornelius and Katharina Unruh lived on West Railway St.

Childhood memories are charming to an eighty-one-year-old me, when the recollections date back to my third, fourth and fifth years of life. My memories of Hepburn are few but vivid. They begin when I was two and three years old. Many of them have converted nicely into children's stories that I have jotted down for my grandchildren, along with illustrations.

All roads in town were dirt roads. I loved visiting Grandma Unruh. From my parents' home on 1st Ave. South, I peddled my bicycle west to Heritage St., crossed the train tracks and turned left along West Railway St. and arrived at Grandma and Grandpa Unruh's house on the right. It was easy. Very little vehicle traffic. One of Grandma's treats for me was a slice of freshly baked bread with melted butter on which she sprinkled white sugar. Highly nutritional. Grandma spoke no English. She wanted to learn. She spoke only the German dialect (Plautdietsch) with which I became familiar. I never learned to use it in speech. Grandma insisted that I speak English to her. It saddens me still that I did not become fluently bi-lingual.

In the tiny town of Hepburn everyone knew me ... well, they knew the Unruhs. I was the small blond-haired Unruh kid. From my tricycle I waved at people on Main Street, through store windows and to drivers in trucks as they passed by. I do recall a few people. I remember Mr. John Sukkau. I called him 'Sooky.' When I was with him, I called him "Barber." That was the man's profession. His house and barn were visible across a large field from our house. From our porch I called, "Sooky." We did this often. He called back and invited me over. There was a grain mill inside his small barn. He sat me on a sack of grain in a corner, out of harm's way. I watched him grind quantities of wheat and other grains. As I watched him, I popped grain kernels in my mouth until they were soft enough to chew. I vividly recall seeing Mrs. Sukke killing chickens. Her name was Mary. One at a time she caught the birds, placed their necks on a wooden block and brought a small axe down on them. The heads would fly off still making squawking sounds. To my amazement one or two chickens ran headless for a few seconds before dropping. That was a childhood shock, but it was a lesson in how rural living was done. I had no idea where roast chicken came from before that. Every visit to Sooky's place was educational.

Prairie economy was bleak. New post-war industries in the east were hiring employees. Prairie families began the exodus either to British Columbia or to Ontario. In 1947 Mom and Dad gathered their belongings and made the ambitious move to Ontario. They chose St. Catharines, in the beautiful Niagara Peninsula with its peach, cherry, and apple orchards and acres of grapes. Mom's mother Marie and stepfather Abraham Willems had already settled in St. Catharines with several of their children, Les, Gladys, Ruth, Esther, and Ruby, all of them teens or older and some of them married.

ST. CATHARINES, ONTARIO 1947-1961

Mom was pregnant with my brother (Murray) when we arrived. I was four and one-half years old. Mom and dad rented a wooden, uninsulated two-room shack on undeveloped Geneva Street for a few hot summer months. Dad found any kind of work to make ends meet. As mom's baby's birth drew nearer, Ed (Edwin) and

Alma Willems graciously arranged for us to stay with them for a few weeks. Edwin was Mom's stepbrother, so he was my uncle. Ed and Alma had a three-year old daughter named Marilyn and Alma was also pregnant. On September 7, 1947, Mom gave birth to a baby boy to whom mom and dad gave the names Murray Dennis. Shortly after Murray's birth, Aunt Alma gave birth to a son who received the name Gerald, Gerry as we came to know him.

On the special day of my brother's birth, September 7, 1947, my father bought me roller skates, the kind that were strapped to a pair of my shoes. We walked to Montebello Park and there on the vast wooden floor of the green and white covered pavilion, I learned to skate as my father watched. We crowned the day with ice cream cones, one of Dad's favourite things to do.

During the first week of Murray's life, Dad rented an apartment for our family. Mom came from the hospital with her infant son, to a new home of our own, a massive three-bedroom apartment on the third floor of an apartment building on St. Paul Street. At ground level was a shop, and we entered a door from the sidewalk to begin our climb up six flights of stairs. Suit cases, boxes, baby carriage, groceries all came arduously up the stairs. Dad had already furnished the apartment with beds and bedding and table and chairs and assorted other furniture, all used or donated by friends and relatives and all of it carted up the never-ending staircases.

I had my fifth birthday on September 13, 1947. For some reason my parents felt it appropriate to gift me with a gold signet ring with the letter 'R' and a small sparkling stone. I loved it. It turned rather easily on my ring finger. I was forever pushing the ring back over my knuckle. Five years old, and old enough for school. It was my kindergarten year. I remember Mom walking with me for several blocks to show me where the school was and to introduce me to my teacher. We walked from St. Paul Street to Welland Avenue. I remember her returning in the afternoon and walking home with me. Just a couple of days of this oversight and once I knew my way, Mom expected me to walk alone. These were long city street blocks with intersections I must cross. Crossing guards were non-existent. No other children walked with me. Coming home one day I noticed some road construction, an excavation, a deep hole with fencing around it and water in the bottom of the hole. Curiosity and childhood are synonymous, and I crowded close enough to inspect the hole, into which my signet ring suddenly slipped from my finger and dropped into the muddy water. I was heartbroken, and I remember considering running away and never returning.

My father was first employed at Ontario Paper Mill in nearby Thorold, then at Thompson Products, pumping out General Motors car parts for the burgeoning North American post war automobile markets. Lastly, he worked at Anthes Imperial (furnace manufacturer) where he remained for well over forty years. I spent the impressionable years of my boyhood and youth in this city. I loved the city. It holds much of my life, memories, graves of loved ones, and still is home to much loved family members.

My Introduction to Church

Being a father must have motivated Dad to consider church attendance. Calvary Church on Lake Street was appealing to Dad. Many attendees were blue-collar factory workers like my dad. And perhaps there was affinity because it was not Mennonite. And perhaps because it was not Mennonite. Many of his new church friends had a Mennonite background yet they were attending this non-Mennonite church. Uncle Ed and Aunt Alma Willems attended the church. So did Ruth and Esther and Ruby. In fact, Grandpa and Grandma Willems also attended the church until they settled into Scott Street Mennonite congregation where the German language was used. Church attendance became a steady feature of my life. I remember two pastors from those earliest years, first Rev. Charles Tourney (founding pastor) and then Rev. Archie McGilvray (a Scotsman with an intriguing accent).

Rosedale Gardens and Grades 1 & 2

Ken Grimwood, the choir director, told Mom and Dad that his father's rental home in Rosedale Gardens was available. Mom and Dad moved us there. I loved that small, detached bungalow with a room of my own, and a back yard and soon, a new black spaniel puppy named Skippy. I spent my first and second grades at Consolidated School on Queenston Rd. I liked my teachers, especially Miss Brown in grade 2. I was teacher's pet, seriously. And I had a girlfriend in grade 2, sort of; kissed her in the cloakroom. Her mom told my mom. Both women had a chuckle.

The school and our home were located near Victoria Lawn Cemetery. The gravesites of both sets of grandparents, Unruhs and Willems are located at that cemetery. To and from school I passed a barn where a man engraved tombstones. I was a curious kid. The man invited me to come in to see how he did his work. Then he asked me whether I went to church. I said yes. He asked, "Do you know this song?" He sang a song I had never heard, but I know it now.

"Jesus wants me for a sunbeam, to shine for him each day. In every way try to please him, at home, at school, at play. A sunbeam, a sunbeam, Jesus wants me for a sunbeam. A sunbeam, a sunbeam, I'll be a sunbeam for him."

Four decades later, when Grandma Marie Willems died, the Willems family asked me to officiate the graveside service in that cemetery. In answer to the tombstone engraver's question, "Yep, I went to church." Though Calvary Church was a thirty-minute drive on Sundays, our family made the trip because that was 'our' church. Dad's work at Anthes Imperial was a long drive too. This house was a pleasant place to raise a family, but it was far from the city core.

Dad, Murray, Ronnie, Mom

10 Clark Street in St. Catharines

Before the start of my third grade in 1950, we moved back into the city to a two-story rental home at 10 Clark Street. Mom and Dad sub-let the second floor to two sisters, Mary Pankratz and Elizabeth Janzen, and Mary's twelve-year-old daughter Betty. I admired these women so much because they survived Stalinist butchery in Russia that had killed their Christian families. I didn't understand such violence, but I saw a result. Mary's left elbow was healed but it had a protruding bone because a communist soldier on horseback smashed her against a stone wall. Why? Because she was a Christian. Yes, that left its mark on me.

The Clark Street house was next to the St. Catharines Transit Barns, a vast maintenance yard for city buses and trains. When those barns were built, rodents found other places to live. Our home was infested with large black rats that burrowed in earthen tunnels in the crawl space under the floors, and sometimes we heard them inside our walls. Previous renters had dealt with the rats by shooting bullets into the walls, noticeably riddled with holes. The back yard had a couple of tall trees, which I loved to climb. I concluded trees were made for climbing.

I now began grade 3 at Central School at the age of eight where Mrs. Robinson was the principal. I had a serious crush on Terry Lynn Emas, and it was mutual. I was even invited to her birthday party. Life felt good. I had friends on Clark Street. Ronnie and Jamie Barr were sons of the minister of the Presbyterian Church at the top of the hill. Eddie McArthy's family across the street had purchased the first television on the block and neighbourhood kids were invited to watch some shows such as Sagebrush Trail and Hopalong Cassidy and Howdy Doody Time. Joey Daniel and his sisters Geraldine and Pat lived around the corner on Raymond Street.

This home was closer to Calvary Church, and closer to Dad's work at Anthes Imperial Canada. Although he did a variety of jobs in the plant, from the foundry to overhead crane operator, most of his forty plus years with that company, he spent on an assembly line screwing small pieces into home furnaces. He was proud that his salary was based on "piece work" because his output meant he earned more than the hourly rate.

This was the pre-TV era and at our Clark Street home we listened to Hockey Night in Canada with Foster Hewett, the Shadow, and Fibber McGee and Molly. I finished grade three at Central School and completed grades four through seven at Robertson School located at the top of Clark Street and around the corner on Church Street.

When Christianity Became Personal for Me

I was ten years old. One Sunday night in 1952 my father attended church by himself. My dad was a good dad. A good man. On a child's scale of 1-10, he was a 10. My Mom had been a professing, baptized everyday Christian since she was a young girl on the Prairies. That night in response to the pastor's public invitation, my Dad put his faith exclusively in Jesus Christ. His decision fascinated me. It caused me to seriously consider what I was doing at church. Those were years when children attended Sunday School that preceded the morning service that they also attended, usually sitting with their parents. Children like me sang every song and listened to every word. No handheld devices to occupy us, other than pencil and paper. Sure, sometimes I was listening but not hearing.

Did you know that cute blonde headed boys steal things? My neighbourhood friends and I were routinely stealing candies from Mr. Yurchuk's corner store. I suspect I was the ringleader. That is, until one evening later in 1952 when my remorse and anxiety overwhelmed me. We had returned from church after Pastor McGilvray preached about sin and punishment and hell. Alone in my bedroom, kneeling by my bed, (that's the posture of contrition we were taught), I said sorry to God. I made a personal commitment to Jesus Christ. I excitedly announced this to my folks. The rest of my life has demonstrated that the childhood faith was authentic. I was ten years old. Now as I write, I am 81 plus.

Church Life

Mom popped a roast into the pressure cooker, and it would be done by the time we came home from church. On summer Sundays our family walked the long, long walk from Clark St. to the Lake Street site of Calvary Church. We were unmistakable churchgoers in our dress clothes. My assembly-line dad in a sweat-stained T-shirt five day a week, walked with shirt and tie and impeccable suit. Come to think of it, Murray and I were also in suits.

Music in the church was typically hymn singing led by one song leader with organ and piano instrumentation, and customarily a special music segment by choir, group, or soloist. Occasionally I was asked to sing a solo. It was easy. I sang with a clear boy soprano voice. Something else. Pastor McGilvray named us, 'The Golden Bells Trio', consisting of Betty Pankratz, Ruby Willems, and Ronnie Unruh. I sang high tenor. These were early lessons in Christian service.

These were also the years at Calvary Church when Christian

Service Brigade (CSB) thrived. With its post WWII military style formation and uniforms, CSB appealed to boys, and I enjoyed the games, was impressed by youthful leaders, and became comfortable with the talks about living for God.

Life Was Like This

St. Catharines was a hockey city, with the St. Catharines Teepees, a farm club for the Chicago Black Hawks. Saturday skating was something I loved at Rex Stimers Arena, many blocks away. I often went there on my own. Unlike today, the freedom of movement for a child was carefree and enjoyable. We walked or cycled everywhere as kids. On my bike, I owned the city; could go anywhere. The city Library was several blocks from home, and I obtained books each week and was an avid reader. Perhaps I learned independence to a degree because doting parents were unheard of. Parents were busily making a living. We knew we were loved. Yet deciding to take clarinet lessons in the summer and attending Youth for Christ meetings on a Saturday night at the St. Catharines Collegiate were choices I made and attended on my own.

I had a cute younger brother, Murray, three years of age, who tried to hang out with me more than I wanted him to do. When I was eleven years old, my youngest brother Neale Bryan was born on October 12, 1953. We lived in the Clark Street home for one more year before moving a few blocks west to James Street where we lived for just two years.

The James Street House

On James Street I was in grade seven. Our home was a newer two-story rental house. I made a new friend across the street. Jimmy Wong was two years older than me. Jimmy and his father operated a laundry in the basement of their tiny home, washing and ironing sheets for hotels. His home was constantly filled with steamy air. Jimmy didn't have a lot of spare time to play but sometimes he came with me to Christian Service Brigade for boys and to Sunday school. I felt I was acting like a missionary. The church informed us about missionaries and when missionaries returned home for a break they often spoke to children's groups. I acquired a downtown paper route for the St. Catharines Standard with fifty deliveries each day. My rolled newspapers were loaded into a large wire carrier on the front of the bike. While riding the bike I became skilled at tossing them accurately onto a house porch to land at the front doors of homes.

The Move to 531 Bunting Rd.

After two years on James Street, Mom and Dad were able to purchase their own home on Bunting Road. It was 1954 and dad was 40 years of age and mom was 36. The house was a modest bungalow that had three bedrooms, one bath, an unfinished basement, a good size yard and a gravel driveway. Despite very modest incomes, Mom and Dad saved enough money for a down payment. The house cost was $10,000 with a down payment of $1000, and a mortgage payment of $100 each month almost to the day that Dad retired, ultimately paying three times the original listed price. After living thirty plus years in this house, Mom and Dad eventually sold it for $67,000.

It was exciting to me to move outside the city to a suburb and the first house of our own. This new home was located between Linwell and Scott Streets and near the Welland Ship Canal and locks one and two. A Great Lakes freighter makes its way between Lakes Erie and Ontario through a system of eight Welland Canal locks. This freshwater shipping system is part of the greater St. Lawrence Seaway containing 16 locks that move a vessel from Lake Superior to the Atlantic Ocean. The elevation change from Lake Superior to sea level is 601 feet (183 m). Each lock can accommodate a 740-foot-long ship. A lock fills with approximately 91 million litres of water (24 million gallons) in 7 to 10 minutes. Lock One was located at Port Weller with its dry docks for shipbuilding and repair, a 20-minute bicycle ride from home. Lock two was closer to our home where Scott Road crossed the canal.

Grandma and Grandpa Willems had also moved from Center Street in downtown St. Catharines (known affectionately as St. Kitts), to 64 Beamer Street, a ten-minute bike ride from our new Bunting Rd. home. I would peddle there frequently. Zweiback, delicious double buns, one small ball on top of the larger roll, were always a reason to go to Grandma's place.

Murray and I celebrated birthdays as we began a new school year in September 1954. Murray was 8 years old in Grade 3 and I was 13 in Grade 8, at Maplewood Public School on the southwest corner of Niagara Street and Linwell Road. Neale was not yet in school. I still had my paper route in the city downtown core. After school each day, I peddled five miles to the city and delivered the fifty newspapers and peddled home. For some years I had been experiencing pains in my lower abdomen. I found I could overcome the pain by doubling over on the ground and pushing into my lower abdomen with my hand. An attack of pain could happen any time of day. Little did I know that I was relieving a hernia that would rupture one day while I delivered papers. It happened on a Saturday. Fortunately, it was on Saturday when my parents drove me around the route in their car. We were planning on going somewhere immediately after I finished the papers. As I hurried from one house to the next, I was stricken by another attack. I knelt on the ground breaking out in a sweat and in great pain. My parents realizing this required attention, rushed me to the hospital where I was surgically repaired. Hernia treatment then was not the one-day, in-and-out and back on your feet variety. I was kept immobile in hospital for two weeks after which I could hardly straighten up or walk.

On most Sundays, Murray and I travelled to Sunday school with Uncle Bill and Aunt Ruth Low and our cousins, Deanna and Doug who lived close to us. My mother and father came to church one hour later. As I grew older, I listened more carefully to sermons. So did Murray. I remember Murray and I returning from church on a Sunday and then role-playing at home in the basement, each of us taking a turn at being the preacher and the audience. I particularly remember a retired missionary named William Pape who was an interim pastor for a short term. His blue eyes and warm voice and charming stories held my interest. Through my teen years I found the teaching of Pastor James Vold to be exceptional. This was all God's ground work in preparing me for something larger than my own plans.

High School Years and God's Call to Me.

I attended grades 9-13 at Grantham High school. Like many youths I found teen years to be fun but mostly disturbing and perplexing. So many predictable body and attitudinal life changes occurred. My voice did not change until I was into my sixteenth year. I sang as a boy soprano in Niagara Music festivals, taking voice lessons from Mr. Arthur Hanneson. Not until I was seventeen, did I make a significant stature sprout, growing several inches in a year. When that happened, the natural speed I had as a child transferred to my growing physique, and I excelled on the track. My highest achievement was being the second leg (runner) of a championship relay team that won numerous races in the 4 X 100 and 4 X 200-yard races in the Southern Ontario Secondary School Association region.

High school class curriculum options were categorized as either academic or commercial, the latter having all the shop classes. I don't know why, but I selected the academic which meant languages, French, Latin, English literature, necessary maths and sciences, and art. I didn't know then that the languages were preparation for a career with words, researching, writing, and speaking. I was not a good student. I knew more about art than my art teacher. I had no idea what I wanted to do with my life, so I focused upon a career in graphic art. That was making sense when I failed grade 12 and had to repeat it. Yet God was always reaching to me in many ways.

I was seventeen years old and in grade eleven when my friend Roger Poirier and I were baptized by immersion in water by Pastor Vold. My mother later related that Pastor Vold told her, "God has his hand on Ron." I was unsure about that, and I couldn't know what it might mean. I was preparing to enroll in the Ontario College of Art (OCA) in Toronto. I knew OCA would challenge my faith and my morality, but I was also becoming serious about my walk with the LORD. When we lacked youth sponsors, Ron Schindel, Linda Poirier, and I ran the youth program for our peers with Bible studies, discussions, and prayer. Ron Schindel and I led meetings at a senior's home each month, taking turns directing singing and preaching. Then a climactic event occurred.

Earlier, I mentioned five missionaries killed by Waorani

(Auca) Indians in Ecuador. The Waorani were also sometimes known as Huaorani, or Waodani, In 1960, four years after the murders, five of my friends and I drove with our Sunday School teacher from St. Catharines to Chicago, to the University of Illinois, the site of the1960 Urbana Conference for young Christian senior high school and college age adults. Our small individual worlds expanded over one weekend as we assembled with 10,000 people in one location. The compelling attraction for me was a movie called 'Through Gates of Splendour.' It told the true story of two courageous women who lived with the Wourhani tribe after the killings. Those women were Rachel Saint (Nate's sister) and Betty Elliott (Jim's wife). As the movie ended, Rachel and Betty and one of the killers, stood right there in person to speak to us about what had been happening in the Waorani community over the past several years. They told us how the Waoranis had been fearful of white people whom they saw only occasionally. The whites whom they confronted were armed employees of oil companies. Indians had died in such encounters. They had become so fearful that they had rejected the missionaries' attempt at friendship. Over time the Waoranis learned that the white missionary women were non-threatening and were peaceful. Elementary communication was replaced with language as both groups learned from one another. The story of God's saving plan and the life of Christ and his purpose was shared. Watching and hearing that story of dedication and faith impacted me. Evangelist Billy Graham preached a powerful message and then appealed to young men and women to step up and fill the gap left by the five martyrs. I was one among thousands who said yes to God for service. For Ron Schindel and me, these were decisions that led to our applications for Bible training. We came home, applied, and were admitted to London College of Bible and Missions (LCBM).

LONDON COLLEGE OF BIBLE AND MISSIONS, LCBM, 1961-1967

During the months before we went to Bible College, I worked as a lineman on locks 1-8 of the Welland Canal, the western section of the St. Lawrence Seaway. I and three other lineman and a lockmaster assisted massive great lakes freighters to enter, to cable-up to pylons, and exit the locks. We handled several ships during each shift. With free time between ships, to play cards or nap, it was enjoyable work, more like recreation.

Ron Schindel and I dated two nurses who began to attend our church. Ron S. was a goner. He loved June Thompson from the first moment he met her. The fall term for the 1961- 62 school year was coming up. Ron owned a 47 Plymouth coupe, and we drove like exhilarated free birds to our new world, or at least our new chapter. In Alloway Men's Residence Ron and I shared a room with two other men. The women's dorm was directly across Queen's Ave. That was of interest to me but not to Ron S. His heart was still back in St. Catharines. Ron and I were somewhat codependent. We both worked in the Simpsons shoe department; did the same Christian service and attended the same church. What we didn't share were good grades. At the end of the year, my grade point average was dismally failing, and I dropped out of school.

In 62-63 I was back in St. Catharines, living with my parents, and working at Commercial Photo Copy. I drove a VW Van to deliver blueprints to architectural firms. I bought a '52 Pontiac coupe. It lasted the year. My Uncle Les Willems gave me his VW Beetle in exchange for a painting I did for him. The painting was a portrait of an elderly Russian woman with a beguiling smile. My salary of $50 per week was not much, but I saved enough money to return to college.

I truly wanted to succeed, and I had decided that I wanted to serve God. I returned in 63-64 and I was introduced to Christine Langlois. My initial interest was put in cold storage because she was popular and was going steady with another student. In that year, I concentrated on academics and found that I could achieve A's and B's instead of D's and F's. By 64-65 I loved my college experience, voice lessons, Choir, good friendships, classes, pin pong, and an afternoon part-time truck driving job. Ron Schindel was married to June Thompson.

The school year 65-66 was even better because I found myself dating Christine, and I loved her … no doubt about it. Holding hands, we walked the snow-covered streets of London at night, after classes and afternoon jobs.

We sang together with Dave And Sharon Gast - a college mixed quartet, doing college promotion by singing Christian music at church functions. I was increasingly comfortable with God's call for me to become a church pastor, and I was becoming a competent communicator.

During the summer of '66 I worked for Eastland Bros. of Niagara Falls. We paved country roads with layers of slurry and gravel. Lorne Eastland drove the slurry truck and I stood on a platform at the rear of the truck with a large wheel that I turned to open and close the spray valves. A gravel spreading machine followed. It was a dirty job. I was dressed in coveralls and cap because the spray came back at me all day long. On hot days, the heat of the large tank of hot oil and from the road and the sun was intolerable. My brother Neale took over for a couple of summers when I moved on.

1967 A Summer To Remember

And the end of the 66-67 school year, I returned to my parents' home in St. Catharines and to a summer job. It was my second summer working for the Eastland Brothers paving.

I was engaged to Christine. I had proposed to her on New Year's Eve 1967 when she visited my family and I during the Christmas break. I drove Christine to Niagara Falls. Snow was on the ground. Coloured lights played across the face of the Falls. I asked her to marry me. We set August 12th as our wedding day. We planned to marry and then to move back to London, rent an apartment and complete our college education. During the summer, while I was in St. Catharines, Christine was living at her family home in Point Claire, Quebec.

On June 6, 1967, when I returned from work at the end of the day, I was surprised to find my Uncle Neale and Aunt Agnes Unruh. They had made a cross Canada car trip from British Columbia. That is so memorable for me since it was only the third time that I had seen Uncle Neale, and it was the last time.

Also, in June I learned that my pastor James Vold was leaving our church, Calvary Church, to move to a congregation in Philadelphia. He was our spiritual shepherd through my teen years. God used his preaching to teach me and to inspire me. He was a man with a remarkable memory. He read several books each week and preached without reference notes.

I was working during the days, preparing in the evenings for a sermon I would preach on June 25. I borrowed a commentary from Pastor Vold on Tuesday June 20, and he told me to keep it, and then told me to come into his study where he proceeded to gift me with scores of books. He loaded my arms with volumes, and I made trip after trip to my car.

Later that evening I had already forgotten about the books for my burgeoning library and was thinking only of Christine. Days passed, and on June 23, Christine travelled by train from Pointe Claire, to visit me. I wrote a note in a diary, "It is 10:30 pm. How does 'thank you' sound? Praise God from whom all blessings flow. Christine comes by train in two hours – my wonderful sweetheart."

The next day, Saturday, the 24th, Christine and I visited a florist, a jeweller and a photographer and made final preparations and arrangements for our wedding. Then on the 25th she sat in church as I preached my sermon to be best of my limited ability and experience. Listening to me preach was something Christine did for decades to follow. How affirming it has been to hear her say long after I was no longer preaching, that she missed the teaching I had provided all those years.

Christine and I were married on Aug 12, 1967, and in '68 Christine graduated with her Bachelor of Sacred Music degree, and I was completing a Bachelor of Theology.

COLLEGE MOVE FROM LONDON TO TORONTO, 68-69

At the conclusion of the 1968 year, Christine graduated with Bachelor of Sacred Music degree. I still had part of one year remaining to complete my degree. We learned that LCBM and Toronto Bible College (TBC) had finalized a merger agreement under a new title, Ontario Bible College (OBC). The kicker for us was that the merge would be located on the Spadina Avenue campus of TBC in Toronto.

Christine and I had a decision to make. A call from Rev. George Bradford, pastor of Park Royal Bible Church (an Associated Gospel Church) in Mississauga helped us to decide to move. In exchange for my pastoral assistance, the church paid for rental of two rooms at Mrs. M. Stoll's home nearby. We would have a place to live.

Christine was pregnant as we made the move to Toronto in August 1968, and our first baby was due in January 1969. We arrived in our '56 Chev with all our possessions loaded into the trunk and rear seat. One of the two upstairs rooms we used as our bedroom, and the other as my study, soon to be a nursery. We were given use of the kitchen to prepare meals and upon rare occasions shared a meal with Mrs. Stoll. The most expensive item we owned was Christine's piano, and Christine taught several students. That income, $30.00 per week purchased my GO-Train and subway tickets to school each day. We had to eat. We marveled at God's provision of other income almost on a weekly basis through thoughtful donors. That entire year was characterized by such charity.

Under the new title, Ontario Bible College, all aspects of the educational experience, from faculty to student body was integrated. Each class year had co-presidents, one from each partner school. I was co-president of the class of '69. That same year my brother Murray enrolled and was in the Freshman class. He had attended Briercrest High School years earlier and then had become an employee at A&P Supermarket in St. Catharines and was being groomed for managerial positions. In Toronto, Murray lived in a rooming house with other students. He was at school for only few weeks when he took an interest in a young woman named Diane Dibbley. Having already studied at LCBM in London, Diane was in her second year of studies. Diane and Murray hit it off and the relationship developed and within a year, on May 30, 1970, she became Mrs. Diane Unruh.

Cari Was Born

On January 14th, 1969, Carinne May Unruh was born at Mississauga General Hospital. I remember taking Christine to the hospital at night and occupying a chair in a waiting room, aptly named, because I was there hour after hour. I was allowed to visit her in labour only occasionally. This was an era when the father was not permitted to stay with his wife or be present through delivery. Early on that morning our doctor stepped into the waiting room doorway holding a pink-blanketed infant girl with fuzzy white hair and deep blue eyes. She was gorgeous. I was overwhelmed to think that Christine and I had produced this wonderful life. My parents visited us in the hospital the next day and I recall my father standing with me proudly peering through the nursery window at a room full of baskets holding babies and seeing our white-haired one, his first grandchild.

Graduation and an Invitation to Pastor a Church

I graduated in the spring of 1969. I was one of two students selected to give a graduate address at the Spring Commencement Ceremonies held at Varsity Arena. A TBC student named Anand Chaudhari, delivered the other testimonial. He later returned to his native India to teach and to found Rajasthan Bible Institute. Unknown to me, some people in attendance, heard me, and passed my name along to their friends, Ken and Frances Maley in Smiths Falls. Their church was searching for a pastor.

Meanwhile, I obtained a job with Sears Canada, driving 24 ft. and 28 ft. box trucks in downtown Toronto. I delivered product from warehouse to the downtown store. Other than the time-consuming commute from Mississauga to Toronto each morning, I enjoyed the job throughout the summer. We also moved from the Stoll residence to a fourth-floor apartment in a high rise building in Mississauga.

In June of 1969 I received a letter inviting me to candidate for the position of pastor of Calvary Bible Church in Smiths Falls.

17 THE TWO OF US IN SERVICE TOGETHER

The Churches That I Served

FROM 1969 TO 2001, I WAS LEAD PASTOR OF FOUR CHURCHES, three in Ontario and one in British Columbia. We forged lasting friendships with thousands of congregants. Serving as the president of the Evangelical Free Church of Canada from 2002 to 2008, was the privilege of a lifetime. I could collaborate with district leaders and 150 congregations spanning six provinces. Mine have been deeply fulfilling years. Always I benefitted from the wisdom, spirituality, and friendship of those with whom I worked. Here are the experiences that define my pastoral journey.

CALVARY BIBLE CHURCH IN SMITHS FALLS, ONTARIO 1969-1974

We were waiting on God for the next step. Meanwhile, in 1969, at age 27, I was driving a Sears truck in Toronto. Christine and I were in a fourth-floor apartment in Mississauga. We were adoring our white-haired infant daughter. I received a letter from Calvary Bible Church in Smiths Falls. The church was asking me to candidate for the pastoral position. Smiths Falls was an unfamiliar town to me. The town had a population of 10,000. It was a six-hour drive from us. There were several churches in town including Presbyterian, Baptist, United, Pentecostal, Salvation Army, Free Methodist, and Anglican. All I knew was that Calvary Bible Church was a member of the Associated Gospel Churches (AGC), the same denomination as my home church in St. Catharines and the church I interned at in Mississauga.

"Don't Go!" AGC President Don Hamilton and AGC General Superintendent Jack Hockney, cautioned me not to go to Smiths Falls. Calvary Bible Church had a troubled history. The men told me, "You will be a lamb going to a slaughter." The church had hired and released three pastors in five years. The reasons were never disclosed to me. It seemed toxic. Nevertheless, in July 1969, Christine and I visited, felt welcomed, and developed a connection with the congregation. We felt a calm conviction that God wanted us to be there. The members approved us and called us to come. Christine and I believed it was God's will. In September 1969, with our infant daughter Cari, Christine and I moved from Mississauga to Smiths Falls. Christine was pregnant with our second child. Our beautiful son Jeffrey was born in February 1970. I had a son. He was beautiful to me. I was so glad for his sage arrival. God gave me a daughter and a son.

Love Them. This was a diverse congregation of 70 people, a few school-aged children, some teenagers, and mostly older adults. Our arrival marked a turning point. The church had grappled with issues caused by strong-willed individuals, but with the guidance of God, Christine and I became examples of respect, Christian kindness, and love. Our youthful energy drew other young adults, and I eagerly embraced a multitude of roles, from Sunday School Bus ministry to preaching, visitation, and even orchestrating an eight-day evangelistic crusade. Christine, equally dedicated, balanced motherhood with leading teenage Pioneer Girls, typing and printing the church bulletin, leading an occasional choir, and teaching piano students for a little extra income. The church flourished, growing to 120 worshippers, and tripling Sunday School attendance to 180.

Evangelism. Besides my expected pastoral duties, I wanted to mobilize and equip people to share their faith with others. I attended training sessions with Evangelism Explosion and Campus Crusade For Christ. I then selected two elders, Ken Maley and Clarence (Rick) Richey to visit people together with me. The Lord honoured our efforts immediately. Jack and Joan Mandeville were the first couple whom we visited. They put their trust in Jesus Christ after two visits with us and became stalwarts in the church. Mac and Nancy Davies' three daughters attended Pioneer Girls. We arranged to visit the parents. The diagnostic question "Why should God let you into his heaven?" evoked this response from Mac. "God shouldn't let me into heaven. I'm too wicked a man." That was like an open door for me. I explained God's loving plan for personal salvation, and both Nancy and Mac prayed to receive God's forgiveness and to become followers of Christ. Mac and Nancy and the three girls were baptized in following weeks. Donnie and Chloe McCracken had a nominal church background but were not attending church anywhere. Our clear presentation of the gospel was something they had not heard before and after a few visits, they made a genuine commitment to Christ and were baptized as believers.

The principle of training two who each would train two more sounded promising but one of the faults of my youthful zeal was impatience. After six months my two colleagues did not feel ready to train two others, so I gave up on the program. Only much later did I learn how disappointed these men were about this decision. That half year of visitation had been one of the highlights of their spiritual lives. Reflecting on these efforts, I learned patience but realized the absence of systematic discipling follow-up for those making commitments to Christ. I lacked the time and strength for more. Regrettably, some who made life decisions fell away due to the absence of proper spiritual grounding. Although a full-time pastor in every other sense of the term I was also a youth pastor by choice because I saw so much potential in young lives. I loved the young people of this church. Because I was young and energetic, I met with them weekly, and I took them to every youth rally and function available to us.

Prayer. At our prayer gatherings in that church several names of relatives were recurrent. I challenged our people to covenant to pray specifically for the salvation of four men, two were husbands of two of our church members; another was a brother, yet another was a son. Over the course of one year, we saw three of these men come to Christ one by one through different circumstances. The fourth, a husband, resisted the Gospel.

The Record News

Very soon after arriving in Smiths Falls, I noticed that the town newspaper had one religious column in its weekly publication. It was written by a United Church writer in Toronto and didn't reflect the view of many town citizens. I walked into the publisher's office to tell him I would write a better piece. That began my weekly column called 'To The Point,' that ran each week for the five years I was there. It was marvellous discipline for me, and it kept me current and developed my writing habit.

Charlie Paul. Charlie, now with the Lord, had been a hotheaded irritant but became my right-hand man. Something I had done during the week annoyed him. Following the next Sunday church service, he delivered a stinging insult to me and left. That might have become a large problem. I was shocked and worried. This became a teaching moment for Charlie and me. David selected five smooth stones to go to battle against Goliath. I found five suitable Bible passages to speak brotherly love to Charlie. At Charlie's home, I asked him to sit with me in my car. With his permission, as I read the verses, Charlie's anger disappeared into tenderness. He admitted his action had been unkind and he apologized to me. We became a productive duo. I cherish the memory of Charlie Paul's comment at the Elders' meeting on the night that I submitted my resignation. He said, "We are sorry to see you go Ron. You have taught us how to love." Several years passed. I lived in Peterborough. Charlie still resided in Smiths Falls. I had begun a Master's program in Toronto and was sitting in class one afternoon when to my astonishment, Charlie Paul entered and sat beside me one Monday in 1976. He took in the lecture, and we spent hours later catching up with one another's lives. Charlie had cancer and had little time left. He had driven for six hours to say farewell to me, and then to drive home again. His love and our connection has blessed me at every recollection.

The Smiths Falls church received good return on the eighty-five dollars per week stipend that we were paid. After five years of tireless effort, we decided to embark on a new pastoral journey, leaving behind a congregation reinvigorated with hope and joy, forever grateful for the transformative impact of our time there.

FERNDALE BIBLE CHURCH, PETERBOROUGH
1974-1981

Peterborough, Ontario is a charming, medium size city. Trent University, Eastern Pentecostal Bible School, and many thriving companies were located there. Ferndale Bible Church enjoyed a good reputation within the city and within the Association of Gospel churches (AGC) of which it was member. Two pastors whom I respected, Rev. Carl Crate and Rev. Carl Friedrich, preceded me at Ferndale Bible Church and owned distinguished ministries there. Christine and I welcomed the invitation from members of Ferndale Bible Church, for me to become their pastor.

A board of Elders consisting of a pastor and four lay elders led the church. It was a vibrant, contented, and growing congregation of 150 people in a relatively new church building that had a seating capacity of 200 people. The basement had four large rooms and a kitchen suitable for social events, and for programmes for children and youth as well as adults. There were many young families, and young families were added during our early years. Our children Carinne and Jeffrey were five and four years of age as we arrived. This church was the right place for our own children. There were many school age children. Our family fit well. Across a gravel parking lot, a parsonage on a large lot became our family home for seven years. Both buildings are in a residential neighbourhood. Cari and Jeff attended a local public school. Christine was devoted to Cari and Jeff, and these were important developmental years for our children.

Ferndale Bible church was financially sound. My salary was satisfactory. Christine and I found ourselves part of a young congregation with an eagerness to experiment with methods and enjoy a community of believers. Ministry was fun. Christine's musical training and ability was needed and appreciated. She organized Sunday worship music and led the church choir.

Of the four churches that I have pastored, this was the only church of the four that had an untroubled recent history. Nonetheless, my peace-making proficiency was tested early with a deacon who angrily left a Deacon's meeting one night. Following the meeting I drove to the deacon's home. As I had done with Charlie Paul in my first church, I had five carefully chosen scripture passages. I was as confident as Old Testament David with his five smooth stones going out to meet Goliath. I invited my friend into my car to talk. We talked for a long time, resolving nothing until I asked his permission to read the Word of God. Again, I witnessed the authority and power of the Word of God. As I read, my friend wept, and the defenses came down. This enthusiastic deacon and I became co-workers and good friends.

Making Disciples. It was at this church that I learned disciple-making skills. I discovered that one on one discipleship takes an investment of time and one's own heart. Some cases stand out as examples of the joy I experienced.

Gary Welch was not a Christian when I met him. His home was located directly across the street from the church and the parsonage. His wife Lynn and three children were attending church, but he held back. I remember some Sunday mornings when Gary sat on the steps of his home, cigarette in one hand and a can of beer in the other. We became casual friends. As we spent time together, Gary asked serious questions and eventually asked Christ into his life. He started to attend church. He agreed to meet with me each Thursday morning for three years for study and prayer. He grew. He changed. He overcame. He made mistakes and grew further. I remember him rejoicing when he successfully stopped smoking. His spiritual growth was evident to others as he was elected to the elders' board and then to chairing it. He led his father to Christ before the man died. Such was Gary's growth.

I recall **Jim and Vicki Baldry**. Vicki was a Christian believer and a regular church attendee. Jim was a holdout. At an adult social function, Jim and I became acquainted. We sat together and chatted. I sensed his interest in spiritual things but also his reluctance to get involved with church. He agreed to have me come to his home to answer his questions. On my second Tuesday night visit, I showed him from scripture how he could know the forgiveness of his sins and the assurance of eternal life. Jim knelt with me by his living room sofa and invited Christ to be his Saviour. He stood up and excitedly said, "It feels like I've taken off a heavy coat." His enthusiasm was immediate and sweeping. He hurriedly called his brother Steve and his mother and told them what he had done moments earlier. Within two weeks he had witnessed to his family, leading his mother, his brother Steve, and Mary, Steve's girlfriend to trust in Christ. I began a lengthy follow-up study with Jim. He was employed as a hospital nurse, but he became restless and briefly moved into financial planning. Then, he felt that God wanted he and Becky to go to Briercrest Bible Institute for Bible training. Jim graduated and was hired by BBI, eventually becoming its Dean of Students. His brother Steve also went for theological training and became the senior pastor of the celebrated Philpot Memorial Church (AGC) in Hamilton, Ontario, and then Chedoke Presbyterian Church, and currently MacNab Presbyterian Church in Hamilton.

Richard and Anne Kinch lived directly across the street from the parsonage. Anne was a schoolteacher and Richard was a rising young executive with Ethicon, a Johnson and Johnson subsidiary. They were young, friendly, open, and impressionable. They did not attend church anywhere. In fact, they never did come to our church. We were in each other's homes, shared meals and evenings of conversation and day trip excursions. Richard and Anne admired the way we raised our two children, Cari and Jeffrey. When their first son was born, they named him Jeffrey. Christine babysat Jeffrey for two years. Then a daughter was born, and she was named Shannon Christine, as a tribute to my wife. We did not aggressively witness to Rich and Anne. We built relational bridges. It was easy. They are so likeable. Then in our last few months at the church and in the community, we had a weekly Bible study with Ann and Rich. We left Peterborough uncertain of their spiritual status. But good seed had fallen on good ground. Many months later, Anne wrote to Christine to let her know that she had accepted Christ as her Saviour. They both became active in a United Church in their community (The United Church in Canada is of Methodist heritage). Upon their retirement from their careers, both invested themselves in an exciting ministry that was Anne's brainchild. 'Our Children Africa – Emancipation through Education' is a Canadian organization supporting children in Ghana. It provides access to free quality Africentric education with emphasis on literacy, leadership development, and reproductive health education. This is effectively helping to remove barriers so that they can escape the cycle of poverty and reaching their full potential. https://ourchildrenafrica.com

I met **Don MacMullen** at a Toronto Blue Jays baseball game. I was doing a summer master's level course in Toronto. My friend George Bradford was also enrolled. Eric Hartlen, a member of George's church, invited us to a Blue Jays game. Eric and Don were already seated when we arrived. In recent months Eric had been sharing his faith with Don. As God would have it, Don lived and worked in the city of Peterborough where I pastored. Following my study week Don and I began to have coffee regularly. He was a hungry reader and he was reading the Bible when he started attending our church and meeting with me to discuss his questions and concerns about Christianity. Then one Sunday morning he prayed to receive Jesus Christ as His Lord and Saviour. A successful K-Mart store manager, Don gave up his career to go to Bible college. Upon completion of his studies, he went for a short-term overseas mission trip, met the young woman who became his wife and settled back into the business world. He earned an MBA, became a highly successful business owner and publisher, and an influential witness for Christ for many years.

This and That
Cluster Headaches was the diagnosis I finally received for crippling headaches I endured since childhood. In Peterborough they intensified in frequency and strength. pain. Sufferers call them 'suicide headaches.' I wanted to die. They are rapid onset, ripping pain in one eye and side of head, every day for many hours, for weeks at a time. There was no cure, but some relief from Chiropractics.

Ecuador. Our college friends, musicians Dave and Sharon Gast were missionaries in Ecuador working at radio station HCJB (Heralding Christ Jesus' Blessings). Years before, the four of us sang as a group. Chas Fisher, a Christian businessman surprised us one day. He was a board member of the mission, and he sponsored our family to travel to Ecuador for a two-week ministry trip. Hosted by Dave and Sharon, the four of us had recording sessions at the radio station, sang in local churches, and travelling to numerous missionary settlements.

Master of Divinity. I began and completed 5 years of studies at Ontario Theological Seminary in Toronto. This was done through attendance at all day Monday classes and two-week summer courses, and numerous research papers. In the spring of 1980, I graduated with my Master of Divinity degree and was asked to give my testimony, soft valedictorian speech. Gordon Johnson, chairman of the Board of Ontario College and Seminary was present and heard me. That was important.

The congregation was healthy, and the attendance increased from 120 Sunday worshipper to 200. There was no reason for a significant adjustment, but sometimes you never cannot anticipate events.

Two Jobs that We Turned Down.

I Didn't Become Director of Pastoral Studies, Ontario Bible College

In 1975, while at Ferndale, I joined the M.Div. program at Ontario Theological Seminary, the graduate division of Ontario Bible College in Toronto. The program required Monday in-person classes and a two-week session each summer for five years, which I completed by the spring of 1980. Meanwhile, I was invited to direct the Pastoral Studies Department by the Board and faculty of Ontario Bible College. I underwent meetings with the search committee, board members, and faculty, and received the formal invitation from Dr. Victor Adrian, the college president. However, there were challenges. The salary offered wasn't enough for us to live near the school in Toronto. It necessitated residing north of the city in an apartment, which we were not keen about. Despite feeling prepared for the role and desiring to work with the next generation, the financial constraints posed a concern. We decided to pray over the decision for two weeks. After conversations with faculty members and sensing tension between the faculty and administration, we chose not to accept the position. We concluded that remaining in pastoral work was where God intended us to be, leaving the future in God's hands. We were unaware that Toronto would be in our future. God would handle the details.

We didn't go to Alaska.

How different life might have been if Christine and I had accepted the opportunity in Glenallen, Alaska. In the summer of 1980, Phil Armstrong, previously with Far Eastern Gospel Crusade (FEGC), visited us, extending a three-part role involving pastoral work, part-time Bible instruction, and a radio talk show host position. Christine would have been engaged in music instruction across church, school, and radio. While my son Jeff welcomed the idea, my daughter Cari wasn't enthusiastic about the potential move. Their approaching teen years influenced our decision. Despite the honor in the invitation, after careful consideration, we declined.

The Decision to Leave Peterborough

Yet, unexpectedly, we relocated to Toronto after seven years in Peterborough. During Fairhaven's Bible Conference, where Christine provided music, I stayed back in Peterborough. One evening, I noticed four cars parked in the church lot, all belonging to our lay elders. Investigating, I found them discussing, to my surprise, the possibility of my resignation without any formal review. Their decisions appeared influenced by a new, highly influential elder on the board. Despite the shock, I remained composed and calmly stated our intention to seek God's guidance for our next steps. I then informed Christine and assured her not to worry. Remarkably, the very next morning, Gordon Johnson from Wishing Well Acres Baptist Church contacted me, inviting our consideration of the lead pastor position at their 300-member church. It was a reassuring sign, and I eagerly informed Christine about how God was guiding our path.

I preached and was interviewed at WWABC, then was called to be lead pastor, affirming God's call to continue pastoring. We remembered the Lord's guidance to live in Toronto, and we accepted the invitation, arriving in October 1981.

In September 1981, we received the shocking news of our friend Phil Armstrong's tragic plane crash off the coast of Alaska, resulting in the loss of all lives on board. Phil, a well-known and respected figure in the international missions community, was 62 years old.

We fondly recall church retreats, choir concerts, New Year's Eve events, and the love and warmth of the people who enriched our lives. Our lives were enriched by this congregation's love and guidance.

One unforgettable Church Anniversary Sunday stands out, when the Ferndale congregation invited Christine and me for a special evening. I preached, Christine and I sang, and people expressed their appreciation for our years with them. It was a humbling and touching experience.

WISHING WELL ACRES BAPTIST CHURCH, 1981-1991

Upon my arrival in 1981, Wishing Well Acres Baptist Church (WWABC) in Agincourt, North Toronto, was approaching its twenty-fifth anniversary. The church represented Agincourt's multi-ethnic community, with most attendees being Caucasian, 15% Asian, and 15% from the Caribbean Islands. The congregation spanned a broad economic spectrum, from tradespeople to executives, and included both affluent members and those relying on our church food bank. It featured a diverse age range, including seniors, working adults, young adults, students, and children. The church held conservative, Calvinistic, Baptistic beliefs, treasured its history, embraced traditional hymns, and was cautious of modernity.

WWABC stood as a flagship congregation within the Fellowship of Evangelical Baptists in Canada (FEBC) due to its founder and pastor, Dr. Will Whitcombe. Dr. Whitcombe, an educated and visionary leader who had been associated with Dr. T.T. Shields of Jarvis Street Baptist Church, initiated this congregation in 1956 while he was a professor at Central Baptist Seminary. The church, situated on Sheppard Avenue and named after the nearby Wishing Well Acres community, expanded steadily. With time, the church grew, acquiring additional properties and constructing a building with a sanctuary for 400, a gymnasium, a kitchen, classrooms in the basement, staff offices, and housing for returning missionary families.

Dr. Whitcombe led the congregation for two decades until his retirement. He was succeeded by Rev. Gordon Heath from Scotland, along with his wife Greta. Adjusting to Canadian life proved challenging for the Heaths, and after three years, Gordon resigned, and they returned to Scotland to pastor a church and be with their family. Although this decision surprised WWABC, the church quickly moved forward with capable leaders. Rev. Gordon Rendle, an experienced pastor in his sixties, served as the associate pastor, while his wife Helen, an exceptional women's Bible study leader, offered valuable contributions.

At the age of thirty-nine in 1981, I took on the role of senior pastor, tasked with revitalizing the congregation following the unexpected departure of the previous pastor. Dr. Whitcombe, the founder, and former pastor, met with me several times, seeking to understand my approach, beliefs, and vision for the church he held dear. His inquiries were not intrusive but rather a reflection of his affection for the church and its people. I welcomed the interactions, and I believe he found comfort in the continued well-being of the church he had nurtured over the years.

Our First Home Purchase

For twelve years, we lived in parsonages without home equity. Only in our last four years at Ferndale did the church contribute to a housing fund. Moving to Toronto offered an opportunity for home ownership, despite high bank loan interest rates exceeding 18%. With a $25,000 loan from the church and mortgages arranged by our real estate agent, Ian Griffiths, son of Dr. Gerald and Kitty Griffiths from Calvary Church (AGC), we could make our dream of owning a home a reality. The loans came with 14.5% and 15% interest rates. Ian wisely advised us to maintain our initial monthly payments even after rates dropped during renegotiations, allowing us to clear our debts quickly.

After exploring various houses, we found a suitable one at 11 Foxhill Rd. It was a solid brick, twenty-year-old three-bedroom bungalow located two blocks from the church. Jeff was excited about the possibility of renovating the house, as he was keen to help. With Cari at 12 and Jeff at 11, this move was favorable for their transition into their teen years. They quickly made friends through various church programs, including Pioneer Girls, Christian Service Brigade, Sunday School, and Youth programs. Don and Sandy Symons and Steve and Debbie Poole served as lay sponsors for the Youth program, providing guidance and support to the young people. Cari and Jeff, along with their friends, formed a supportive community that lasted from pre-teen years through college age, fostering a close-knit group.

My Work and My Colleagues

Rev. Gordon Rendle, my gracious colleague, a gentle, prayerful veteran in his early sixties, managed congregational visitation. Our ten-year partnership in service was harmonious. Within a year, the Deacons Board conducted an audit, noting that my forthcoming decade held prime performance potential, shaping the church's vision. In 1982, we added Mark Jaynes as the third pastor, responsible for leading young adults, youth, and Christian education. Mark's remarkable 41-year tenure stands out as an enduring feat. At nearly 100 years old, Rev. Gord Rendle remains a cherished figure.

My roles included visitation, counseling, weddings, funerals, and administration, providing a platform to enhance my organizational and leadership skills with multiple staff. Guiding a large city church taught me diplomacy, peacemaking, and nurturing young adults to become leaders. Officiating numerous weddings allowed me to witness their lives unfold, especially through glimpses on Facebook.

Preaching was my primary focus at WWABC, nurturing me into an effective communicator of God's Word. The congregation embraced expository preaching, valuing my approach in teaching the purpose and content of biblical books, aiming to let the voice of God resonate through the ancient texts.

I led two Sunday services and a Wednesday Bible study. I had a book allowance and access to seminary libraries, purchasing commentaries every quarter to plan my sermons. I often visited the Reformation Book Store. Each September, I spent a week alone at the Johnsons' cottage to read, pray, and plan sermons. Christine would join me for a weekend. This routine helped prepare my preaching schedule for the following year, ensuring I lived up to the commendation of Rev. Bob Holmes, a church member. During this time, I occasionally lectured on homiletics at Ontario Bible College.

Once again Christine stepped forward to oversee music ministry in the church. The church had a Sunday choir and a director. When the director decided to take a break, Christine became worship leader and choir director. Her leadership skill enhanced the effectiveness of music allied with the teaching theme.

I found encouragement in the retired ministry veterans at WWABC. Their mentorship through examples, conversations, and gentle counsel was invaluable. Rev. Bob Holmes, a retired pastor, offered his wisdom, as did 80-something-year-old Rev. Syd Kerr, who still preached at times. Dr. Roy Lawson, then the General Secretary of the Fellowship of Evangelical Baptist Churches in Canada, attended the church. Rev. Jim and Anna Rendle were members. Jim taught at Central Baptist Seminary and pastored various churches, including Glencairn Baptist in London where Christine attended during her college years.

Great Friends and Sad Happenings

At WWABC, strong and lasting friendships were formed. Marguerite Davies, chair of the international Missions program, and her husband Keith, a deacon, visited us after three decades, just one of many friends to stay in our B.C. home. Gordon and Ruth Johnson were among those who cared deeply for us, especially Ruth, who became a close confidante to Christine. Our home was open to many church friends who reciprocated the hospitality. I recall meetings with the Deacons' Board chairs: Gord Johnson, Ron and Vi Hartwick, Jim and Elsa Breadner, Dave and Ann Eastwood. Each month, I discussed and planned with one of them, usually over lunch.

Moments of sorrow and growth are etched in memory. The drowning death of Jim Wilson, Eunice Burry's passing when she left behind a grieving family. Praying for Andy Mann before he passed remains somber recollections. On a Sunday, informing the congregation of 21-year-old Drew Mann's tragic vehicle accident that occurred during the hour that we were in church. I recall heartfelt discussions with Jim Kernohan about his daughter Lorrie's blindness, a source of profound anguish for him. These experiences offered poignant insights and life lessons for me.

A Crash, Mine

For the first seven years of my term the church was well attended with 400 Sunday morning attendees and 200 at night. that plans for expansion emerged. With no room to spare, plans for expansion emerged seven years into my term. We raised $200,000 in cash and notes for the project. Yet, obtaining city approval for the 240-seat addition took two grueling years, while construction costs doubled. With the approval, a crucial business meeting was held but faced challenges. Scheduled in the summer, the meeting coincided with many members' vacations. Older members on fixed incomes were apprehensive about the now $350,000 project costs. The seniors were in the majority. The approval failed. The setback was more emotionally shattering than I anticipated. I had never experienced an internal response like this. It revealed the depth of my investment in the church's future. Seeking guidance, I turned to Dr. Roy Lawson who suggested taking three months off. Despite the sound advice, I resisted because I viewed it as a sign of weakness. However, my emotional turmoil was undeniable. During a particularly challenging Sunday service, I walked home overwhelmed with fear and anxiety. I confided in Christine, expressing my reluctance to return. Dave Eastwood, the Deacon chairperson, arranged a meeting with the deacons, and the outcome was a three-month leave. I was emotionally fragile. No one is ever ready for this vulnerability.

During the quiet weeks, I received inquiries from various churches, a surprising turn. Reflecting with Christine, we realized my work at Wishing Well Acres Baptist Church was complete and that the disappointment may have been a nudge to consider leaving the church I cherished. Cloverdale Baptist Church was the first of five to reach out. I have a policy to address churches in the order of their queries. We visited Cloverdale, spent a week engaging with the congregation, preaching, and conversing. Following that visit, an invitation to lead emerged. Wishing Well Acres Baptist Church allowed me to conclude my tenure well, with two months of pastoral duties and then a gave our family a heartfelt farewell evening.

The idea of a daring new start in British Columbia at age forty-nine held allure. Leaving Toronto meant departing from deep connections, family, and a lifetime of educational and ministry experiences. I could only justify the impact that such a move could have upon my own family and extended family as well as upon myself, by trusting that God was doing something in which I was to play a significant role. All that God has invested in Christine and me, was for such a time as this. I didn't want to overlook what might be an important opportunity.

CLOVERDALE BAPTIST CHURCH 1991-2001

I REMEMBER ASKING MY FATHER FOR HIS THOUGHTS ON OUR DECISION.

Christine and I considered the enormity of this cross country move across four provinces. At 48 and 49, we sought this new adventure and B.C. was intriguing. However, our parents were still alive, and we were leaving them. It was uncertain when or if we would return. We were leaving our siblings and their families. That would forever be the downside. Special occasions like birthdays, Thanksgiving, and Christmas would never be the large family gatherings to which we were accustomed. We pondered where our children might choose to settle after their graduations. My father, at 78, quietly said, "If God has called you, then you must go." His words brought a sense of release. We journeyed into an unknown chapter with a congregation we hardly knew.

The New Chapter Began This Way

Bob and David Dobson were our college friends. We had no contact with them for two decades. David was pastoring Ladner Baptist Church in B.C. In 1989, Bob and Donna Dobson, along with their two children, and later, Bob's parents Ron and Lillian Dobson, relocated to Cloverdale. Bob left his position at the Toronto Board of Education to assist Dr. Doug Harris at Northwest Baptist College. When Bob and Donna joined Cloverdale Baptist Church, it was facing challenges, but the congregation remained hopeful and open to new vision. Within two years, Bob was elected as an elder and tasked with chairing the Pastoral Search Committee.

In spring of 1991, Christine and I attended a Fellowship Baptist Church Convention in Winnipeg. We were delegates for Wishing Well Acres Baptist Church. Also attending were Bob Dobson and Dave Heppell from Cloverdale Baptist Church. They were seeking potential candidates for their church. After speaking with General Secretary Roy Lawson, the men were recommended to consider me. They approached us and explained the church's recent troubled history and its need for a senior pastor who would provide sound teaching, stability, and healing.

Following the conference, Christine and I earnestly pondered the life-changing prospect. Feeling a sense of peace, we decided I should pursue the opportunity. We journeyed to B.C., spending a week in Cloverdale. We felt it crucial to include our children, Jeff and Cari, in discussions about the move. Jeff, already at Trinity Western University, adored British Columbia. Cari, in Winnipeg, was involved in a music program. When she joined us, we had a significant evening of prayerful conversation about the potential shift to the West.

During the candidating week, Christine and I attended various functions, engaged with groups and individuals, fielded questions, spoke at a large banquet, and delivered a Sunday sermon. Upon returning to Toronto, we were content with what we had achieved during our week in the West. Within two weeks, I received a phone call conveying the congregation's invitation, which I accepted.

1991. Buy and Sell. The Dream House.

Christine prayed that our house at 11 Foxhill Rd., Agincourt, would sell within one week. God answered that prayer even though other homes on the street were listed for several months. We flew to Cloverdale, B.C., to house shop, looking at several areas and house styles. Located only five minutes from the church, we purchased the house of our dreams. It was a one-year-old 2750 sq./ft. two-story home with a detached double garage on a one third of an acre lot. It was spacious and perfectly accommodated large gatherings. We flew home and prepared for our move.

With our possessions in a van already en route, we left Agincourt, Ontario to Cloverdale, British Columbia at the end of summer 1991. We came to this wonderful house that I dubbed the Rose House because of the stained glass rose insert in the front door, and subsequently, the large bed of roses that Cari and I planted and that flourished for years. The house served us so well as a family home for twenty years. It was the home into which our newborn grandchildren came and where we enjoyed their early years.

Where on Earth Were We?

The lower mainland region of B.C. covers the southwest corner of British Columbia and serves over 60% of the provincial population. This area includes Greater Vancouver, coastal and valley rural areas with diverse environmental and economic opportunities. Cloverdale, situated twenty-five miles southeast of Vancouver in the Fraser Valley of British Columbia, is now part of the Surrey city. While traditionally seen as agriculturally based, it was evolving with the emergence of businesses in industrial areas. Trinity Western University is located in Langley, and Cloverdale Baptist Church is at the eastern end of Surrey, bordering Langley.

The Church Started as a Prayer

Cloverdale Baptist Church originated as a prayer request turned into reality. It evolved from a home Bible study and soon saw a surge in participants, fostering the idea of establishing a Bible-based church in Cloverdale. In 1929, several families commenced worship services in the Liberal Hall, led by local pastors. The Home Missions Committee of the Regular Baptists proposed that the group affiliate with them. By March 10, 1931, the group of twenty-two members was officially recognized as a Baptist congregation. That year, they acquired a city lot and constructed a church, actively engaging with the community, visiting homes, and extending invitations that welcomed new believers.

The Church Continued to Grow

In 1961, with increased membership and resources, the congregation acquired one acre of land at 17400-60th Avenue. A new church facility was constructed and dedicated to the Lord on October 11, 1962. By 1972, with a membership of 171, classroom additions were completed to accommodate the expanding Sunday school, coinciding with the era of bus ministries that brought children to the church.

Twenty years passed and in August 1981 the congregation moved to the 12.8-acre site on 64 Avenue and constructed a new 22,500 sq. ft. building and parking lot on a five-acre footprint. This church included an auditorium seating 550-600 people, a gymnasium, Christian education facilities, a smaller chapel/fellowship room and a kitchen. Seven acres remained unoccupied. By the late 1980's Sunday morning worship attendance filled the auditorium to capacity and the whole multi-age enterprise was enthusiastic and energetic. Then suddenly it wasn't.

Conflict Occurred.

Sometimes the Christian Church itself becomes the arena where the timeless contest between evil and good occurs. I have witnessed this myself. It's disheartening. Yet, if the Church is the mainstay of truth-telling about redemption and liberation from evil, it's easily comprehensible that evil will assault the church, either from outside or the inside. It was insidious how this happened to Cloverdale Baptist Church in the 1980s.

During the 1980s the church was a vibrant ministry centre with valued activities for all ages. With a full-time pastoral team consisting of three pastors, Rev. Michael Brown served as senior pastor. He had established a reputation as a good and gentle leader and a praiseworthy preacher. The large church auditorium was constantly filled with 550 eager Sunday worshippers.

At times, Christian churches that preach deliverance from evil become arenas for the struggle between good and evil, a scenario I've witnessed personally, and it's disheartening. Sometimes, these conflicts arise from within, not outside. Cloverdale Baptist Church faced such a divisive battle three years before Christine and I arrived. The Vineyard Movement, an evangelical neocharismatic renewal movement, gained influence in the region, creating tension in various churches, including Cloverdale Baptist. The conflict centered around the use of charismatic practices, particularly speaking in tongues, causing a rift between charismatic and non-charismatic factions. The progressive, young charismatics were proselytizing aggressively, alarming the more conservative, non-charismatic members who feared the church's potential transformation.

For months, Pastor Brown attempted to reconcile opposing beliefs within the congregation. His conciliatory approach eroded confidence in him, especially amid his wife's cancer battle and with all his children in their teens. This led to his resignation in 1989. Meanwhile, Pastor Wasyliw, with his gentle demeanor, worked to comfort the fractured community. Eventually, bewildered and disappointed, many left the church, resulting in the departure of half the congregation.

Christine and I Arrived and We Began.

On our first Sunday in autumn 1991, roughly 200 people, a fraction of the congregation after the earlier split, gathered in the 500-seat auditorium. It felt noticeably empty. After the service, we discovered the worship leader had accepted another job. Christine stepped up, leveraging her musical expertise to lead worship from the second Sunday. She retained this role for our entire ten-year tenure, recruiting, training vocalists and musicians, and starting a School of Music. In 1994, she established this music school, offering week-day lessons by seven teachers of various instruments. Christine was also involved in the Music Leaders Fellowship, a network providing support and guidance to worship leaders of Fellowship Baptist churches across the provinces. The Lord blessed us for a long time.

I Loved What We Were Doing

Sunday March 15, 1992, six months after our arrival, was the tenth anniversary of the 64th Ave. church building. Original charter members Helmut and Emily Seiler represented the congregation as they put a match to the mortgage certificate for the building. This was a symbolic gesture indicating the full payment of that debt, and everyone then praised God for his faithfulness in helping this congregation achieve this objective.

Together with the pastoral team, elders, deacons, and volunteer workers, we built relationships, firmed up our mission and reignited vision. Dennis Wasyliw was Associate Pastor and Rod Heppell was our Youth Pastor. Tom Fairgrieve was our pastor to seniors. Church life was filled with a Daycare program, a School of Music, a Skate Church to reach youth, a highly effective youth program, High Power Soccer camps in the community, a Seniors program, a young adult worship service called Lampstand, and a growing Sunday attendance. Within 18 months the fractured congregation of 250 became 400 people, and in 24 months (1993), 500 people. Soon the auditorium was tightly accommodating almost 600 worshippers. Early in my ministry at Cloverdale, I enrolled in a Doctor of Ministry program with Trinity Evangelical Divinity School in Chicago, Fortunately for me, many professors came to Trinity Western University to lecture which saved me so much money. For a six-year period, my elders allowed me to develop disciple making throughout our church programming and that well documented effort became my D.Min. project which culminated in 1998. During these years, Dennis Wasyliw resigned, and Bob Dobson was hired as Associate Pastor. Rod Heppell married Anne and they became missionaries. Jack Ninaber became youth pastor. We became a solid team. I submitted my dissertation in 1998, flew to Chicago to defend it, and graduate with a Doctor on Ministry degree in 1998. I also served as Pres of the region for Fellowship of Evangelical Baptist Churches of BC and Yukon for four years and was an adjunct prof at Northwest Baptist College. Christine was adjunct prof in music at NWBC at the same time.

A full house and creative people of faith birthed two initiatives. First, in 1995 the launch of a new congregation in Murrayville. Second, a proposal for a new sanctuary seating 1200 people to be added to the existing building using the courtyard as a large glass-topped lobby. Concurrent with that, the remaining seven acres were to be invested with three, three-story saleable multi-unit condominium buildings and one subsidized apartment building. A large park accessible to the entire surrounding community would centre all of this. That proposal remained in the planning stage for a long time.

We launched a new church.

Cloverdale Baptist Church had a history of planting daughter churches, a robust characteristic of the congregation. CBC had played a crucial role in establishing four early daughter churches: Northwest Langley Baptist Church, Aldergrove Baptist Church, Newton Baptist Church, and North Surrey Baptist Church. From

Newton Baptist, a vibrant granddaughter congregation, Parkland Fellowship, emerged. Although North Surrey Baptist Church operated successfully for many years, it eventually closed. In 1995, Jet Takaoka, our pastoral intern, was invited by the Home Mission Commission of the Fellowship of Evangelical Baptist Churches (F.E.B.C.) to establish a new church in the same building.

The concept of launching a new church was initiated by Dave Heppell, a farmer and dedicated elder and evangelist. After identifying a potential location in Murrayville, we embraced the idea. The congregation supported it, established a church planting fund, and assembled a core team of 18 adults. A church planting coach provided guidance for a year, and we hired a pastor to be on our staff for six months, before moving with the new church. Declaration Sunday in November 1995 the Core Team of 18 adults and their children stood at the front of the church. I asked those in the congregation who sensed God's calling to join the 18, to stand up. Many stood. On a Sunday in December, we commissioned a pastor and 100 people (some of our best workers) and gifted them with $100,000. In January they began in a rented school auditorium located in Murrayville, five miles east of Cloverdale. Within a few years they Southridge Church dedicated a new church building seating a congregation of 900. This planting experience in 1995 was an essential part of our discipleship focus and is one of my fondest memories.

People care was happening at our church. One story stands out, emphasizing why I'm grateful for my pastoral calling. The narrative revolves around Tamar Lisette Turner, the daughter of Allan and Judi Turner, who also had a son named David. I had no prior acquaintance with this family until that fateful Sunday, March 30, 1997. Judi, Tamar's mother, stood outside our church, a stranger to me but drawn by the church's proximity to her neighborhood, and prompted by her daughter's desire to speak with a pastor. Inside my office, Judi gathered the strength to share the heart-wrenching news that Tamar, aged 28, had been diagnosed with stomach cancer, leaving her unable to eat and rapidly losing strength. My own daughter was the same age, intensifying the emotional impact of the situation.

Tamar was engaged to be married and had a simple request –

she wanted a Bible. Over the subsequent weeks, we delved into Scripture, prayed together, and she immersed herself in the New Testament. She was building her own treasury of comfort. Her questions found answers in the Bible, leading her to accept Christ as her Savior. Tamar also fervently prayed for her parents' salvation, which eventually became a reality. The family's newfound faith became a source of solace.

Miraculously, Tamar's condition improved; she regained her appetite and strength. On Mother's Day, May 11, they attended church together, Allan, Judi, Tamar, her fiancé, and his parents. Tamar was flourishing at home, and all three family members had embraced their faith. I had the privilege of baptizing them, and they officially became members of our church. Summer months were a blend of hope and wonder, and harsh reality as Tamar's ongoing battle with cancer remained. Eventually, her health deteriorated, leading to her readmission to the hospital. On October 17, 1997, she peacefully entered Christ's presence. Allan and Judi, now part of our church family, had found comfort and a life in Christ through this profound journey.

Suddenly, Leadership Broke Down and Hearts Were Broken

The church operated with a plurality of elders, lay and ordained. That was a refreshing change for me. In my previous church I often felt burdened by sole responsibility. Yet, I expressed my desire to guide the church in the areas of my experience and education. One elder, Heinz Volkmann, a farmer, reassured me with a simple yet insightful statement: "We are all equals, but we know that the cream always rises to the top."

Initially, our Elders had beneficial day-long and weekend prayer and planning retreats. However, the board's composition changed, with more corporate-oriented members who viewed pastors as employees rather than part of the leadership team. The elders made unilateral decisions to ask the youth pastor to resign and alter other pastors' roles without consulting us. We were shocked, and the youth pastor and his wife were devastated. We questioned the decisions and their process. I promised Christine that I wouldn't let myself be an emotional casualty. I didn't realize the challenges that awaited me.

The pastors sought counsel from the denomination's regional director, but it was unhelpful. The youth pastor, pressured, resigned publicly, causing shock. The Board Chairman adopted a corporate leadership approach, monopolizing a public meeting and leaving the team silent. This meeting left things unclear, and discussions remained deadlocked.

The Elders Board sought advice from the regional director, who ill-advisedly recommended their collective resignation. This announcement heightened the congregation's distress and unfairly implied the pastors' responsibility for the discord. This led to demands for answers. During a public meeting, five of the six elders accused me of non-cooperation, deeply affecting both Christine and me as the elders were our friends. However, one elder broke ranks, revealing that crucial decisions had been made privately by the elders, including asking the youth pastor to leave and changing the pastors' job descriptions. The perception of a united eldership was shattered, leading to the departure of all but one elder from the church.

The congregation had nothing to do with the dysfunction. They appreciated the pastors, and they loved us. They were understandably perplexed. I was deeply disheartened. We had such high hopes and fine ministry plans. I chose to resign three months later, believing that my ability to maintain a reputable ministry was compromised. For those months, I kept my sermons practical, relevant, and pointing to the future. I had no intention of harming what I had been building for ten years. I concluded my service on September 15, 2001. Bob Dobson, the associate pastor contemplated resigning but ultimately decided against it, becoming a crucial source of strength for the church as it embarked on a path to recovery in the ensuing months and years.

The church was fortunate to hire Dr. Doug Harris as interim pastor. The respected past president of Northwest Baptist College, his mature and peaceable spirit was restorative and inspiring. Although I was gone, Christine continued to direct the School of Music until the end of the school year in 2002. The new board of elders asked Christine and a worship team to lead worship on a Sunday to which they invited me. On that occasion, seven months after I resigned, the board chairman, expressed the congregation's gratitude to Christine and me, for our ten years of service to them.

He then presented us with a monetary gift of $8,000, freely given by the congregation. Through the experiences I learned lessons, too late to fix things there, but beneficial for what I would do next.

Cloverdale Baptist Now

Some plans belong to God, and some are set aside. My successor, Rob Godard, was hired four years later. New leadership opted to sell the seven grassland acres to a townhouse developer. With that revenue the church approved the demolition of the old church building and the construction of state-of-the-art 1000 seat auditorium with suitable Christians education and food facilities. So many new memories will be made in the years to come.

For many of us, it is appropriate to be thankful for lives that were changed in the earlier years, for the relationships that were deepened and healed, and for the Spirit of God blessing the vision and faithfulness of his people.

PRESIDENT OF THE EVANGELICAL FREE CHURCHES OF CANADA

On Sept 15, 2001 at the age of 59, I informed my congregation that God had told me I had pastored my last local church. I did not know what that would mean for me. October 14 was my final Sunday as pastor of Cloverdale Baptist Church. I had a wonderful time reminding the congregation of all the things that God had done in people's lives and I named them.

In the following days, as I spent time with the LORD, I fashioned a new Life Mission Statement which read, *"Believing as I do, that the local church is the ideal context for perfecting life change and personal transformation to which God calls sinners, I am resolved with God's help, to invest myself, my heart, experience and knowledge in the work of God's Kingdom by encouraging and developing Christian leaders to build healthy churches.'*

That seemed an audacious statement given that I had just stepped away from church in distress. Yet, dark times are learning experiences. How would I convert the lessons I learned in 34 years of pastoring into transferable and beneficial encouragement for others. And where was there a need for me? Would such an opportunity be available for me?

Then This

A few weeks after leaving Cloverdale Church, I received a letter inviting me to submit a resumé for the position of President of the Evangelical Free Church of Canada (EFCC). I was surprised and honoured, but I knew little about EFCC, so I declined.

The Evangelical Free Church of Canada (EFCC) is a western-based denomination of 150 churches in six provinces. EFCC and EFCA, its sister group in the U.S., founded Trinity Western University and Seminary. TWU was located 30 minutes from my home. The Home Offices of EFCC were housed in the Fosmark Building on TWU's campus. The Fosmark building also contained A.C.T.S., the Association of Canadian Theological Schools. In 1985 Trinity seminary, together with Canadian Baptist Seminary, Northwest Baptist Seminary founded A.C.T.S. To this consortium was added Mennonite Brethren Biblical Seminary in 1999.

On November 6, 2001, I received a call from Les Braaten, chair of the EFCC Search Committee. He was asking me to reconsider the EFCC president position. It was an informative conversation and I agreed to send a resumé. We arranged to speak again and did so Nov 14 in a one-hour conversation. Les assured me that the Search committee was already praying for us and that I was the only candidate they were currently considering. An interview was scheduled for December 14, 2001. I studied the history, purpose, and vision of EFCC. Christine and I now prayed with expectation that God was up to something important.

At the Best Western Hotel in Langley on Dec. 14, the EFCC Search Committee warmly welcomed Christine and me. We were informed that EFCC had suffered a leadership crisis. A moral failure of a top officer had caused erosion of confidence among churches and staff. Restorative work was needed. We were told that the job as president would be demanding and would entail team building, vision communication, encouragement, and promotion for the sake of finances. Considerable travel was required, often by air, as much as 45-50% of my time.

We spent two hours with the Search Team. As Christine and I returned to our car, we held hands and I told Christine, "This thing is going to happen." An ineloquent expression of the sense of assurance I had that God was in this. From that moment until I was elected in July 2002, my spirit maintained resolute confidence. Nonetheless, the Search Committee doing due diligence before they would recommend me, had me meet many groups of leaders during the early months of 2002. National Conference in July 2002 was held in Lethbridge, Alberta. Again, a rigorous schedule of questions and answers and then a vote of approval.

Elected and Busy

As the summer of 2002 ended, I was getting accustomed to my responsibilities. I started attending district conferences all over the country as the newly appointed president, feeling like a stranger in those settings. After these conferences, I made the decision to fly to Calgary, rent a car, and embark on a journey across the provinces, AB and SK, visiting every town and city where there was an EFCC congregation and donors. Despite facing winter storms, I met with pastors and church boards to introduce myself and discuss matters. In the spring of 2003, District Superintendent Clint Heigh accompanied me as we traveled to churches throughout the Canadian Pacific district, reaching as far as Fort McMurray.

In early 2003, our financial department uncovered a substantial deficit that had gone unnoticed until then, a situation that was severely debilitating. It became evident that we lacked the necessary funds to sustain two executive positions. Given my status as a newcomer to the organization, I offered to step down from my role. However, I was informed that this wasn't the preferred course of action, primarily because I had been elected to the position. Instead, Terry Kaufman, the Executive Director of National Ministries, who was an employee by hire, made the decision to resign in June 2003. He subsequently assumed the role of Senior Pastor at Emmanuel Evangelical Free Church in Steinbach, Manitoba.

Losing Terry, who had been my invaluable right-hand support since I took on the role, presented a significant challenge. I found myself faced with a task for which I had no prior training or experience – fundraising. Remarkably, within two years, we successfully eliminated the crippling deficit. We did this with the help of my treasurer Kenneth Tsang and the Board and through a combination of budget reductions, tireless effort, and the restoration of donor confidence. From that point on, we managed to maintain a positive financial position in each subsequent year.

Christine was not employed by the EFCC, but she became integral to what I did in ministry. Her volunteer spirit and commitment to serve God helped her to find and identify where God could use her. After discussion with Women's Ministry leaders and at their invitation, Christine invited Marilyn Carlaw and Donna McClun to join her as a ministry team whose purpose was to be an encouragement to Pastors Wives. As time passed, this effort received a large and enthusiastic response. This work complemented what District Superintendents wives were doing in their districts.

Highpoints Along the Way

The two denominations, EFFC and EFCA, played significant roles as founding bodies of Trinity Western University (TWU) during its early years as a college. During Dr. Neil Snider's presidency at TWU, from 1998 to 2001, he and his wife, Marlie, attended Cloverdale Baptist Church where I was lead pastor. When I was elected as president of EFCC, I considered it a great privilege to serve as a member of the TWU Board of Governors, as did Dr. Bill Hamel, the president of the Evangelical Free Church of America. Neil and Marlie became good friends of ours before and during my time as EFCC president. It was a tremendous honour for me to officiate at the memorial services for both Marlie, who passed away on June 11, 2005, and for Neil's mother, Anne Snider, who departed on November 10, 2010.

EFCCM, now called Serve Beyond is the international ministry arm of the EFCC serving in the birth and growth of healthy churches internationally. Our EFCC European missionaries invited Christine and me to join them in Ukraine for a retreat that was held on June 16-20, 2004. This was a great treat for us, and these friends were so much fun. We flew into Dnepropetrovsk and after some days there, we travelled by a 3-car caravan into Crimea to a retreat centre. I was a guest speaker each day and Christine and I sang.

ANACEFC. Approximately 20% of EFCC's churches are Chinese congregations. I wish I spoke Cantonese. An affiliate of both the EFCCanada and EFCAmerica is called The Association of North American Chinese Evangelical Free Churches (ANACEFC). It exists to unify, equip, and develop healthy churches. I have attended their gatherings, and I enjoy my many friends in our Chinese churches and Anacefc.

IFFEC. During my 6 years as President, Christine and I attended one general conference in Chang Mai, Thailand. IFFEC means International Federation of Free Evangelical Churches. It brings together a worldwide community of about 700,000 people in 34 countries. It was stimulating for us to see the commitment to God and His Word around the world.

Merger Talks. One morning, I received an unexpected call from Bud Penner, the president of the Associated Gospel Churches of Canada (AGC). Bud conveyed the AGC Board's request to initiate merger discussions with the Evangelical Free Church of Canada (EFCC). I was familiar with the AGC. My family home church and two churches that I pastored were affiliated with AGC. The EFCC was well acquainted with the AGC. There had been two significant merger discussions in the past 35 years. Cooperation had been achieved but no merger. The EFCC Board agreed to meet because at this point, it was evident that the proposal wasn't for merger in the traditional sense, but rather AGC becoming EFCC. Uniting predominantly western and eastern groups of churches was exciting in theory. Both Boards agreed to present the concept to their national conference delegates. At the AGC convention in Niagara Falls, delegates enthusiastically endorsed the prospect of AGC becoming part of EFCC. In a Calgary Hotel 30 participants from both groups met with facilitator, Dr. Paul Magnus. It became apparent that the two merger teams had different ideas as to what the AGC "joining" the Free Church meant. Based on all previous discussions, we saw it as more of an adoption to create a changed entity. AGC saw it as a marriage to create a new entity. We concluded that the core of what made the Free Church the Free Church, would be changed perhaps beyond the point of continuing to be recognizable. We made the decision to conclude the talks. We parted with great respect for each other and an enduring friendship.

Distinguished Alumnus. Very unexpected was the notice that I was to receive an honour from my Alma Mater where I earned my master's degree. In the spring of 2006, Christine and I were invited to fly to Toronto to the campus of Tyndale University. Tyndale is the new name for the Ontario Bible College and Seminary. On that occasion, I was honoured by the Ontario Theological Seminary, from which I had graduated in 1981. I was awarded the Distinguished Alumni Award by Dr. Janet Clark, Academic Dean of Tyndale Seminary.

Grand Mal Seizure. In autumn of 2006 while visiting Cari and Tim in Edmonton, I suffered a severe seizure. Paramedics arrived and I awoke hours later in the hospital Emergency ward. The episode was an anomaly that has never repeated. However, it profoundly affected me. I was unable to drive my car for four months. Specialists did tests to determine a cause and a forecast. At work, I functioned well enough, yet a noticeable impairment was evident. My short-term memory was scrambled. Although two years remained on my term, I made a wise decision and informed the governing Board that I would retire in 2008.

New Statement of Faith. One of the primary projects for my final two years was the championing of a new Statement of Faith. This was a joint project of the EFCC and EFCA, primarily researched and drafted by Greg Strand, outstanding theologian from EFCA. I and other board members travelled to districts to present the 10-point statement and answer concerns. It was convincingly endorsed by delegates in 2008.

Biannual national conferences were held in Lethbridge 2002, Winnipeg 2004, Abbotsford 2006, and Edmonton 2008. Each conference was an elixir of fun, restored enthusiasm, cooperation, team productivity, and good spirit. Election of new executive leaders were held in 2002 and 2008 Conferences. In 2002 that leader was me, and in 2008 it was Bill Taylor. 2008 was my swan song. I knew when I began, that at my age, I would serve for a brief window of time. I had given 6 years to the work, some of the greatest enjoyment of my life in Christian ministry. I loved it all. As I stood to give my final report, the delegated rose to applaud. Caught off guard by their affirmation, tears came to my eyes. Best of all, Christine and I look back at those years and remember that everywhere we went, others gathered around us, laid their hands on our shoulders, and prayed for us. EFCC will always feel like home.

Marie Fast Doerksen Willems

Edward (Ed) and Tina Unruh, 1942

Ronnie and Mommy, downtown Hepburn, SK., across the street from Tina's and Ed's Café. 1945.

Ed Unruh, newly enlisted, 1942 … the palm tree motif seems unusual because he was stationed in the Yukon most of his term.

18 CONCLUSION

In summary, I must say thank you to the LORD, that I have been allowed to pastor four much-loved congregations and thereby gain equipment and the desire to lead a movement of churches. I could not have planned such a full and rewarding life and career. I will always be grateful. Categorically stated, none of these events or experiences over the past 50 years would have been possible or as enjoyable without the companionship and gifts of Christine who is largely unsung but who is herself distinguished in my eyes and of those who love her.

Christine and I never envisioned where we might be fifteen, twenty, thirty, or fifty-six years later. Yet here we are thirty-two years in B.C. Even as I write, British Columbia is home to us. Our children and grandchildren are our compelling reasons for staying here. As Christine and I have aged, we have missed so much our extended family, our parents, our brothers, and their children and all the family events and celebrations that we have forgone through the years. We are grateful that we have been able to regularly visit them, even annually for many years.

To all my family, old and young, I sincerely hope that portions of this book will have been enlightening and inspiring for you.

ABOUT THE AUTHOR

Ron lives in beautiful British Columbia, Canada, together with his wife Christine, and very close to his children and five grandchildren. He drives an MX5 soft-top to saltwater shores at Crescent and White Rock Beaches as often as possible. He is an artist who paints portraits, and mountain, ocean, and vineyard scenery near his home. He spent a lifetime working with words. He has been a spiritual shepherd and pastor to people in several congregations. Along the way he earned master's and doctoral degrees related to his altruistic service. He is a storyteller and perhaps some aspect of this large family story will shepherd you to consider deeply, how you can fully live. Understanding that faith in Jesus Christ, the visible image of invisible God, enabled at least ten generations of five families to endure, survive, and thrive, and it's just the beginning. Hundreds of thousands more global families have become and will yet become forgiven people, living life that God promised would never end.

Ron is the author of:

- *Crandall's Door*, a novel for Young Adults aged 11 plus;
- *God in the Open*, a devotional commentary on Colossians and Philemon;
- *The Eleven, My Interviews with the Apostles*, a narrative and nurture volume;
- *Why? The Riddle of the Human Experience*, a devotional commentary of Ecclesiastes.

Author Website: www.ronunruh.com

Artist Website: http://ronunruhgallery.webs.com

www.ingramcontent.com/pod-product-compliance
Lightning Source LLC
Chambersburg PA
CBHW071212090426
42736CB00014B/2792